CUISINES
of the
Western World

Editor: WILLIAM LAAS
Art Production: THE CHARTMAKERS, INC.
Book Design: CLARENCE LE PEER
Art Director: THEODORE DU BAY
Associate Editors: JOANNA ALDENDORFF
                   NANCY KENNEDY

Travel Photographs: Courtesy of
  Pan American Airways
  Continental Magazine
  American Airlines
  French Government Tourist Office
  Pan American Grace Airways
  National Tourist Organization of Greece
  Turkish Information Office
  Intourist—the Travel Organization
    of the U.S.S.R.
  Danish National Travel Office
  Greek Press and Information Service
  Clarence Le Peer

Some of the text and pictures in this
book have appeared in House Beautiful
magazine during the years 1951 to 1965

Printed in the United States of America
by Western Printing and
  Lithographing Co., Inc.
Library of Congress Catalog
Card Number 65-28281

L. to R.: American Airlines (Mexico); Danish National Travel Office; French Government Tourist Office

CUISINES
of the
Western World

By ELIZABETH GORDON

Editor of House Beautiful for 23 years

GOLDEN PRESS NEW YORK

When you have mastered some of the
techniques of foreign cuisines you
not only broaden your taste experiences,
but the drama of entertaining.
This is cherries jubilee, for ice cream

Contents

"Tell Me What You Eat..."

An introduction to cookery and knowledge of good food as one of the fine arts of living

The food we eat from day to day, whether as cooks or patrons of cooks, at home or abroad, is as much a manifestation of the cultural quality of our lives as the homes we live in, the clothes we wear, the books we read, the music and art objects we enjoy. Food as a part of civilized life and culture is experienced so often each day and throughout the years as to outrank all other arts of living in claiming our attention. What incomparable luck that food also is a fascinating subject and a never-ending pleasure!

My goal in this book is to present a bird's-eye view of the principal cuisines of western civilization, beyond the borders of the United States, in such a way as to alert you to new fields of interest and enjoyment. Plainly, the more you know about food, the more you can appreciate it, both sensually and esthetically. But the array of world foodstuffs, and the literature about them, is so vast that the first problem is one of selection.

One may pursue food as a cultural matter on many levels. There is the gourmet point of view which most people think of first. It means the training of one's palate, one's eye, and one's nose to recognize the subtle differences that distinguish a civilized dish from mere fodder. Only with this sensitive connoisseurship is it possible to develop as a critic or as a cook, and so enter fully into a world of better living.

But one may also adopt the view that knowledge of foods equals knowledge of the world—which is the level of inquiry pursued in this book. The Germans have a proverb, *"Was mann isst, mann ist"*—what man eats, man is. Anthropologists believe that many so-called racial and national differences bear directly upon the foods available and eaten by a people for many generations. Indeed, it would appear that the proper study of mankind is food. Anthelme Brillat-Savarin, the 19th century gastronomist, said: "Tell me what you eat; I will tell you what you are."

"Cuisines of the Western World" is based upon the proposition that foreign cuisines provide a key to understanding foreign peoples. To learn how cookery has been cross-pollinated by exploration (like Columbus looking for India), by trade, wars, colonizers, immigration, religious taboos, even by tourism is as revealing and interesting as more formal history. What people eat and how they prepare it reflects their climate, their agriculture, their wealth, their social system, who they conquered or were conquered by. Both the folk wisdom and the elite culture of any nation are embodied in its culinary practices.

If you like to cook, such knowledge could guide you to better food. For example, knowing that the Greeks are experts with lamb you might

do well to look for a Greek recipe when a fine baby lamb is the meal you plan. If you are not a cook, but perhaps a traveler on international business, you might gain a sharp insight into the country you are dealing with if you could detect in their food practices the difference between thriftiness and plain poverty. Brillat-Savarin said, "The fate of nations hangs upon their choice of food."

Accordingly, our recipes are not presented here in "cookbook" order from soup to dessert, but rather in accordance with cultural characteristics. Neither are they grouped strictly by political boundaries. A second proposition of this book is that there is no truly national cuisine; for example, recipes for a "French" *bouillabaisse* appear cheek-by-jowl with "Greek" cookery. The reason, as you will see, is the niche this famous dish occupies within a basic olive oil cuisine, which had been flourishing for centuries when the French nation was yet to be founded by Charlemagne.

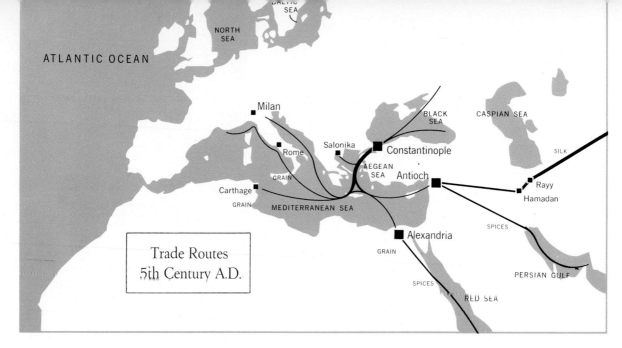

Trade routes during the fifth century concentrated in the eastern end of the Mediterranean, and were primarily for importing spices from the East. Westerners did not know their place of origin, and bought them from Arabs.

The Five Great Cuisines

How much more fruitful to look at the map of the world as if arranged not by nations or even races but by culinary traditions! Such an expanded frame of reference enables you to look upon any food, whether in a recipe or a restaurant menu, on a high level of cultural interest.

So, in this book, the cuisines of the western world are defined by certain common denominators of the author's own choosing. One of these is the prevalent cooking oil or fat. In Europe there is one culinary world of olive oil, that of the semi-arid Mediterranean region; and quite another world of butter and fat cookery in the cooler, lusher countries where animal husbandry flourishes. This scheme of categories transcends national boundaries. For example, French Provence in the use of olive oil resembles *southern* Italy and Spain more than it does the rest of France; whereas *northern* Italy by the use of butter comes closer to Paris in cuisine than to Rome or Naples—or to Provence.

Within each region are sub-regions (at least four each within France and Italy alone), and within those in turn one may find thousands of local variations. A virtue of the system chosen here is to show how cuisines tend to be more alike than unlike. Food practices have jumped borders and followed the sea routes of traders or conquerors. You find Indonesian curries in the Netherlands, brought back by Dutch colonials from the East Indies. A traveler in Venice cannot help being reminded of Chinese food. Surely ravioli is a sister of the *won ton* we meet in Chinese soups

and spaghetti and vermicelli are twins to the *mein* of China and *suomen* of Japan. Marco Polo found them in Asia in the 13th century.

Sometimes the common denominator in food practices will be a dominant cereal or legume. Especially where cookeries have become interwoven by the movement of peoples, the basic starch or vegetable protein—so closely related to the fertility of the land—stands out as the chief cultural signal. It is used in this book to characterize the corn-and-beans cuisines of Latin America.

From this point of view, the world divides into only five uniquely different cuisines, and the western world into only three:

1. Olive oil (also nut oils such as peanut oil): Southern France, southern Italy, all other countries bordering the Mediterranean, tropical South America, and some Caribbean islands.

2. Butter and fat (especially lard and the fats of fowl): The rest of Europe, including the sour-cream cuisine of the Slavic countries, plus most of the English-speaking world such as the United States and Australia.

3. Corn and beans (plus rice): Mexico, Central America, some Caribbean islands, and Spanish-speaking South America. However, in these countries Europeanized foods are favored by the wealthy classes.

4. Rice and seed oils (plus the soybean): The Orient, mainly China and Japan.

5. Curry: A rather arbitrary label for the complex spicing that distinguishes the cuisine of India, Pakistan, Indonesia, Malaysia, Thailand, and parts of Africa fronting on the Indian Ocean. Clarified butter *(ghee)* is the dominant cooking

fat, along with seed oils, and rice is the dominant cereal as in the rest of the Far East.

What It Means to You

While of course there are many other food practices, not all are worthy of attention as "cuisines." The first three culinary cultures are the subject of this volume. You may be asking yourself, "But what is the down-to-earth, tangible pay-off of considering cookery as an area of culture?" Here are half a dozen rewards, as real as you could ask:

1. The vast difference between eating merely to assuage hunger and dining in full awareness of the food itself. The person who is culturally interested in his food is more truly alive and alert. Nothing affects the quality of life so much as our diet, our daily pleasure in it, and what it does for us nutritionally. To this may be added the pleasures of the mind that come with added knowledge.

2. Once cooking becomes more than reading a recipe and following it slavishly, you begin to cook superbly. Cooking ceases to be drudgery. You begin to realize that many a recipe may be less than superb—because the person who created it did not have tastes sharpened by years of tasting the best. With knowledge of world cuisines, you view any recipe merely as a starting point for your own creativity. You improve upon it as you go along. You may even transpose it from one language to another, as a musician transposes in key. This is what the "born cook" does (and you can tell I think that cooks are made, not born).

3. You become a better shopper, screening the best available out of the huge variety of foods on the market shelf. You get a better focus on price, for you know when to pay for extra quality and when not to pay for a false value buried in the price. For instance, peak-of-the-season plenitude brings both peak flavor and lowest prices. Out-of-season means poorest flavor and highest prices. The knowledgeable gourmet eats in season.

4. The cultured cook commits no clichés in entertaining, such as the ubiquitous buffet of baked ham, potatoes au gratin, and green salad; nor does he delude himself into thinking he can achieve distinction by calling in the city's most expensive caterer. (As one wedding-weary guest remarked, "You can taste the rubber stamp.")

5. With a sensitive awareness of the cultural values, you see food for what it really is, without prejudice, preconception, or snobbery. A Frenchman would not be so blind as to insist upon caviar at $44 per Russian pound when other equally good roes, such as the mealy gold of poached mullet eggs, may be bought for 30 cents a pound. His critical faculties would not be warped by price, "imported" status, or any value except whether the food tastes good. Once you adopt this purity of approach, you become just as gourmet about a snack as about a banquet, just as choosy about brands of tomato juice as about vintage wines.

And you can order a meal with greater assurance in a restaurant. You know how to run your eye down the menu and fairly estimate the sophistication and capabilities—sometimes even the nationality—of the chef, and to choose those dishes likely to be the restaurant's best.

6. Finally, knowledge of cuisines adds a new dimension to travel. It is, in the truest sense of

By the 15th century, Europeans had explored all the oceans, except the Pacific, and had brought back many new foods.

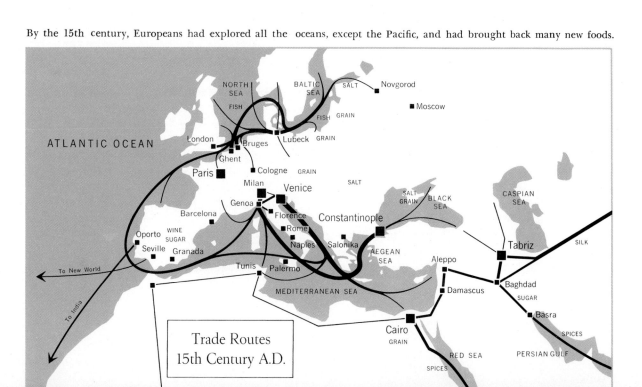

Trade Routes
15th Century A.D.

Viewed in culinary terms, there are two Europes divided by the two different types of cooking fats that prevail. In countries touching the Mediterranean, olive oil is normally used. Elsewhere the fats from animals and fowl are most common.

the word, your passport into hidden delights, your introduction to people, places, and things which the less informed tourist never sees. The American who travels around the world looking for "a good cup of coffee" or "a decent steak" might almost as well have stayed at home. Even if he does set out to taste his way around the world, he may have to work at it. Except in a very few countries—notably France, Italy, and Scandinavia—the public eating places catering to tourists conspire to keep the visitor innocent of the fine specialties of the land.

No one would consider leaving Paris without tasting at least a few French dishes. But how many have come away from Haiti without ever having tasted black rice—dark as caviar, with the inky juices of the tiny wild *jonjon* mushroom lending an earthy mountain fragrance as delicate as the truffles of Perigord? How many, having sunned on the beaches of Barbados, have also tasted its flying fish and dolphin steaks and dove peas—which, because "dove" rhymes with "rove,"

from French *daube* or braise, reveals more quickly and pleasurably than a history book that this very, very British island was once French?

Or let us say you have traversed a thousand, two thousand miles to some tropical paradise. On a ride through the countryside you have seen strange tropical fruits. In the markets you have seen baskets piled high with curious and wordrous vegetables. Now you are back for lunch at your luxury hotel. On the menu is written, "Noted for Continental Cuisine." You know you are in for it—a poor imitation of fourth-rate so-called French cooking, prepared by a chef who may have forgotten everything he learned in a Swiss hotel school twenty years ago.

You should have seen the way the eyebrows of the maître d'hôtel at a famous restaurant in Mexico disappeared into his hairline when I asked

The monastery at Daphne, Greece, contains some of the greatest Byzantine mosaics. It is only 2 hours drive from Athens, with tavernas along the way serving delicious food.

10   *Introduction*

for the whitefish of Lake Patzcuaro instead of a "thermidor" made out of lobster he told us proudly had been flown down from Maine. Or when we ordered the celebrated goat cheese of Oaxaca and a bottle of Mexican rosé wine. He said, "We serve here only imported cheese and wines. Frankly, I have never heard of the others."

The Camaraderie of Cookery

I don't mind an admiration of French cooking, but I don't believe we should rule out admiring the best that can be produced elsewhere as well. Indeed the French are experts at recognizing any good food for exactly what it is and adopting it as their own. They have what Gertrude Stein called "pure vision," so necessary to great cooking. It lets you know whether to serve the strawberries whole or to slice them well sugared, when to turn up the heat under a boiling egg or to turn it down so the white is not leathery. If you know how much fat to cut off the steak before you broil it, the exact instant to turn a pancake, the right herb to sprinkle on a roasting lamb— then you are operating with skill. Without such knowledge you can only stumble along, trusting to luck.

The devotees of food as culture are a merry company. You find them everywhere. Some are rich, some are pension-poor; many live in cities, some on farms and ranches. Perhaps one generalization may be permitted: Usually they are the most interesting people, often the most successful; a warm-hearted, kindly, aware folk. This makes it all the more fun to be one of them.

You find their haunts in restaurants, grocery stores, and open-air markets. A decade ago they gathered at the old Fortnum & Mason's in London, now at Hediard's in Paris, or at Charles, the Vendome, and Maison Glass in New York. You find them at the Farmer's Market in Los Angeles, or prowling among the delicacies at Marshall Field's in Chicago, or scrutinizing the mushrooms in Chinatown and the interesting sausages in a Spanish, Italian, or Hungarian neighborhood.

You'll feel a thrill of recognition when in a strange land you encounter an old, old friend wearing another name. You'll feel inordinately proud to meet *aioli* in Provence and say to yourself, "Why, I know you. Originally from Greece, the ancestor of mayonnaise, which most people think came from France." Then when you get home, you make this garlic mayonnaise and while pounding the garlic in your mortar you think long thoughts about your trip, and wonder whether the Greeks got their version of *aioli* from some civilization still older than ancient Greece.

The purpose of this book is not to turn you into a scholar who can argue with other scholars about whose recipes influenced whom. Rather its aim is to help you to think (and cook) in a new, less restricted way, unhedged by national or regional habits or prejudices. Its aim is to broaden your working scope and your culinary horizons. It should help you free-wheel in the kitchen, to get the best out of the best restaurants and the most out of foreign travel.

Acknowledgments

For some of the background information in this book and for all of the recipes I am indebted to a number of leading experts in foreign cookery. Some were writers of articles for *House Beautiful* during my editorship, as gratefully acknowledged where quoted in the text. Also, while deferring to scholars on matters of historical or anthropological fact, I have made my own interpretation of these facts as related to the art of cooking, for which I accept responsibility.

It will be observed that I have omitted some areas entirely, notably the United States and its principal culinary parents, England and Germany, whose food practices are largely familiar to American cooks. Such a book as this cannot be an encyclopedia, but rather a guidebook to favorite but unfamiliar dishes in those regions an American might like to visit or wish to emulate. The recipes tell you what these dishes are, why they are favored, and how to make them. In addition, the book contains several chapters on Continental methods of cookery as you might practice them at home, and an alphabetical list with explanations of *haute cuisine* terms you might encounter on a French menu or in foreign cookbooks. For more exhaustive research into various specialties of this fascinating subject, I refer you to selected source books.

Cooking is fun, especially when it has a higher purpose than easing hunger pangs. And thinking of food in these worldwide terms makes some of the best dinner conversation there is.

When cooking shifts from being a necessity to an informed art, the kitchen itself goes through a transformation and changes from a utility room to a place with personality.

L. to R.: Turkish Information Office: C. L. LePeer (Italy): Pan American Airways (Spain): Greek Press and Information Service

World of Olive Oil

The first of the two Europes was the Mediter-ranean half, indebted to the Near East for its wonderful ways with cooking food

5,000 Years of the Olive Tree

How it spread via cultural bridges to create a modern cuisine

Western cuisine, as we know it, traces its ancestry directly back to ancient Greece and, beyond the Aegean Sea, to still older cultures in lands we now call Turkey, Syria, Lebanon, Israel, Jordan, Iraq, Egypt, Crete, and Cyprus. It was here, in the Near East, that a cultural stream originating in Asia and in Egypt flowed westward to create European civilization. It was here that the peoples first learned to grow food rather than gather it where nature grudgingly provided it. That discovery was the basis of man's progress out of savagery and barbarism, as well as the beginning for the civilized art of cooking.

Archaeologists and anthropologists tell us that early man in the temperate zones of Europe could not, by himself, have progressed from nomadic food-gathering to sedentary food-growing. He must have learned the trick from the peoples of the eastern Mediterranean. His first flocks of sheep and seeds of grain had to be brought by migrant shepherds and cultivators moving westward. For, when northern Europe was still tundra or ice-sheet, some of the now arid zones of the Near East were grassy steppe. While the Stone Age European was still hunting game in the forests with the aid of half-wild dogs, his fellows in the Near East had already learned to cultivate the prairie grasses as a source of food. When cultivated, these became barley and wheat. Wild sheep and cattle roving there were fit for domestication. As herdsmen and cereal farmers, men emancipated themselves from nature's whims by creating an assured supply of foodstuffs.

The particular foods they were able to grow in their warm but gradually desiccating climate determine the character of Mediterranean cuisine. It is fascinating to trace the course of events which

led to the dominance, in the cookery of this region, of the oil of the ubiquitous olive.

In the fertile valleys of the Nile, the Tigris-Euphrates, and the Indus, men won a further victory over nature through the science of irrigation. For the first time since "Adam delved and Evë span," man could produce a large surplus of food. So he unleashed the first population explosion. As farming replaced nomadism, it settled the tribes in place and supported growing numbers increasingly concentrated in great cities. Such was the dawn of organized, literate civilized life.

The island of Crete, favorably situated for trade and travel between peninsular Greece and both Asia Minor and Egypt, played a pivotal role as a cultural bridge as early as 2800 B.C. The Cretans developed their High Minoan civilization on an economy fed by fishing, the breeding of goats, cattle, and pigs, and cultivation of cereals and fruits. They seem to have been the first to domesticate the olive tree. Olive oil became a principal Cretan export to the other lands bordering the Mediterranean Sea.

After the destruction of Minoan sea power (1400 B.C.), the seagoing Phoenicians from Syria took over as the principal cross-pollinating influence. Interested in trade and profit more than in conquest, these great sailors carried both olive trees and vineyards as far west as the Iberian peninsula. So, 3,000 years ago, the foundation was laid for Spain's position today as the world's largest producer of olive oil and the chief exporter of sherry wines.

Meanwhile the land bridge via Asia Minor and the narrow Hellespont, along which Persian armies marched, carried Eastern culture into

Greece and the Balkans. When the Greeks in their turn pushed back across the Aegean islands to create a Hellenic empire, they found in Anatolia (now Turkey) an economy resting on the cultivation of wheat, barley, millet, vegetables, vines and fruit trees, plus the breeding of cattle, sheep, goats, and pigs. Promptly they adopted many of these foods as their own.

All civilizations owe much to borrowing from others, which is the premise of this book as it relates to cuisines. The ancient Greeks were demonstrating what biologists call hybrid vigor. It was in Greece that the lore of cookery was first set down in books, by philosopher-cooks like Timbron the Athenian, by Archistratus, and by Soteriades the Sage. The Romans, much later, imported Athenian cooks as well as tutors for their children. And as the Roman Empire expanded throughout the Mediterranean world, this Greek-bred cookery went with it.

All of Mediterranean cuisine still rests upon the use of olive oil and of the cookery knowledge brought originally by traders or settlers from the east. Since these lands were similar in climate, the same foods flourished everywhere although different regions might handle them in quite different ways. With some exceptions, as in northern Italy, the Mediterranean climate favors the olive tree but does not provide good year-round grazing for meat animals. The protein of the people was more likely to be fish, chicken, and eggs. Any four-footed animals were apt to be killed young, since large herds could not be sustained through the long, dry summers. Goats and sheep, which can live on the poorest grazing, became dominant.

Baby lamb, kid, and veal are common meats in all these countries—as well as in non-Mediterranean parts of France where vineyards replaced the pasture acreage. Also significant in the preference for olive oil, the scanty fats of these animals are not particularly palatable, although their milk makes excellent cheese.

The spice trade with the Orient added another fillip to olive oil cuisine, as well as the strongest motivation for cross-pollination of Mediterranean cultures. Not until the year 1488 A.D., when Bartolomeu Dias managed to sail around Africa, were Europeans able to fetch the spices where they grew instead of from the Arabs of the Near East, who kept their sources secret. And it was the frantic race for the "Spice Islands" that led Columbus and other explorers from Spain and Portugal to discover the New World.

The trade route maps in this book show more clearly than words how ideas and foods migrated from east to west. As ship building and navigational knowledge progressed, the explorers and traders went farther and farther. By the end of the 13th century every major city from Gibraltar to the Levantine coast had its mariners and their chronicles to marvel at, their imports to finger and to taste. The result was a complicated mosaic of influences, and it is amazing, in some ways, that the different peninsulas developed any distinct differences in food practices.

What did happen was a shift of the center of culinary creativity from Greece and Rome to the Iberian Peninsula, during the 15th and 16th centuries. In less than 50 years following the discovery of the New World, the Spanish and Portuguese brought back new foodstuffs that changed the course of cookery even more than had the importation of Oriental spices. Look at this list to appreciate how much they broadened and enriched European cuisine: corn, several varieties of beans, sweet potatoes, white potatoes, peanuts, chocolate, sugar, turkeys, ducks, rabbits, tomatoes, vanilla, avocado, squash, melons, pineapple, bananas, papaya, limes—and the capsicums, improperly called peppers because some of them had a hot bite like the pepper of the Orient. They include such diverse varieties as cayenne, chillis, pimento, sweet bell peppers, and paprika. It was by a similar, romantic confusion of names and places that Columbus thought America was the backdoor to Asia, that the Caribbean islands came to be called the West Indies, and the natives of the New World, Indians.

According to a scholar in this matter, Betty Wason, in "Cooks, Gluttons and Gourmets," turkey and sweet potatoes were the first of the New World foods to be adopted. "A chocolate drink was an immediate sensation in Spain, but more than 100 years had to pass before it gained acceptance in the rest of Europe . . . The progress of the tomato was even slower, until an adventurous chef at the Spanish court tried combining tomato with olive oil and onions."

To this day, amusingly enough, a high percentage of recipes from any Mediterranean country seem to start with, "Brown some onions in olive oil and add tomatoes." The culinary cultural stream in the 16th century reversed direction from westward to eastward. Nevertheless our survey of this civilized art in southern Europe begins with the principles evolved in Greece.

The Cookery of Classical Greece

*In the beginning, it was the Greeks who
established the civilized food practices still followed today*

Ancient Greece did more than amalgamate all the influences and foodstuffs then known as she rose into a great civilization. The strong philosophical tendencies of the aristocratic classes provided a discipline that is necessary if an epicurean practice is to be formed. Classical Greek cooks believed in moderation, simplicity, and respect for the materials—which later became the basis of France's culinary tradition.

They had a recipe for almost every dish and every technique known today. If you study culinary history you cannot believe that the *haute cuisine* rose full blown out of the courts of the Louis' with a slight assist from Catherine de' Medici and the Renaissance cooks of northern Italy. With all due homage to the Duke of Béchamel, one can't accept the tale that this basic sauce named in his honor was invented by his cook or in his chateau—not when Athenaeus (*c.* 228 A.D.) described so accurately the white sauce invented by the Greek Orion. Our ubiquitous brown sauce (call it gravy or *espagnole*) is ascribed by many authorities to Lampriades. Agres of Rhodes first taught the boning method of dressing fish—the cutting of filets so expertly practiced today by deft headwaiters. As for the "French" fish sauces, scholars for more than 20 centuries have looked for the lost recipe of the poet Menander, who wrote of a fish sauce delectable and ambrosial past belief.

Of course neither did Greek gastronomy rise shining like the goddess Venus out of the blue Aegean Sea. Many of the most prized fruits, nuts, vegetables, sherbets, ices, and juleps came from Persia. The delicate art of making flaky pastry (called *phyllo*), for which the Athenians were famous, probably derived from Egypt or Anatolia. Greek pastries remind you of Hungarian strudel or French puff paste.

Modern Greek cooking is as different from ancient Greek as the language. In many instances other countries, like France, come closer to the classic ways. The French, for instance, use saffron to flavor their *bouillabaisse*. Originally saffron was a Greek product, much esteemed by the ancients, and well known today in Macedonia and Asia Minor. According to Nicholas Tselementes, in his book "Greek Cookery," *bouillabaisse* is "a real Greek recipe" introduced to Marseilles when it was a Greek colony. The fish stew (without saffron) is called *kakavia* in Greek, from *kakavia-kasarola*, meaning pot, and was translated into French as *bouillabaisse*, which is made in a *bouillotte* or pot.

What about mayonnaise made by the addition of oil, drop by drop, to egg yolk and vinegar? And the strong garlic flavored *aioli* of Spain and France's Provence? In basic principle and method they differ practically not at all from *skorthalia*. The Greeks use this redolent forerunner of mayonnaise on fish, boiled potatoes, fried zucchini, or squash.

SKORTHALIA SAUCE

6 or 7 cloves garlic
1 tablespoon salt
4 cups olive oil
2 cups moist bread crumbs
½ cup red wine vinegar

Peel garlic cloves and place in mortar. Pound with pestle while slowly adding salt. Pound until

garlic is reduced to a pulp. Add bread and olive oil alternately, a little at a time while pounding. When thoroughly blended, add vinegar to mixture slowly while stirring with a wooden spoon until mixture becomes a smooth, soft paste. If mixture is too stiff, add a little cold water. If too soft, add a little more bread. Four medium boiled and peeled potatoes may be substituted for the bread.

Olives and Loaves

Probably the single taste most provocative of Greece is that of Greek olives. They bear little resemblance to what has come to be the typical olive that we obtain in supermarkets and groceries.

Lawrence Durrell writes, "The whole Mediterranean, the sculpture, the palms, the gold beads, the bearded heroes, the wine, the ideas, the ships, the moonlight, the winged gorgons, the bronze men, the philosophers—all of it seems to ride in the sour pungent taste of those black olives between the teeth. A taste older than meat, older than wine. A taste as old as cold water."

Greek olives are withered and shrunken, looking unloved though shining with the olive oil in which they have been preserved. But they have a taste so superior that once you have met it you are spoiled for all other olives, except perhaps those from Jerusalem, which you are unlikely to meet unless you go to Lebanon or Jordan.

In this country, they are best bought out of wooden barrels or tubs, in Greek grocery stores or gourmet shops who know their business. There are several canned brands, but the quality may vary from can to can.

Only one person in a hundred seeing a crusty white loaf, round or oval, would call it anything but French, Italian, or maybe Cuban. But there is a great deal of evidence that very early in their history, the Greeks graduated from flat Oriental bread baked on hot stones. Athenaeus writes that Megalarte and Megalomaze taught them how to knead flour and bake it in ovens. They also baked bread under ashes like the ash cake of our own South, over charcoal on spades like our hoe cake, or between two pieces of iron,

Greek cuisine pays infinite attention to basics such as the quality of bread, olives, salad greens — even cold water.

like waffles. Sometimes they used a bell or cover of some metal with a rim around the top and live coals over it, like the original Dutch ovens. Nor was yeast any mystery to them. They had many different types of leaven, and we are told that they used "9 pounds, 6 ounces of leaven to 12 bushels of flour."

The Athenians took particular care to place their baking facilities near a mill so that the various processes the grain had to undergo "should take place with ease and promptitude." This helps to explain why they became the most skillful bakers in the world. Athenian loaves were "of a whiteness that dazzled the eye and a taste most exquisite." Even today it is difficult to find anywhere in Greece a loaf of bread that is not delicious, and no Greek would dream of a meal without his bread.

The good grain-mother Demetria was lavish in her cereal gifts to the citizens of Attica, who made artful use of barley, millet, wheat, kasha, and oats not only in breads and pastries, but also in various types of porridge, to serve like the modern polenta as an accompaniment to meat. Often whole cooked grains were seasoned with savory meat drippings and combined with mushrooms or truffles, both of which were much revered.

Poetry in Vegetables

About the middle of the second century A.D., certain explorers saw in Africa in the plains of Getulia "asparagus in excellent quality and of very beautiful growth, being no less than 12 feet high." The Romans cultivated this plant with extreme care and at Ravenna, we are told, they raised asparagus, each stem of which weighed 3 pounds.

But the Greeks many hundreds of years before had reveled at the start of spring in the thin, bright green stalks of a wild grass that grows abundantly even now on the rocky slopes of Greece, Majorca, and certain sandy islands in the Rhone and Loire rivers. As in our own day, the connoisseur knew that asparagus must be ever so briefly cooked. There was a saying, "Let it be done quicker than you would cook asparagus."

So you must cook your fresh asparagus only about 8 minutes; frozen asparagus no more than 2 or 3 minutes; after that it returns to grass, wilted at that.

Of all the sauces contrived by man perhaps the

most bewitching companion to asparagus, as well as to other vegetables, soups, and meats, is *avgolemono*. Simple and straightforward as a Doric column, there are only three ingredients: eggs, lemon juice, warm water or meat broth. Yet the blending is masterly. It's less an act of cooking than a poetic transmutation.

Hollandaise may be a *nouveau riche* descendant of the patrician *avgolemono*. The Greeks could never have made hollandaise, for they had no butter as we know it. It remained for the blue-eyed Saxons, Normans, and men from Flanders to enrich cooking in this way. *Avgolemono* should never have been "buttered up" in my opinion.

AVGOLEMONO SAUCE

Break 3 whole eggs into the blender; add a tablespoon of water, the juice of 1 large lemon (about 3 tablespoons). Blend 1 minute. While blender is still running, pour into the center 1 cup warm stock. Blend 1 minute longer. Flavor with salt and pepper to taste.

Place in a small saucepan and heat, stirring constantly until the sauce thickens and coats the spoon. Then remove immediately from the heat, stir two or three times more, just for good measure. Wonderful to serve with asparagus, broccoli, or cauliflower, with a delicate fish or, as the Greeks do, over meat balls or stuffed vine leaves.

We must remember that garlic and dried beans anciently were the food of slaves and common soldiers. So there are many bean and lentil recipes in Greek cooking. Here is a main course bean dish:

BEANS AGORA

*1 pound lima beans, black-eyed peas, or
kidney beans   2 quarts water
3 cloves garlic, minced
1 cup celery, chopped
4-5 medium onions, thickly sliced (optional)
1 cup carrots, chopped
Salt and pepper
2 sprigs parsley, chopped
½ cup olive oil
3 ounces (½ can) tomato paste
Bay leaf, crumbled
¼ teaspoon oregano
¼ teaspoon thyme*

Soak beans overnight and cook until tender as directed on package. Drain. Sauté vegetables and garlic in olive oil; add tomato paste. Add the water, salt and pepper, parsley, bay leaf, oregano, and thyme, and simmer until vegetables are tender and most of the liquid has cooked away. Add beans, mix well, and cook 10 minutes longer. Allow to stand ½ hour before serving. Serves 6 to 8.

PYRAMID SALAD

The basic ingredient of all Greek salads is lettuce, and the pyramid salad is comparable to the French chef's salad. Generally, the pyramid is started upon whole lettuce leaves laid upon a deep platter. More young lettuce is shredded and piled high, then the pyramid is decorated with sliced cucumber, green peppers, Greek anchovies or any other plump anchovy filets in olive oil. Onion slices appear here and there. There is a studding of Greek olives and slices of *feta* cheese, a kind of cream cheese made of goat's milk and preserved in brine. You can buy it put up in cans.

When the work of art is finished, sprinkle with oregano, which the Greeks call "joy of the mountains." It can be fresh and finely chopped or dried oregano, which has been soaked for perhaps half an hour in olive oil. Instead of a pyramid, you may use the same ingredients in a tossed salad. Whatever else, don't omit the cheese. For it is a tradition, as ancient as the Acropolis, that a Greek meal must have eggs in the first course, cheese in the third.

The typical Greek salad dressing is a little more tart than the French. They use one or two parts of oil to one of vinegar (or lemon juice), instead of the Gallic two to four parts of oil. Strangely enough, though Europeans ridicule the American use of sugar in salad dressings, the most ancient Greek recipes often included a small amount of honey (they had no sugar), salt, a touch of dry mustard, and such herbs as oregano, fresh thyme, parsley, fennel, or anise.

The Arts of Pastry

Though the Greeks have always been noted as pastry artists, their baked dainties are generally served between meals rather than as dessert. To the ancient as well as the modern Greek, dessert consists of fruits and nuts laved in wine or with juices added. Combinations of fruits, arranged to afford an interesting contrast in flavors, colors, and textures, were so popular in Macedonia that they are still known to us by the French word *macédoine*.

LOUKOUMADES
(Honey puffs)

Loukoumades are of many types. In the *tavernas* frequented by working men they are often made of yeast dough, but there is an aristocratic version which antedates by a thousand years the *beignets soufflés* of France, the *seppoli* of Italy, the *churros* of Spain, and our own cream puffs.

To make an excellent quick version use the recipe for cream puffs on the package of Flako pie crust mix. The recipe calls for ½ package, 2 eggs. I use a full package and 4 eggs. Very authentic it is, too, because this mix, like the ancient Greeks', uses lard! For flavoring, use ½ teaspoon of grated lemon peel or ¾ teaspoon lemon extract.

Loukoumades are not baked like cream puffs but are fried like doughnuts in deep seed or nut oil. Just drop by the teaspoonful into hot Wesson oil and fry, a few at a time, at 375°F. for 3 or 4 minutes or until they turn golden and float on top. Drain on paper towels. Sprinkle with sugar, honey, or cinnamon.

TRAHANA

Greece has its version of pasta, a dough made of flour, sour milk or yogurt, and eggs, which is sun-dried for 3 or 4 days. They call it *trahana*, and use it mainly in soups. (Hungary has a very similar product, *tarhonya*.) The best recipe I know is from "Constantine Cooks" by Constantine Hassalevris.

2 eggs
3 cups yogurt   ½ cup salt
8 cups sifted flour
Cold water

Place eggs, yogurt and salt in large bowl. Mix thoroughly. Sift flour in slowly while continuing to mix. Add more flour or some cold water, whichever is needed to make a stiff dough. Knead all ingredients thoroughly. Roll dough between palms into balls size of a walnut. Set on a clean tablecloth, cover with dish towels and let stand for 2 days. Roll out flat on a floured board, set on tablecloth, cover with dish towels and let dry for 2 days. Then rub dry dough between hands until it crumbles into bits and pieces. Set on covered tablecloth again for 2 or 3 days. Store in covered

jar. Will keep fresh for months; boil as needed.

This pasta can be obtained, occasionally, in Greek grocery stores. Its flavor is really unique. If not obtainable, the trouble it takes to make is well worth the effort. An interesting blend of the yogurt cookery of the Middle East and the pasta techniques of Italy and China, *trahana* shows how ideas get around.

With the Greeks the material is the thing, rather than tricks of cookery. Greek gourmets know exactly where the best cheese is to be found, the best olives, oil, and oranges. They know about special figs to go along with an herb-flavored, smoky ham (rather like the Italian *prosciutto*). They know where to find the most fragrant melons and also when to look for them. Like their forebears, they speak not of "wine" but of the wine of Lesbos, Chios, and Samos. Nothing is too plain or ordinary to deserve attention. Cold water is as ceremoniously tasted and commented upon as an old brandy.

The Greeks were and are sharp shoppers and observers. It is part of being an epicurean to care, to be willing to take time to procure the best available. Also, we can learn to take thought about utensils. Certain dishes, so the Greeks insisted, were best prepared in bronze utensils, some needed silver, some cast iron. Sensitive cooks, ever since, have felt the same way.

LAMB WITH GARLIC AND OLIVES

3½ lbs. shoulder of lamb, boned, trimmed of fat,
and cut into 1-inch cubes
1 cup black olives, pitted
2 coarsely cut or whole garlic cloves
⅔ cup tomato purée
1 cup chopped parsley
1 large onion, chopped
1 teaspoon basil
½ cup chopped celery leaves, or
1 teaspoon dry celery leaves
½ teaspoon oregano
½ cup dill, chopped
½ teaspoon monosodium glutamate
2 teaspoons salt
½ teaspoon sugar

Mix all ingredients together, reserving half a cup of parsley. Place in a heavy pot which can be tightly covered. Place in a 350° oven for 1 hour. Reduce heat to 300°. Continue cooking 30 to 45 minutes longer, or till meat is tender. Skim off fat before serving. Sprinkle with remaining chopped parsley.

BAKED LAMB AND POTATOES

3½ lbs. shoulder of lamb, boned, trimmed of fat
and cut into ½-inch cubes
⅔ cup tomato purée
2 large onions, chopped
2 cloves garlic, minced
1 teaspoon basil
2 teaspoons salt   Pepper to taste
½ cup parsley, chopped
3 pounds potatoes, peeled, then cut into thin
matchsticks
¼ cup olive oil

Combine all ingredients except potatoes and oil. Mix well together with your hands. Place in a casserole—preferably one which is broader at the top than at the bottom. Press mixture down firmly. Arrange potatoes evenly on top of meat. Sprinkle with oil. Place in 400° oven about 1½ hours. Occasionally, baste potatoes with meat juices from casserole. Potatoes should be very crisp when casserole is ready to eat. If this needs to be held over before serving, set oven very low and leave casserole in oven.

GREEK PILAF

This is a kind of Mediterranean *rijstafel* built around a central dish of kidneys on a mound of rice, with its trayful of separate accompaniments and two complementary dressings: one mild and one very hot.

1 or 2 or more pork kidneys per person
Rice   Olive oil
Lemon
Salt and pepper

Small quantities of bacon; onion; watercress; cucumber and sour cream; olive oil, lemon juice, tomato, and parsley dressing; chili pepper or fresh red pepper dressing.

Cook an adequate quantity of white rice. The grains must be separated and bone dry. Then grill the pork kidneys. Skin and trim them, split lengthwise without completely separating the halves, stick them on a skewer, sprinkle with a little olive oil, and cook them under a hot broiler for a few minutes until well-browned but quite rare. Put them at once, uncut, on top of the rice,

---

WHAT TO ORDER
Menu-Hopping in Athens

SOUPS

SOUPA TRAHANA—meat stock filled with the
Greek pasta made of eggs, flour, milk, and yogurt
SOUPA AVGOLEMONO—rice soup with
egg and lemon juice
KAKAVIA—the original bouillabaisse, and similar
except that the Greeks do not use saffron in it

MEAT

KOTOPITTA—chicken pie
KEFTETHES—fried meat balls (beef)
YOUVARLAKIA—small meat balls
SOUDZOUKAKIA—sausages from Smyrna
ADJHEM PILAF—rice pilaf with mutton
ARNI SOUVLA—meat grilled on skewers
STIFADO—beef with onions
CEPHALONIAN—lamb pie
DOLMATHES—grape or cabbage leaves stuffed
with chopped meat

VEGETABLES

MOUSSAKA—eggplant casserole, with
or without meat
KOUNKIAR BAYENDI—eggplant purée
with cubed meat

SALADS

TARAMA SALATA—fish roe salad

DESSERTS

MOUSTALEVRIA—wine pudding
RIZOGALO—rice pudding
GALATOBOUREKO—cream pie
BAKLAVA—piled flaky pastry filled with
ground almonds and honey
KATAIFI—a pastry, like shredded wheat with
a cream or chopped almond filling
KOURABIEDES—butter cookies, with or
without almonds

which should be hot as hot; sprinkle with a few drops of olive oil, squeeze a little lemon over them, add salt and pepper, and serve at once.

With them serve the following accompaniments, prepared beforehand:

A small hors d'oeuvre dish full of crisp fried bacon, crumbled into bits.

A small dish of raw onions sliced paper thin.

A small dish of fresh watercress, plain but coarsely chopped.

A larger dish of diced cucumbers, unseasoned, but covered with ice-cold sour cream.

A small bowl of a mild dressing made from olive oil and lemon juice mixed with one small peeled tomato chopped fine, a teaspoonful of very finely minced onion, salt, black pepper, and chopped parsley.

About an eggcup full of a very hot condiment made by setting aside a few spoonfuls of the mild dressing (before the parsley went in) and mixing it with a teaspoonful of finely chopped red pepper or chili pepper.

At the table a good bed of rice is put first on every (hot) plate. Then a grilled kidney, still uncut, goes onto the rice. Now everybody helps himself according to taste. The bacon and the watercress are lightly mixed into the rice; some onion rings are sprinkled on top. Then the mild dressing is stirred and a spoonful of it is poured over everything. Now the grilled kidney is cut into and its juices perfume the whole dish. A dab of the hot dressing is cautiously put on the edge of the plate, and the ice-cold cucumber and cream at the side are resorted to for contrast and refreshment.

For a party, a more elaborate display can include the following additions: Cooked ham, rather fat, cut into strips. Fat salt pork, simmered for an hour until it becomes very mild and tender, diced. Hard-cooked eggs, coarsely chopped. Plain boiled chick peas in small quantities. Strips of sweet pepper, grilled and skinned, or raw. Small young stringbeans, plain, and very underdone. Paper-thin slices of eggplant or zucchini, fried crisp. But no chutneys. No pickles.

On Concocting and Serving Bouillabaisse

Although the recipes that follow are in the French rather than the Greek style, I include them here because in *bouillabaisse* we clearly see a bridge between ancient and modern taste in food. Historical evidence indicates that this masterpiece of fish cookery traveled around the shores of the Mediterranean with those pioneer civilizers, the ancient Greeks—perhaps on the heroic voyages of Odysseus himself. It survives today almost unchanged in basic, centuries-old approach to a feast.

A *bouillabaisse* should be made for at least six to eight people, so that a variety of fishes may be included without waste, and because it is the kind of important festive dish that is most fun to eat in large quantities with good friends. Here is a recipe from around Toulon, adapted loosely to our potentialities, by a famous Provençal cook called *Mère Terrats:*

BOUILLABAISSE MERE TERRATS

Pick out freshly caught fish both large and small. Scrape, clean, and wash them carefully, cutting the larger ones in slices. For 6 people, get at least 4 pounds of fish. In a large cooking casserole put 1 tablespoon of good olive oil for each person, and lightly brown 1 large and finely chopped onion in it. Add 3 or 4 chopped tomatoes; a *bouquet garni* of fennel, parsley, and bay; 3 or 4 peeled and crushed garlic buds; salt and pepper, and a scant teaspoon of saffron. Lay a few slices of potato on the onion and herbs in the casserole, and on top of them put the fish, shaking to mix slightly. Add 1 cup of boiling water per person ("... and one for the pot," Madame Terrats says, of course).

Put the casserole on a very hot fire and force to the boiling-point. It should boil hard for about 15 minutes. Arrange the various fish gently on a platter, with about half the sliced potatoes on them. Mash the rest of the potatoes into the bouillon to thicken it, and pour over slices of crusty bread in a big shallow dish or in soup plates.

Mother T.'s recipe is very simple and depends mostly on quickness. Personally, I prefer a thinner bouillon and more good bread. A slightly more finicky recipe is the one given by the great Provençal chef, Reboul.

BOUILLABAISSE OF CHEF REBOUL

Scrape and prepare 3 platters of fresh seafood. Separate (1) the shellfish such as lobsters (cut in quarters) and crabs; (2) the firm-fleshed fish such as haddock or rockfish, cut in slices; and (3) the

very delicate fish. They go into the casserole in layers in that order, the first two at the same time.

Put 3 chopped onions, 4 mashed garlic buds, 2 tomatoes peeled and chopped, a faggot of thyme, fennel, parsley, and bay, and the rind from ¼ of an orange on the onions and herbs. Add layers of shellfish and firm fish, sprinkle with about 3 ounces of good olive oil and barely cover with boiling water. Season with salt (discreetly if the fish is from the sea), pepper (freshly ground), and saffron (about a teaspoonful). Bring to a violent boil as fast as possible. (On an open fire the casserole should be half enveloped in flames, M. Reboul says firmly.) After 5 minutes add the tender-fleshed fish and continue the very rapid boiling for exactly 5 more minutes. (M. Reboul is very firm about this, too. He believes that the violent boiling keeps the bouillon perfectly amalgamated with the oils and perfumes, which otherwise would separate.)

Pour the liquid over 1-inch slices of good fresh crusty bread which has been dried out in the oven rather than toasted. Put the various kinds of fish gently on a hot platter, sprinkle with finely chopped parsley, if you wish, and serve forth.

M. Reboul is almost ferocious on the foolishness of putting firm and tender fishes together and boiling them all like mad for 15 minutes, and I agree with him:

"Unfailingly," he says, "a slice of delicate whiting which has been boiled for 15 minutes alongside a quartered lobster will be nothing but a mush . . ."

Sometimes, to get a rich *bouillabaisse*, the tails and heads of the fish are used for making a broth first. This involves lengthier preparation, complete with strainings, and so on. It is delicious, but heavy, unless it will be the only dish of the meal, together with a compote of fresh fruits.

In Provence a sauce often served with a *bouillabaisse* is called a *rouille*, because it is mixed in the plate with some of the hot bouillon from the soup. You find it in such excellent restaurants as Noah's Ark on the little Golden Isle of Porquerolles, or at La Méditerranée in Paris, or in private homes. The sauce is often served in a big shell or a good old-fashioned gravy boat, and the whole production, for that is really a good word for it, is called *une bouillabaisse rouillée*.

ROUILLE PROVENCAL

Mash 3 garlic buds and 2 or 3 red peppers (fresh or dried) in a mortar. Add 3 tablespoons of fresh white bread crumbs soaked in milk and then pressed dry, and 3 tablespoons of olive oil. Work all this to a smooth paste with a pestle. Add about 3 tablespoons of the bouillon and serve with the *bouillabaisse*.

BOUILLABAISSE FOR INLAND COOKS

Since not everyone lives on the seacoast, here is a "chain-store" version of *bouillabaisse*, one that you might call Inland, U.S.A. Every single ingredient can be kept on hand in your kitchen or in the freezer, and all except the saffron, perhaps, can be bought in any market.

Have on hand 3 pounds of frozen fish fillets such as haddock, sole, or any saltwater fish, thawed and cut into 1 inch pieces; 6 frozen rock lobster tails, thawed and halved in their shells; 1 pound of cleaned raw shrimp, fresh or frozen; 1 can (10-ounce) of whole clams in their juice or 1 dozen fresh clams in shells; and the following ingredients:

1 cup chopped onion
1 clove garlic, minced
½ cup olive oil
1 can (16 ounces) whole tomatoes
1 bottle clam juice
2 bay leaves, crushed
¼ cup chopped parsley
1 tablespoon salt   Dash freshly ground pepper
1 tablespoon lemon juice
1 teaspoon saffron

In a large kettle, cook onion and garlic in oil, stirring about 10 minutes or until onion is tender. Add fish fillets, lobster, tomatoes, bay leaves, and 2 quarts water, or 1 quart each water and dry white wine. Heat to boiling; reduce heat; cover and simmer gently 10 minutes. Add shrimp, clams, and remaining ingredients; simmer gently 10 to 15 minutes longer. This makes about 12 servings.

At serving time bring to the table in a tureen or a casserole. Or follow the classic pattern and arrange the fish on a hot platter and serve the broth separately, placing in each soup plate a toasted or oven-browned crust of garlic-rubbed French bread.

Bouillabaisse, commonly thought to have originated in Marseille, is more likely to have been born in Greece or Crete. Now it has migrated to all lands with sea fishing.

Eggplant is a much-liked vegetable
in all the countries around the
Mediterranean. This is with Parmesan cheese.

How to Add That Fine Italian Touch

*Your cooking will bloom with the ways
of a cuisine that may not be at all what you think*

To anyone in search of gastronomic adventure there is no land, with the possible exception of France, that offers fare so richly varied yet so simple as the food of Italy.

To appreciate what Italian cooking is we must begin with what it is not. The Italians have not one but many cuisines. Every one of the provinces, some smaller regions within a province, and the great cities have their own dialects in food as well as language. Each has its own idiom, its own special wine or cheese, its own highly individualistic way of combining and flavoring.

Many of us think of "Italian food" as spaghetti, along with macaroni or ravioli, veal scallopine, tomato sauce, garlic, pizza pies, and Chianti wine. These have been made popular by the southern Italians and Sicilians who emigrated to America in great numbers and whose restaurants, naturally, reflect the food preferences of their homeland regions. But the familiar Neapolitan style does not by any means cover the culinary gamut of the rest of Italy—the herb-scented, wine-flavored, cheese-enriched entrées; the delicate yet hearty soups of egg and broth, the meat and fish expertly grilled or crisply fried, the incredible selection of sausages, the vegetables so knowingly prepared and with such restraint that they look and taste as fresh as they did in the sunny fields.

When you go to Italy, take in all those lovely tastes along with the sights. It's worth a special trip to Genoa to sample the minestrone, which has little relation to our American style. It is made of navy beans, herbs, olive oil, cheese, carrots, celery, and escarole. In Rome, be sure to experience the delight of Roman artichokes cooked in deep oil in a special straight-sided copper pan,

according to a recipe that is said to have been brought by the Crusaders from Jerusalem.

When you can tear yourself away from Rome you must go to Venice to taste the *scampi* or prawns, the crabmeat, mussels, and whitebait which are as characteristic as gondolas. You may get an indulgent smile from the head waiter on the roof of the Royal Danielli if you ask for *risi e bisi* at lunch—rice and baby peas cooked in broth, diced bacon and onion, and a sprinkle of fresh Parmesan cheese so fragrant that the whiff of it covers the table. This dish is of noble origin. We are told it was served to the Doges in the days of San Marco.

In Florence, although you've been warned not to expect American steaks and chops on the Continent, you must order *bistecca* at Sabatini's. It's three inches thick, marinated in olive oil and cooked over charcoal. Or order a quartet of meats from the spit (baby kid, lamb, pork, and beef), brushed as they turn with branches of rosemary, sage, or oregano.

In Fiesole taste mushrooms that grow under the chestnut trees. Find in the mountains of Piedmont the famous fondue made of *fontina* cheese, egg yolks, and white truffles. It makes the Swiss fondue seem rude by comparison. Discover the red oranges of Sicily, the confections of Naples—the elaborate candies and pastries, the *cassate* and *mantecati*—direct and exquisite ancestors of many fancy desserts of the modern world.

Not a single one of the four widely familiar "basics" of Italian cookery—sauced pastas, tomatoes, olive oil, garlic—is used in all areas. There is a broad belt through northern and central Italy where spaghetti is rarely eaten. Egg noodles and

a few delicate, filled dumplings are served, usually in broth. Rice is the starch of Venetia and the Po valley where it grows in profusion. Corn meal *polenta* is widely used in Lombardy.

The influence of the Orient is evident in north Italian dishes where ingredients are thinly slivered and very quickly cooked (as in *fegato Veneziano*), and also in the stir-fried greens of Emilia. These ideas were brought home to Italy by her great maritime traders, especially those of Venice and Genoa. All the pastas seem to be a Chinese invention found in Cathay by Marco Polo.

The tomato, and particularly our long-cooked tomato sauce, is a prima donna in the south of Italy where it was introduced by the Spaniards, who found the bright fruit-vegetable in the American land of the Incas. Italians call them *pomadori*, which the French translated as *pommes d'amour*, or love apples; but it seems likely that the term meant "apple of the Moors." Many other Spanish and Moorish influences are discernible in the foods of Sicily. There is even an Italian version of North African *couscous*.

In a delightful introduction to what might be called Italy's Fanny Farmer—"The Talisman Cook Book" (Crown, New York)—Dr. Mario Pei, philologist of Columbia University, writes of "the two great civilizations of Italy: the wine and olive zone and the milk and butter culture."

In Emilia, Lombardy, and Venetia the olive groves, so distinctive in the south, do not do well, but herds of cattle do. So the northern Italian cooks with butter instead of with olive oil. The farther north you travel, the better the butter and the more lavish its use.

As for garlic, the Sicilian and the Calabrian are mad for it. They even slice it on bread for sandwiches. Highly redolent custom! But nearby, geographically as well as gastronomically, begins Basilicata, the land of basil, whose name in Greek means kingly or royal. A Byzantine legend tells how it was revealed to St. Helena, mother of Emperor Constantine, that she would find the True Cross in a spot where a heavenly perfume filled the air. She did find it on a hillside covered with sweet basil.

Less obvious than garlic, the fragrance of basil, mingled with the aromas of onion, oregano, marjoram, and thyme, pervades a great deal of Italian cooking.

Egg noodles Alfredo, a deceptively simple saucing with cheese, butter, garnishes (and sometimes cream) has spread from Rome around the world because of its perfect flavor.

The Italian appetite is infinitely varied and imaginative. Here are just a few from hundreds of possibilities for meal beginnings. Ideally, they are served with vermouth instead of cocktails.

Melon and Prosciutto

As soon as the melons and the green figs appear, Italian gourmets give up all other forms of appetizer in favor of these fruits served with the thinnest possible slices of ham. The renowned hams of Parma are considered most appropriate, but many types of smoky, long-cured Italian *prosciutto* are used. In the vicinity of Bologna, for centuries the synonym of most excellent pork sausage, a pungent salami often takes the place of ham. No matter how peppery the meat, a mill filled with peppercorns is always on hand.

Cantaloupe is classic, but honeydew, Persian, or casaba melon, even papaya, are good too. Generally the melon is sliced into thin wedges with seeds removed, skin cut away, and melon meat served upon the detached skin. Count on one small cantaloupe and a quarter pound of *prosciutto* to serve four.

Two to four green figs make a portion. They need no preparation other than peeling and may or may not be cut into sections like a flower.

Prosciutto, either imported or made by local packers, can be obtained in all parts of the U.S.A., especially in Italian neighborhoods. Or you can use Westphalian ham from a German delicatessen or a tin labeled Noacks from Holland. Another fine substitute is Jordan's Smithfield ham, now available in quarter-pound packages in perfect thin slices.

Some people place thin slices of ham on top of the melon; others merely arrange the fruit and meat side by side on a platter or on individual plates. Serve with a knife and fork so that each mouthful will include a taste of both.

STUFFED TOMATOES, ROYAL DANIELLI

Typical of the many delicious rice dishes of Venice are these stuffed tomatoes. When large, they are often served hot as a luncheon entree. Even more delightful are small tomatoes. Chill well for an appetizer.

A cup of rice should make enough filling for 4 large tomatoes, 6 medium-size, 8 tiny ones. Cook 1 cup of Uncle Ben's converted rice or Carolina pre-cooked long grain rice in 2 cups tomato juice along with ⅛ teaspoon cinnamon, 1 tablespoon chopped parsley, a few grains of garlic powder, ¾ teaspoon salt, ½ teaspoon pepper, and to add richness, 2 tablespoons butter or olive oil.

Cut tops off ripe tomatoes, scoop out, remove seeds and cut the tomato pulp into small pieces. Combine with cooked rice. Place the mixture in the tomatoes, sprinkle with two tablespoons olive oil. Cover each tomato with its own top, place in a well-oiled or buttered baking dish and bake uncovered at 400°F. for 10 or 12 minutes or until the tomatoes are well heated and puffy.

EGGPLANT MARINARA FROM CALABRIA

Calabria is a land of glorious vegetables as well as seafood—world famous for broccoli, cauliflower, and eggplant which grows in many sizes and colors from white purple-striped to a midnight hue. A delicious antipasto that keeps for weeks in the refrigerator is made this way:

Cut a large eggplant into half-inch cubes. Leave the skin on. Cover with water and cook uncovered about seven minutes. Drain very well, then place in a large bowl along with ½ cup white wine vinegar, 1 teaspoon salt, ½ teaspoon pepper, 2 cloves garlic put through the press, 1 teaspoon fresh chopped oregano or ½ teaspoon dried oregano, and the same amount of basil. Cover and let stand in the refrigerator overnight. Before serving add one cup Italian olive oil. Mix well but lightly so as not to break the cubes and serve with plenty of crusty bread. Makes 8 appetizer servings; 4 to 6 main-dish portions.

Generally either soup or an entrée is served at the start of a meal but rarely both. In many homes one of the following hearty soups often is the complete meal at lunch or supper time.

ZUPPA PAVESE

The name, some people will tell you, comes from the word *pavese*, meaning peasant; but others insist that the soup was named for Pavia, a town in Lombardy. When you're tired, when your appetite needs tempting, when you're hungry but can't think of a thing you want to eat, *pavese* is the answer.

First, toast and butter four thin slices of crisp French or Italian bread. Better still, brown it in 4 tablespoons of butter. The bread should be gilded on both sides. Have ready a quart of rich, boiling hot chicken broth or beef bouillon (the richer the broth the better the *zuppa*). Place a slice of bread in each soup plate; break an egg on top of the bread and sprinkle it with a tablespoon of grated Parmesan cheese. Pour a cup of boiling broth into each dish; the heat of the broth cooks the egg just right. Of course, you may use two slices of bread and two eggs per portion as is usually done in Italy. Together with a salad and a bit of dessert, this makes as fine a lunch or supper as anyone could wish.

"LITTLE RAGS" SOUP
(Stracciatella)

In the most sophisticated restaurants in Rome or in a modest trattoria you find *stracciatella*, a broth of a soup with delicate shreds of egg. It is not unlike the Chinese egg-drop soup, except that it has more body and richness, probably because of the cheese.

Traditional Italian directions say that you must beat eggs together with semolina and cheese for at least 5 minutes with a silver fork. To serve 4 generously, use a quart of rich broth and bring it to the boiling point. Meanwhile whip 3 eggs, 1 tablespoon cream of wheat or cream of rice, 2 tablespoons grated Parmesan or Roman cheese. Add the mixture to the hot broth slowly, stirring constantly. The egg will cook and break up into delicate shreds. Continue stirring while you let the soup simmer 3 or 4 minutes.

MINESTRONE FROM GENOA

To most people who think they know a minestrone when they taste it, this one from Genoa will be a surprise because it has a wonderful lightness and delicacy. It makes mere cabbage taste ambrosial.

Shred half of a small cabbage. Any cabbage will do, but the green cabbage that we call Savoy is quite superior. Pare and dice 4 small potatoes and 4 small zucchini or summer squash, unpeeled. Once, when we could find no squash we used small, firm cucumbers that were seeded. Also listed among the ingredients: about 4 tablespoonfuls of peas, shelled; a package of quick-frozen green beans cut into pieces (not Frenched); a large can or 2 to 3 cups of cooked dried white beans; 2 stalks of celery, and 4 quarts of water. All this is brought to a boil, simmered gently for about an hour.

That is the basis for your soup but the drama is yet to come: the *pesto*. Made from time immemorial with mortar and pestle (whence the name), *pesto* is now made admirably with a blender. Simply put into the blender 4 tablespoons olive oil, 2 tablespoons softened butter, ½ teaspoon salt, 4 tablespoons Parmesan cheese grated or cut into small pieces, 4 tablespoons fresh basil leaves. Blend one or two minutes and add 6 cloves of garlic put through the press.

In Italy, *pesto* is stirred into the soup five minutes before it is taken from the stove. This amount makes about 4 quarts of soup, about 8 main course portions. It tastes better the second day and freezes well, especially before the *pesto* is added.

VENETIAN PEAS AND RICE

Risi e bisi is a colloquial name for a dish that is as famous as the square of San Marco. Sometimes it is as thick as a *risotto*. Sometimes it is unmistakably a soup. It is unrivaled when made with fresh tiny peas no bigger than caviar.

Melt ½ cup butter in a deepish pan; add 2 tablespoons olive oil and 1 slice chopped bacon, if desired. Brown in this mixture 1 medium-size onion, finely chopped. Add 2½ to 4 cups of hot broth or bouillon depending upon the desired thickness of the finished dish. Add 1½ to 2 cups of fresh peas. Cook 2 minutes. Add 1½ cups rice. Cook uncovered until rice is tender and a little soft. Season with salt, pepper, and at least 2 tablespoons of grated Parmesan cheese. Makes 4 to 6 servings.

Frozen peas may be used. Treat the frozen peas exactly like the fresh. Additional cheese and fresh chopped parsley or other herbs are often passed at the table.

If the soups are solid, the entrées are light in the warm weather menus of Italy.

Florence and two other Tuscan towns, Fiesole and Assisi, are famous for mushrooms that grow in autumn underneath the chestnut trees. To enjoy them fresh you must go there in October, but any time in the year you can have dishes made of the plump dried fungi of Tuscany. These, by the way, can be found in many Italian-American markets in the States including Manganaro Foods, Inc. (488 Ninth Ave., New York, N. Y.), who will ship all kinds of Italian delicacies to any part of the United States.

TUSCAN MUSHROOMS ON TOAST

Soak ¼ pound dried mushrooms in warm water to cover for at least one hour; drain and press out the water. Cut into small pieces or thin slices and cook in 1 tablespoon butter and 1 tablespoon olive oil about 5 minutes; season with ½ teaspoon salt, ¼ teaspoon white pepper. Add ½ cup white Chianti wine or dry sherry and continue cooking uncovered about 10 minutes longer or until mushrooms are quite tender. Serve on toast.

TUNA AND BEAN SALAD

Before the American "invasion," salads like these would have been served as a part of the antipasto. But now in Italy, as well as in our own country, you will find salads doing the honors as the principal dish for lunch. A glass of wine and hot crusty bread improve the picture enormously.

Drain a large can of red kidney beans or pinto beans or garbanzos. Add ½ cup red wine vinegar, ½ teaspoon marjoram, 1 teaspoon basil, one tablespoon fresh parsley chopped, 1 clove garlic put through the press, 1 medium-size can of tuna fish (about one cup) broken up into large flakes, ½ cup olive oil, 1 scant teaspoon salt, ½ teaspoon pepper. Mix well and let stand covered in the refrigerator at least 4 hours. Just before serving, garnish with crisp romaine or escarole and lay several filets of anchovy on the top. Makes 6 servings.

GIANNANI'S PICKLED BEEF

In Milan there is Giannani's, a restaurant which many connoisseurs consider one of the finest in the world. Here you will find many specialties *alla Milanese* including a renowned pickled sliced beef — an extraordinarily fine summer-time standby which must be made at least 12 hours ahead of time. It improves as it mellows in the refrigerator. In Italy, boiled meat is generally used but sliced roast beef is even better. The thinner the slice, the more delicate the dish.

Place 6 or 8 slices of cold beef in a shallow dish. Cover with a marinade made by browning 2 finely sliced onions in 3 tablespoons olive oil. Add ½ cup red wine vinegar, 1 teaspoon sugar, 2 cloves garlic put through the press, 1 bay leaf crumbled, 1 tablespoon chopped parsley (preferably Italian parsley), a very slight sprinkle of rosemary, 2 fresh sage leaves or ½ teaspoon powdered sage, ½ teaspoon salt, ¼ teaspoon pepper. Cook uncovered over high heat about 10 minutes, or until almost dry; add 1 cup white wine, 1 can condensed consommé, ⅔ cup water, cook 5 minutes.

Nowhere in the world has pasta been raised to so whimsical and fanciful an art as in Italy. Scores of shapes and sizes exist.

Pour this hot over the sliced beef. Cover and let stand in the refrigerator about 12 hours. Serve with pickles, olives, pickled peppers, small canned mushrooms, and artichoke hearts in oil. Provide a pepper mill, a small vial of olive oil, crisp bread, and celery or *finocchio* (fennel).

GREEN SAUCE

Allied to the *pesto* of Genoa but much lighter on the garlic is a sauce that comes from Tuscany, a perfect accompaniment for cold fish, meats, chicken, or turkey. You will use it dozens of times during the warm months.

Place in the blender 4 tablespoons olive oil, 2 tablespoons vinegar, 4 anchovy filets slightly cut up, 3 or 4 sprigs of parsley (just the leaves), 2 tablespoons of capers, 6 small sour gherkins or pickles, a medium-size boiled potato cut into half-inch cubes, ½ small onion cut into cubes, and no more than ½ clove of garlic. Blend one minute. Season to taste with salt, if needed, and perhaps a dash of pepper. This makes about 2½ cups of sauce.

"LEAP IN THE MOUTH"
(Saltimbocca)

Several regions including Rome and Milan claim as their specialty a veal cutlet preparation with the intriguing name of *saltimbocca,* a dish so good that it fairly leaps off the plate into the mouth. You must have *thin* veal cutlets. Each piece should be 3 or 4 inches in diameter. Sprinkle the veal lightly with salt, pepper, and powdered sage, and wrap a strip of cooked ham or Italian *prosciutto* around each cutlet. Brown on both sides in butter for a few minutes until the veal is well tanned, then put the slices on a shallow serving dish. Add a couple of tablespoons of hot water or white wine to the frying pan and scrape up all the good, flavorsome browned bits. Pour over the meat in the serving dish. Add a little more butter and heat well over a low fire. You may count on a pound of veal cutlet to serve 3 or 4 persons.

The Italians are almost as adept as the Japanese at deep-frying foods so they are no more than veiled in crust and devoid of any trace of grease. Their *fritto misto* and assorted "fruits of the sea," *frutti di mare,* are exquisite examples of this art. Less heralded, perhaps, is their ability to grill fish or meat and keep it from drying out. This recipe can be used for butterfish, porgies, or any other small flat fish.

BARBECUED BUTTERFISH

Provide one small fish for each portion. Clean, wash, and dry well. Place fish in a china or glass dish and cover with a sort of French dressing made of 1 part lemon juice, 4 parts olive oil, salt and pepper to taste. Cover and let stand at room temperature about an hour. Grill over charcoal or under an electric broiler about 4 or 5 minutes on each side, brushing occasionally with the French dressing. Serve with quartered lemons or limes and a little chopped parsley.

VITELLO TONNATO

3 to 4 pounds lean veal, cut from the leg
1 large onion, sliced
1 small can (2-ounce size) anchovy filets with oil
1 can (7½-ounce size) tuna with oil
½ large sour pickle
2 cups dry white wine

This is *vitello tonnato,* rolled leg of veal cooked with anchovies, tuna, and white wine and sauced with the same.

Few peppercorns (no salt)
2 cloves garlic, chopped
Several stalks celery with tops, coarsely chopped
1 or 2 carrots, coarsely chopped
Pinch thyme
Few sprigs parsley
Chicken broth, your own or canned

Have your butcher bone and roll the veal, eliminating as much fat as possible, and tie securely. Place the meat with all the ingredients in a heavy kettle with enough chicken broth to cover. Bring to a boil, then simmer until meat is tender when pierced with the point of a small sharp knife. Cool the meat in the broth. When meat is cold, remove, wrap securely in foil or Saran, and refrigerate—overnight, if possible.

Place the kettle with all the ingredients still in it over a high heat; bring to a rolling boil, and boil until you have approximately 1 pint of rich broth. Strain and cool.

SAUCE FOR VITELLO

Combine approximately 1 pint mayonnaise with enough of the cool, strained broth to make a smooth, suave sauce, with the consistency of a thin cream sauce. Combine well with the juice of 1 lemon. At this point, taste the sauce for salt. *Note:* This recipe does not call for salt, because the canned tuna and anchovies usually contribute enough.

Mound cold, cooked rice on a large serving platter, highest in the center, and sprinkle generously with finely chopped parsley. Slice the cold veal very, very thin and arrange, overlapping, down the center of the platter, leaving a ring of rice all around. Spoon the sauce over the meat only, covering it completely, and scatter well-drained capers on the sauce. Serve remaining sauce in a sauce-boat on the side, with a few capers on top.

This splendid dish calls for nothing more in accompaniment than sliced tomatoes, seasoned with salt and pepper and perhaps a bit of dill, and a good dry wine. Serves 12 to 14 or so.

POLLO TONNATO

Follow the same recipe as for the *vitello,* but substitute for the veal 10 or 12 skinned and boned chicken breasts, one for each person. Place all ingredients except the chicken in a large kettle with 4 to 5 cups chicken broth. Bring to a boil; then lower heat and simmer very slowly for about 2 hours. At this point add the chicken breasts, bring broth to a boil again, then simmer for 10 minutes. Take care not to overcook the chicken, or it will be stringy and tasteless.

When chicken is cooked, take kettle off the heat and allow the breasts to cool in the broth. When cold, chill in refrigerator. Put broth back over a high heat and cook down until you have about 1 pint. Strain and cool.

Slice cold chicken breasts very thin with a sharp knife, then prepare sauce and serve as in *vitello tonnato* recipe.

BRAISED VEGETABLES

Braising is a top-notch method of cooking vegetables that is much neglected here. It is a good way to cook almost any vegetable, particularly lettuce, leeks, endive, or fennel.

The principle is simple: The trimmed, raw vegetable is placed in a heavy saucepan with hot fat or oil. The vegetable is tossed in the oil (gently, so that it is not broken) till the outer parts are lightly browned. At this point enough good stock is added, not to cover the vegetable but to come about one-quarter the way up. The pan is then covered, and the vegetable is cooked over moderately high heat until tender. In the course of the cooking, the stock reduces somewhat and makes a rich sauce. A final touch is a generous sprinkling of chopped parsley. (You can use olive oil, butter, or even bacon fat.)

VEGETABLES FRITTO MISTO

Another good but neglected method is the Italian one called *fritto misto*—vegetables fried in a batter. This is a unique way to serve vegetables at a cocktail party. *Fritto misto* can be turned into a complete meal if sliced sweetbreads, brains, or seafood are fried in the same batter. Most vegetables may be used; usual ones are peeled and diced eggplant, cauliflower flowerets, celery root slices, artichoke hearts, onion slices, broccoli flowerets, spinach leaves, or green beans. The harder vegetables— cauliflower, celery root, broccoli, artichoke hearts —should be parboiled for 5 or more minutes so that they lose their initial toughness. Green beans should be left whole. When meats, etc., are added, the dish is *fritto alla Romana.*

Make the following batter:

> 2½ cups sifted flour
> 1½ teaspoons baking powder
> 1 teaspoon salt
> 1 cup white wine or beer

Sift flour, baking powder, and salt together. Stir wine or beer briskly into dry ingredients.

In a deep pan, heat at least two inches of olive or vegetable oil to 375°. With fork, dip each piece of vegetable individually into the batter and carefully place into hot fat. Fry, turning once, till lightly browned. Drain on paper towels and serve at once.

Fruit and Cheese

Sometimes one still hears in Italy a remark that seems to belong to another age: "Don't let the peasant know how good pears taste with cheese." The idea being that some of the lower classes, advised of the better things of life, might make too earnest an effort to share them.

Luckiest of all are those who have tasted pears grown in Tuscany and served with old Gorgonzola mixed with sweet butter, half and half. Roquefort or blue cheese may be used instead.

Apples are glorious with *stracchino,* a pale, soft cheese whose name indicates that it is a little tired. Some scholars say that the name refers not so much to the cheese as to the cows from whose milk it is made. They are weary, poor things, after their trip down from the mountains in upper Italy. Stracchino cheese is not too difficult to get in America. Try at good gourmet shops or order from Phil Alpert's "Cheese of All Nations" 235 Fulton Street, New York. Bel Paese or Oka cheese made by the Trappist monks of Canada tastes very good with apples, too.

Something heartier but utterly delightful: fingers of French bread topped with quarter-inch thick slices of Bel Paese or Münster. Set in the oven or under the boiler just long enough to soften around the edges, not a second longer. This is an inspired accompaniment to pears or apples.

Peaches and apricots have an age-old affinity for cream cheese or cottage cheese of all types and especially Italian *ricotta*.

Here is a Roman idea for the perfect buffet dessert: fresh peaches and plums in a basket lined with leaves accompanied by a bowl of creamed cottage cheese (if you have no *ricotta*), and nearby a series of delightful addenda. These include granulated sugar, a tiny dish of pulverized coffee, a small amount of chocolate, and some cinnamon. You sprinkle them alone or in combination over your individual mound of cottage cheese. And if you want cream, have that too!

Fresh fruits in Italy are so often encountered in lyric ways:
Strawberries are sprinkled lightly with sugar and covered with Marsala wine.
Raspberries of almost unbelievable goodness get a light sprinkle of sugar and, if they need it, a dash of lemon juice; then they are covered with Passito, a wine quite similar to Hungarian Tokay or the familiar Muscatel.
Peaches are sliced with the merest touch of sugar and covered with Cinzano or well-chilled Asti Spumanti, the champagne of Italy.

PEACH CHAMPAGNE

You can try the following at Harry's Bar in Venice, a place which, despite its American name, is one of the best for Italian food. "Juice" a big, soft, very ripe peach in a squeeze-type juicer. Combine one part of the peach juice with two parts Asti Spumanti, very well chilled. Drink from a large frosty-cold crystal cup or champagne glass.

CASSATA ALLA SICILANA
(Sicilian cream cheese cake)

For festive occasions at least one of the famous

and very rich icebox cakes of Sicily deserves an American revival. It is the perfect party specialty.

1 pound ricotta or creamy cottage cheese
4 tablespoons sugar
1 tablespoon vanilla or almond extract
3 tablespoons crème de cacao
2 tablespoons milk   2 tablespoons honey
2 tablespoons chocolate bits
2 tablespoons candied citrus, finely chopped

Place the cheese, sugar, vanilla, crème de cacao, milk, and honey into a large bowl. Mix well until smooth and fluffy. With the traditional wooden spoon this takes at least 10 minutes, with a mixer only 2 or 3. Now add chocolate bits and the chopped candied fruit (any kind you like). This is the filling for your cake.

Now cut a sponge cake into slices ½ inch thick and cover the bottom and sides of a casserole with the slices. Pour the cream mixture into the center. Cover with more cake, crust side up. Let stand in the refrigerator 2 hours or overnight. Turn out on a chilled serving dish and sprinkle the top with confectioners' sugar. You will want to serve only small wedges as it is quite rich.

CAFFE ESPRESSO

No one should dream of serving a meal with Italian accents without *caffè espresso*. The word means "individually made"—that is, expressly for you—and the authentic version is made with steam, cup by cup, in a machine. This brew contains less of the harsh oils than coffee made with water. If you haven't an *espresso* machine, an inexpensive *macchinetta*, sometimes known as a Napolitano, will do very well. Most of these come from Italy and do not include directions for use. Here's how it's done:

First, consider that this pot works "upside down." Place cold water in the section *without* a spout. Fill to just below a tiny hole near the top. Now insert the middle section, unscrew its perforated lid, and fill the basket with dark-roasted Italian coffee such as Medaglia d'Oro. (Amounts are determined by size of pot; approximately 3 level tablespoons coffee per measuring cup of water).

Replace perforated lid. Fit on the last section, with spout pointing down. Set over high heat. When the water boils and steam escapes from the tiny hole, remove from heat. Holding both handles firmly, turn the whole thing quickly right side up. Set in a warm place and allow to drip for a few minutes. When it stops dripping, serve hot

Menu-Hopping in Rome

SOUPS

STRACCIATELLA—chicken broth into
which raw eggs are stirred. Reminiscent
of Chinese egg drop soup

ZUPPA DI PISELLI—split pea soup, flavored
with cloves, tomato, and Parmesan cheese

PASTAS

ARANGINI—rice balls filled with ricotta
cheese, rolled in flour and beaten eggs,
then fried in oil. Eaten hot or cold

SPAGHETTI ALLA MATRICIANA—
spaghetti with pork sauce, made of pig's
knuckles and jowls, tomatoes, and
grated pecorino Romano cheese

SEAFOODS

TONNO VIAREGGIO—tuna fried with
anchovies, tomato paste, white wine, and herbs

BACCALA ALLA ROMANO—dried cod fried
with onion, garlic, tomato, fresh currants,
mint, and pine nuts

CALAMARI E RISO—squid fried with
tomato and onion and served on rice

MEATS

SALTIMBOCCA ALLA ROMANA—veal
cubes wrapped in prosciutto ham and fried
in olive oil with fresh sage

ABBACCHIO AL FORNO—roast baby lamb,
seasoned with prosciutto ham, rosemary,
and white wine

CUORE DI VITELLO—veal hearts cooked with
olive oil, tomatoes, onions, rosemary, burgundy

VEGETABLES

CARCIOFI ALLA MENTA—artichokes
boiled and dressed with lemon juice,
mint, parsley, and garlic

MELANZANA ALLA ROMANA—eggplant
croquettes fried in oil, seasoned with
garlic and grated Romano cheese

DESSERTS

DOLCE DI CASTAGNE—a sweet of chestnuts

FAVE DOLCE ALLA ROMANA—tiny,
bean-like balls of ground, blanched
almonds flavored with lemon rind,
cinnamon, and rose water

SCHIUMETTE DI PIGNOLI—meringues
containing pine nuts

as can be in diminutive heated cups by pouring from the spout.

If you do as the Romans do, you'll add a couple of spoons of anisette liqueur to your coffee. Other cities use a bit of cognac or rum or Strega, a sweet cordial which is said to have some qualities of lover's witchcraft. With any of these variations a slice of orange peel or lemon peel is generally added, then a little sugar to taste.

COFFEE GRANITA

Another way to serve the inevitable coffee is in the form of a *granita*, a kind of half-frozen sherbet, topped with whipped cream.

Melt ¾ cup sugar in 4 cups of water. When the solution is hot and clear add 4 level teaspoons of instant coffee. Freeze to a mush, stirring every now and then. Serve in sherbet glasses or sherry glasses topped with whipped cream flavored with a bit of crème de cacao or anisette. If your *granita* becomes too solid just let it stand at room temperature for a few minutes and the correct consistency will return. Makes 1 quart, about 6 to 8 servings.

Peas and rice, bearing shellfish, is a typical dish of Venice and the surrounding country. In appearance and taste it recalls the visit of Marco Polo to the Orient in the 13th century.

No term in cooking has become so
semantically confused as "French
dressing." In France it means fine
olive oil, wine vinegar, salt, and
pepper. No paprika, catsup, or sugar.

How to Make "Real" French Dressing

*The French don't even have a word for it,
but their principles are both simple and precise*

No term in the food world has gotten so semantically clouded over as the term for seasoning
lettuce (and other crisp greens), commonly called
"French dressing." In different parts of America
it means quite different things. In different types
of grocery stores in the same town it means quite
different products. Even different social classes in
the same town have different versions of what con-
stitutes French dressing.

So what do the French think a salad dressing
is?

A man well-equipped to say was Waverley Root,
an American newspaper man who spent many
years working (and dining) in France, and whose
book "The Food of France" is a definitive source
for the culinary enthusiast. He equated French
dressing with *vinaigrette* sauce, which is nothing
more than 2 parts of oil to 1 of vinegar, plus salt
and pepper to taste. It may be enlivened with prepared mustard or finely chopped herbs, or even a
soupçon of garlic. Some use 3 parts of oil.

In the following Mr. Root put it very well:

Actually, there is nothing called "salad dressing" in France. If you serve hard-boiled eggs sprinkled with salt and pepper, the seasoning is not
called an egg dressing. In France, when a salad is
seasoned with these two plus oil and vinegar, the
condiments are not separately called salad "dressing." Seasoning is part of the salad. It has no
name—in salad, that is. You may come across the
same combination of ingredients presented separately in a sauce boat to go with, say, artichokes,
or cold cauliflower, or leeks. Then it is *vinaigrette*.

But with salad the seasoning is strictly anonymous.

In France salad means, unless definitely speci-
fied otherwise, simply a green plant—whether lettuce or dandelion—and its seasoning. France does
not go in for the elaborate confections that come
under the heading of salads in America. As a general rule, fantasy in salad in France goes no
farther than occasionally slicing a few tomatoes
into the lettuce, or perhaps adding a little crumbled bacon—especially with dandelion greens.

Seasoning salad, in France, is so simple that few
French women or French waiters can tell you
how they do it. The result is achieved by instinct.
Seasoning any dish served with *vinaigrette* is considered a highly personal matter, to be regulated
by the consumer's private taste. Salad never comes
to the table already seasoned. It is a case of every
man for himself. The salt, the pepper, the oil and
vinegar are on the table. You (or whoever is head
of the table) concoct your own blend.

This would seem, therefore, to be an art within
the reach of all. Yet I hear from friends wails of
despair about the difficulties of preparing in the
United States a "French" dressing with the tang
of the original on its native heath. This would
be easier to comprehend with mayonnaise, a ca-
pricious concoction everywhere.

About salad seasoning, all I can pass on to you
is how I used to make it, with success, in Vermont,
a far cry from France. I first shook into a saucer
about as much salt as would be needed on a
couple of hard-boiled eggs. I then shook over the
salt the proportion of pepper that I would use
for those two eggs. I then poured over this two

tablespoons of olive oil and one tablespoon of vinegar.

The only possibility of doing anything wrong in this simple operation comes when you mix the whole together, trying to persuade the vinegar to blend more or less homogeneously with the oil, which it is temperamentally unwilling to do. I use a fork to beat the ingredients together. The secret is not to mix with the tips of the tines, but to press them along their whole length, back side down of course, firmly into the mixture, and rotate the fork while applying pressure to the saucer, a little as though you were trying to get lumps out of it. With the result I flavored my salad with invariably pleasing effect—aided, no doubt, by the fact that the lettuce had just been fresh-picked from my own garden.

The two-to-one proportion of oil and vinegar, classic in France, is often varied with the type of salad. Some call for three parts of oil to one of vinegar. For escarole, three parts of oil to two of vinegar is more common. Lamb's lettuce takes almost no salt. For romaine and water cress, you reduce the proportion of oil.

Some housewives replace the vinegar in their salad seasonings by lemon juice, which in my opinion makes it too thin. But you make it rich if in addition to replacing vinegar by lemon juice you replace the oil by heavy cream, converting your dish into *salade à la crème*. In this case the proportion becomes five parts of cream to one of lemon juice.

You might need to do some experimentation on this—the French *crème fraiche* is not quite the equivalent of either our light or our heavy cream. To me, it seems to fall between the two, closer to heavy cream than to light, but it has apparently undergone some processing which gives it a smoother texture than our cream.

If you have had difficulty with salad seasonings of the French type, look first at your ingredients.

We can neglect, I think, the salt and pepper, though I did know before the war a gourmet so fussy that he kept three varieties of salt, as well as two of pepper, on his table. And of course anyone who uses a French pepper mill to grind the whole peppercorns as they are needed is familiar with the difference this makes.

As for the oil there is no substitute for pure olive oil. In France, peanut oil from North Africa is becoming more and more common, because of the great difference in price. But peanut oil seems either to have no taste at all, or only a banal one.

Olive oil, incidentally, has other qualities be-

sides the gastronomic. It is true that it contains almost 100 percent fat, and no vitamins or mineral salts. But it makes up for this by a tendency to reduce cholesterol. Raw—which of course is the way you get it in salads—it is also recommendable for those whose livers are sensitive. From the point of view of dietary balance, its perfect use is in salads since they are rich in exactly the substances olive oil lacks—vitamins and mineral salts—but are extremely low in nutritive or caloric values, which the oil takes care of.

Olive oil is more complicated than you might think. There are many grades, and I cannot guarantee that labeling practices in the United States are consistent with those in France.

In France, the best oil is marketed as virgin (*vièrge*)—oil produced from the first cold pressing of the fruit. The second pressing, using more powerful presses and the encouragement of warm water, produces second-quality oil, often mixed with some of the first pressing before sale, which, if its acidity is no greater than 1.5 percent, may be marketed under the confusing name of *huiles vièrges fines*—fine virgin oils. This might seem to imply higher quality than the simple term *vièrge*, but it doesn't. In olive oil, virginity is an absolute quality, unimproved by refinement.

For vinegar, I always use wine vinegar. If anyone in your family is subject to dyspepsia or related disorders, you had better, after all, substitute lemon juice for the vinegar. Undiluted lemon juice can be hard on the stomach too; but diluted in salad dressing it loses its potency. And it adds to your salad a concentrated dose of vitamin C.

This covers all the ingredients of the seasoning; but perhaps something should be said about the salad greens themselves, of which the most common is lettuce. It should be chosen young and freshly picked, and after you have bought it, do not keep it too long before eating it. If you must keep it for a little while, wrap it in a damp dishcloth after having washed and then dried it. But in any case, try not to keep it longer than 24 hours.

When you wash your lettuce, it is well to do it successively in several changes of water, or under running water. What you should not do is leave it in a basin to soak. You will thus lose most of the vitamin C, which is soluble in water.

Finally, remember that the greener leaves are richer in vitamins and mineral salts than the pale leaves. The chances are that if your dressing is not working out well, the fault may not be in the ingredients, which are easy to obtain anywhere.

Does your seasoning seem watery? This could be for the very simple reason that there is water in it. After the lettuce has been washed, how do you dry it? The approved method in France is to put it into a spherical basket of open-meshed wire and swing it vigorously to get rid of the water, some of which may spray the kitchen a bit while the rest evaporates. Thus you work in a little physical culture with your salad-making. The lettuce is then pressed firmly between soft cloths, which blot up what moisture is left. Only after it has been completely dried is it ready to be dampened again, this time with the seasoning.

How do you apply your seasoning? In American restaurants, I have often been served what was referred to as salad—usually bits of greens finely chopped in a fairly successful effort to make them resemble hay—over which the dressing had been POURED. This may be an error due to a linguistic habit. When you talk of "salad dressing," you imply a separate entity, which can be concocted by itself and then applied from without. But when you speak of "seasoning," as the French do, you mean an ingredient which is an integral part of the dish, worked into it at the same time that the main dish is made, not conceivable apart from it.

The French cook takes a salad bowl large enough to admit maneuvering and begins by mixing the seasoning in the bottom of the bowl. The lettuce is then placed on top of the seasoning. With the salad spoon and fork, the lettuce is now turned over and over in a bowl until each leaf has been impregnated with the seasoning. This "tossing" of the salad is referred to in French as "tiring" it (fatiguer). It may tire the manipulator, but not the salad, which emerges crisp and crunchy from this treatment.

But don't expect to serve any leftovers at the next meal, for by then the seasoning which has coated the leaves will have wilted them into a soggy mass. For this reason, the salad should be dressed just before, or during, the meal—except for the more resistant curly varieties, like escarole or chicory (French style), which may be prepared in advance.

At this point, let me interject a habit of my own family—and of many French families—which is possible only if you serve the salad when the French do: after the main course instead of at the beginning, as is so often done in the United States. We do not have our plates changed after a roast that leaves gravy on them, or some dish which has bestowed on them the remains of a meat sauce—say, the remainder of a just-con-consumed *boeuf bourguignon*. We put the salad in the plate, adding the remaining gravy or sauce to its normal seasoning (you don't stir it in; just put it on the plate) and find that it greatly enriches the effect.

Another detail apart from the mixing of the seasoning itself: What do you use for a salad bowl? The first requirement is size. It needs to be large enough so that you can toss lettuce and seasoning thoroughly together. It may be porcelain, of course, but the best bowls are of wood. And among the different kinds of wood, the best is olive wood. It is, after all, only normal that the wood of the olive should have a natural affinity for its fruit.

When you use a wooden bowl (unpolished, on the interior, at least), never wash it. Rub it clean with a cloth after each usage. As time goes on, the pores of the wood become even more deeply impregnated with the oil, and each successive salad is that much tastier. Obviously, you should try always to use olive oil, in order not to mix inferior blends into your built-in seasoning.

This brings up the question of whether or not to use garlic. If you employ it often in salads, using the same bowl for all, after a while you will have no choice. On a day when you don't want a garlic flavor, there will still be a faint aroma of it. It will come from the bowl. The remedy, of course, is simple: one bowl for garlic-flavored salads, one for nongarlic salads.

I prefer personally to take my salads made from the less sophisticated greens, such as lettuce, without garlic. But there are some types of salad that seem to call for it, such as the curly variety known in French as chicory (*chicorée*) but here more often as endive.

* * *

How to Buy Lettuce

If you would achieve the same results as Mr. Root, use only the freshest, perkiest lettuce. (No one has ever yet revived an old tired lettuce leaf and made a good salad.) Buy the heaviest, hardest iceberg, the heaviest fullest romaine, the heaviest butter and red lettuce. Solid, firm heads give more succulent leaves. Endive, escarole, head lettuce, and romaine are solid enough to stand storage for a week.

The delicious but tender butter or Boston

(both red and green) lettuce, oak-leaf lettuce, red and green curly lettuce, corn salad (known as lamb's lettuce), and the luxurious-but-worth-it limestone lettuce are all so fragile that they bruise and turn brown quickly. Use them promptly and tenderly.

Keep color and texture in mind when you shop, for you can create exciting mixtures from the market's wealth of lettuce varieties—from dark to pale green to red, from satin-smooth to crinkly, curly leaves. But if you can't find the freshest in anything but iceberg, settle for that and get your color accents with spinach, watercress, parsley, or chives.

You can't wash lettuce too carefully. No dumping it in a sink full of water and hoping the good earth will float out; it won't. Divide your lettuces by type, so the husky ones won't bruise the tender ones. Cut off the end of the lettuce stalk, discard bruised outside leaves, then carefully break off leaf after leaf. Wash each leaf on both sides under running water, running your thumb down the inside grooves to get out every last vestige of dirt. Drain the washed lettuce in a colander.

To prepare lettuce for storage, carefully arrange washed and drained leaves on a clean tea towel, with all leaves running one way. Put your husky and tender lettuces in separate towels. Gather up the ends of the towel into a sort of bag, step outdoors, and swing the towel around in a circular motion, until all the water is flung off. The towel is now just damp enough to keep the lettuce fresh. Store, towel and all, in a plastic bag in the refrigerator.

The Fragrant Bulb

When you use garlic, do so with discretion. There are two approved methods. One is to rub the sides of the bowl lightly with garlic (raw, of course). The other is to put a *crouton* in the bottom of the bowl. This means a slice of round French bread, rubbed with garlic and impregnated with olive oil. Its contact with the salad during the tossing is sufficient to perfume it delicately.

The minute amount added to the salad by these methods is not sufficient to produce any unpleasant effects for those allergic to garlic, a plant that curiously combines good and bad reactions on the human system. The instinct of Mediterranean parents who give their children bread and garlic for breakfast has only recently

been confirmed by scientists, who have discovered that garlic possesses antibiotic qualities. The ancient Romans fed garlic to fighting cocks before a match to increase their force, and the Arabs use it as an antidote to certain toxic substances. It is an intestinal disinfectant; it is considered helpful to sufferers from arthritis, gout, and rheumatism; it facilitates circulation of the blood and reduces hypertension. But it is not easy to digest, and when taken raw may be an irritant for the kidneys.

If, after weighing these pros and cons, you elect to use garlic in your salad, here are a few tips for you: If you grow it in your own garden, don't use it straight from the ground. It must be allowed to age in a dry, well-aired place. The transparent onion skin covering protects the garlic from moisture. Don't remove it or split the whole of garlic into its constituent cloves until you are ready to use it; and then break off one at a time only as many cloves as you need immediately. Even more important, don't use garlic that is too old. You can tell when it has passed its prime by a yellow color when you have peeled it (it should be white), by brown spots on its surface, and by a little shoot of green in the center, where the garlic has begun to germinate. When garlic reaches this stage, its odor becomes unpleasantly strong, it is harder than ever to digest, and it can become more or less toxic.

Salad and Herbs

Aside from garlic, a major heightener of salad flavor can be found in herbs. I grow this list: chives, tarragon, parsley, oregano, thyme, lovage, burnet, rosemary, mints of all kinds, savory, sage, marjoram, coriander, basil, dill, and chervil.

Chop the pungent herbs finer than fine. They're strong and you want to impart only a subtle flavor; keep your guests guessing what it could possibly be. Chop chives and parsley and store in separate containers. The leafy herbs, like rosemary, burnet, mint, etc., should be carefully de-leafed from their stems, washed, minced, then wrapped in foil packets and kept in the refrigerator. Use tarragon leaves whole.

Dried herbs can replace fresh, but remember they are even stronger, so use them sparingly. Just a dash, rubbed well into the palm of your hand and flung over the salad, is plenty.

Your dried herb wardrobe could include Spice Islands salad herbs, parsley, green onion, tarragon, oregano, thyme, and dill. House of Herbs puts out chervil, lovage, and chives. Wagner of Philadelphia also packages an excellent variety.

If you're serving salad with meat, a good trick is to put the traditional meat-flavor herb into the salad. Mint, rosemary, chives, and parsley flavor a salad served with lamb. Dill or the cucumberish burnet flavors a salad served with fish. Rosemary and lovage go with beef, tarragon with chicken. Basil or oregano bring out tomatoes.

Always break lettuce into edible-size pieces. Never cut it with a knife. Tiny leaves are used whole.

Overdressing a salad is worse than underdressing. It takes careful practice and observation to dress a salad perfectly, so that each leaf is well enveloped in its fragrant dressing, enough but not too much. A well-dressed salad should never leave a puddle of liquid at the bottom of the bowl. Toss the greens well with wooden fork and spoon so as not to bruise leaves. This fatiguing,

as the French call it, takes time, for each leaf must be coated, but not drenched with dressing.

The simple French dressing is the standard seasoning for plain greens in most of Europe and Scandinavia and into northern Italy. In Tuscany and southward the dressing may add many variations involving olives, shallots, anchovies, hard-boiled eggs, minced onions, mint, etc. Also as you get away from the area of French influence, salad ingredients combine many more things than only greens, and can become almost whole meals in their heartiness.

As you move toward Greece or Spain you find the proportions of oil and vinegar tend to be half and half, because the oil is heavier. Often vinegar is replaced by lemon juice. There are great differences among oils in flavor and quality, as there are differences in vinegar or even lemon juice. The correct proportion is not some arbitrary number, but what makes the salad taste best to you.

Menu-Hopping in Lyon

(considered by some the gastronomic capital of France)

APPETIZERS

SAUCISSON CHAUD LYONNAIS—
a hot potato salad mixed with sliced
Lyonnaise sausage that has been simmered
in a vegetable stock of carrot and onion

ENTREES

VOLAILLE EN GELEE A LA LYONNAISE—
roast chicken enveloped with a
madeira-flavored aspic

*GIGOT A LA LYONNAISE—*roast lamb
which has first been boiled in water.
Seasoned with tomato purée while roasting.

*QUENELLES DE LOIRE—*forcemeat of lake
pike, made in a complex but delightful manner

*POULET DE BRESSE—*chicken from the nearby
town of Bresse (famous for its chickens)
roasted on a rotating spit and basted
with herbs and butter

VEGETABLES

ARTICHAUTS A LA LYONNAISE—
artichokes cooked in butter

DESSERTS

*BUGNES DE LYON—*pancakes seasoned with
lemon rind and deep-fat fried

*FRANGIPANE LYONNAISE—*tarts
filled with a mixture of crushed almonds,
eggs, crystallized orange flowers

FLAN DE MARRONS A LA LYONNAISE—
puréed chestnuts to which are added sugar, butter, eggs, and a paste of pecans and pistachios,
mint, parsley, and garlic

Paella, Gazpacho, and Spanish Omelets

In the food of Spain, the two Indies meet for a culinary adventure

If you look at the map of Europe, you see several fingers of land jutting out into the well traveled waters of the Mediterranean, subdividing it into smaller seas. Each in its turn has served as a focal point for the blending of cultural practices. The Greek and Italian peninsulas were the earliest to mature in the preparation of food. It remained for the Iberian peninsula, home of the Spanish and Portuguese, to achieve the spectacular feat of melding the culinary lore of the ancient Orient with that of the New World. Here the East Indies and the West Indies come together.

Hence it is not easy to generalize about "Spanish" cookery. Historically, while Rome fell before the onslaughts of barbarians from the north, the Iberian peninsula came under the influence of the Moors. Via North Africa, the Arabs brought the riches of an Eastern civilization, stemming from Persia, directly to Spain. Although similar influences had earlier reached Greece and Italy from the same starting point, the route traveled and the peoples who controlled it made the results very different.

The Moors brought spices such as cinnamon, saffron, mint, and cumin. They taught the cultivation of almond and citrus trees. Then, about 450 years ago, the Portuguese and Spanish navigators broke through the barrier of the Atlantic Ocean to reach its opposite shores, and brought back new foodstuffs which became crossbred with the Mediterranean or neo-Oriental practices already established.

In considering the Iberian cuisines, it is safest to ignore political boundaries and think in such terms as distance from the sea, amount of rainfall, and the like. Thus Spain's Andalusia shares many cooking practices with France's Provence. Two very well informed authorities say that, in cuisine, Spain is not one but many countries. Betty Wason counts six or eight; Elizabeth Cass, who lived and worked there many years, makes 13 different regional classifications.

The embellishment of plain rice into an interesting food runs like a golden thread through all the cuisines that the Orient has fathered. Thanks to the Moors, the *paella* of Spain bears a remarkable resemblance to Persian *pilau,* the *pilaf* of Turkey, the *pillau* of India, and the *pellao* of Pakistan.

In her book, "The Art of Spanish Cooking," Betty Wason describes the *paella* as "essentially a rice casserole to which almost anything that suits your fancy can be added." It has thousands of variations. It may use chicken, shellfish, whitefish, veal, lean pork, ham. It also may include peas, tomatoes, pimientos, dried fruits, garlic sausages, onion, saffron, olive oil, cloves, bay leaf, and stock. Here is a recipe that captures the authentic style and flavor:

PAELLA

Traditionally a Spanish *paella* is both cooked and served in a large iron pan which is carried from the fire to the center of the table so that everyone may help himself. An electric frying pan or skillet will do perfectly. The main requirement is to cook the rice exactly right. It should attain a certain crispness yet never be dry. It must be unresistant but never, never mushy.

Ideally, you should start your *paella* by preparing a broth from two soup bones plus the wings, back, and neck of a chicken. This can be done in 30 minutes in a pressure cooker as against 3 or 4 hours in the usual manner. However you achieve it, you will need 5 cups of broth made from chicken, meat, or clams.

Now for the *paella*. Start with a 3-pound frying chicken, cut as for fricassee. Heat 3 tablespoons olive oil in a deep skillet or *paella* pan. Add 2 peppery hot sausages, sliced (Spanish, Italian, or Hungarian). Then add the pieces of chicken. Cook at 325° F. until the chicken is brown and beginning to be tender. Remove from the pan.

Add 1 large Spanish onion sliced very thin; 4 large tomatoes, peeled, seeded, and sliced. Or you can use canned tomatoes if you drain them very well. Add also, 2 green bell peppers, seeded and sliced very thin. Cook slowly for 20 minutes. Then return the browned chicken to the pan. Add 4½ cups of chicken broth, 2 cups Uncle Ben's converted long-grain rice, and 2 teaspoons salt. Stir thoroughly. Bring quickly to a boil. Cover tightly. Turn down the heat and allow to cook 15 or 20 minutes or until liquid is just absorbed.

In the meantime, put two cloves of garlic through the press. Add ¼ teaspoon Spanish saffron, dissolved in ½ cup hot broth. Add these to the chicken and rice mixture. Incorporate well, using a fork. Cover the pan. Cook about 3 minutes. Uncover. Allow to dry for another 3 to 5 minutes. Decorate to suit your fancy with strips of pimiento and cooked green peas. Makes 6 servings.

ANDALUSIAN GAZPACHO

An iced summer soup called *gazpacho* is probably the Spanish dish best known to Americans. It is sweeping the country as vichysoisse did after World War II. *Gazpacho* might be thought of as a salad, for it has all the ingredients of a salad in it, only floating in liquid or puréed.

You must make it only from native tomatoes—home grown, if possible, or bought fresh from the garden that very day. Hot-house tomatoes will not do at all, nor will those that have been picked green.

Get some red Italian, Spanish, or Bermuda onions. Order 4 tins of pimientos and have ready 2 dozen large ripe tomatoes, peeled by blanching in boiling water, and seeded.

Dice the tomatoes on a platter so that none of the juices will be lost. Cut also into small squares 16 canned pimientos (usually a tin contains 4 pimientos). Combine, including their juice, with the tomatoes. Chop very finely 8 red onions (or just plain onions)—middle-size ones. Add, along with 1 cup of the very best pure imported virgin olive oil, ½ cup red wine vinegar. Stir well.

When it's eating-time, add to each quart of the tomato-pimiento-onion mixture 4 cups V-8 vegetable juice. The soup is much enriched by blending in the canned, flavored juice.

Add also 2 small peeled cucumbers, cut and diced, 2 cloves garlic put through the press, salt, and freshly ground black pepper to taste. You will need quite a lot of salt—more than you think—and, if you wish, you might add a couple of drops of Tabasco sauce. This soup is served icy-cold, so you may toss into it a handful of ice cubes to make a merry chatter in the plate. *Gazpacho* should be served in large bowls or wide soup plates that have been chilled.

One quart will provide full meal portions for 4 to 6 people or a first-course soup for double that number.

This soup varies from place to place in Spain and it has cousins all through Europe and Latin America. Bread crumbs may be added. The Poles use shrimps (cooked), hard-boiled eggs (sliced), sour cream, and cooked beets put through a sieve (bringing it closer to Russian borscht). The herbs may be paprika, powdered cumin, fresh dill, fresh chives, or minced scallions. Some nations put in cooked rice. The Turks use sesame oil rather than olive oil.

In short, a *gazpacho* is infinitely variable, so improvise depending on what you can acquire. But keep tomatoes, cucumber, garlic, oil, and vinegar as the indispensable base. And it's all right to use the blender to purée the solid ingredients. Try garnishing with pitted, sliced black olives, and toasted croutons.

SPANISH OMELET

You could not pretend to cook Spanish unless you had mastered the art of the Spanish omelet. It is not an omelet in the French sense, which is stirred rapidly to make it fluffy and then rolled. A Spanish omelet (called *tortilla*, but no relation to the Mexican corn meal *tortilla*) is not stirred while cooking and is heavily laden with a variety of fillings, such as cooked potatoes and onions, or cooked green peas, or beans, or chipped beef, garlic sausages, cooked seafood, cooked tomatoes, or mild grated cheese.

This omelet might better be described as beaten eggs that are allowed to set firmly while cooking, and sometimes even finished in an oven. The result is solid and firm and can be handled almost like a sandwich. Farm workers take wedges of such omelets with them to the field to eat with bread and wine at noonday, for they are as good cold as hot.

Technique counts here, just as with the French omelet. The most succinct description to be found is in Betty Wason's "The Art of Spanish Cooking." She says:

"Put about a third of the beaten eggs in an omelet pan or a heavy skillet, lifting up edges as eggs set, to allow moist egg to run underneath. When this much is solid, add another third of the beaten egg, lifting in the same way. Finally repeat with the remaining egg. Keep heat as low as possible, using a heat-retarding pad under the pan.

"When a golden crust has formed, loosen ome-let all around edge and underneath with a spatula, invert a plate (of the size of the pan) over the top, then turn out upside down on the plate. Clean out any bits sticking to the pan, rub pan with a bit more olive oil, then slide the omelet back into pan again, moist side down. Cook until solid."

The fillings used are already in the pan, being cooked or warmed, before the beaten egg is added. The fillings get pretty well surrounded by the egg mixture due to the process of lifting the solidifying edges to let more moist egg run underneath. No sauces are used on a Spanish omelet, as restaurants do in the U.S.A. When sauces are used over cooked eggs they are not called *tortillas*.

Another basic in Spanish cookery is a soup of *garbanzos* (called chick peas in the U.S. or *ceci* in Italy). You can buy them dried or in cans. If you buy in cans you don't have to soak them overnight and they retain more of their nutty flavor.

This is another recipe that can vary enormously, depending on what you have on hand. The range is from very plain (meaning with only onion, leek, and a few herbs) to very lavish with

WHAT TO ORDER

Menu-Hopping in Mexico City

(The Spanish influence with a New World flavor)

SOUPS

ALBONDIGAS—meat ball soup

SOPA DE ARROZ—rice soup, with or without fowl, shellfish, hamburger

ARROZ CON JAMON—rice-ham soup

CALDO DE ARROZ CON POLLO— chicken-rice soup

GAZPACHO—minced tomato, cucumber, avocado, and bell pepper in cold tomato juice or broth

MEAT

ASADO DE PLATANO—steak with bananas (plantains)

ASADO DE TERNERA CON PAPAS— pot roast of veal with potatoes

BIFTECS ENCHILADOS—beefsteak marinated in chili powder, garlic, and vinegar and pan-fried in butter

ROPA VIEJA—gypsy stew

GALLINA A LA MEXICANA— Mexican style chicken

GUAJOLOTE CON MOLE POBLANO— turkey with mole sauce

DESSERTS

QUESO DE ALMENDRA—almond mold

QUESO DE COCO—coconut "cheese"

CHONGOS JALAPENOS—little pastry knots in style of Jalapa

GUAYABAS RELLENAS—guava stuffed with apples and nuts

ARROZ DE LECHE—rice pudding

PAN DE AJOUJOLI—sesame seed cake

the addition of carrot, cooked ham, garlic sausage, tomatoes, salt cod, hard-cooked eggs, etc. Also you may or may not purée the chick peas, depending on the consistency that pleases you. Here is a simple recipe from Elizabeth Cass' "Spanish Cooking".

PURE DE GARBANZOS
(Purée of chick-peas)

1 pound chick-peas
2 pints water
1 onion   1 leek
1 bay leaf
1 sprig parsley
1 sprig thyme   6 eggs
2 ounces butter

Cook dried chick peas in water until soft, together with onion, leek, and herbs wrapped in cheesecloth. (If you use canned chick peas, follow directions on can for cooking time.) Remove the herbs, onion, and leek, and pass the chick peas and stock through a food mill or sieve. Reheat and hold on very low heat.

The eggs and butter are gradually beaten into the purée. If added too fast the purée will get too thick. The goal should be for the eggs to be scarcely cooked, as in Chinese egg-drop soup. If the mixture gets too thick, add a little hot water or stock. Will serve 6 people as a first course.

Almonds turn up in cooking throughout the Iberian peninsula, in ways we could well copy.

ALMOND SOUP OF SEVILLE
(*à la* Elinor Burt)

24 shelled almonds
5 cups beef stock
1 cup almond water
½ cup raw white fish, cut in small pieces
1 cup cooked lobster in small pieces
½ cup cooked peas
½ cup cooked ham, minced
2 hard-cooked eggs, sliced
¼ teaspoon white pepper
1 teaspoon saffron
⅓ cup raw rice
Parsley and salt

Blanch almonds in boiling water only to cover. Remove skins and reserve this almond water.

Pour beef stock into a large kettle, and add one cup of almond water. Then add fish. lobster,

peas, ham, eggs, salt, pepper, and saffron. Pound almonds to a paste or grind very fine in the blender (using a little stock as the emulsifier). Then add almond paste to the soup. Bring soup to the boiling point and add rice. Cook until rice is soft. Place a sprig of parsley in each plate when serving. Serves 5 or 6.

Shrimps or crab may be substituted for lobster. Drained canned peas may be used instead of fresh-cooked peas.

Here is a Spanish sweet which could not exist if not for the importation of foreign foodstuffs from other countries—in this case, sweet potatoes brought by the explorers of the New World and almonds brought by the invading Moors. These are stuffed into little pastries.

GLORIAS

1 pound sweet potatoes
¼ pound sugar
¼ pound ground almonds
1 teaspoon cinnamon
6 dessert spoons dry anisette (aguardiente)
½ jigger white rum
¼ pound flour (approx.)
6 dessert spoons oil
Rind of 1 lemon, grated
¼ pound icing sugar

The sweet potatoes are cooked in their skins in the oven and then peeled and sieved. Reheat the purée with the sugar in a saucepan for a few minutes and mix in the almonds and cinnamon. Put to one side to cool.

The anisette, rum, oil, and lemon rind are mixed with the flour until a firm paste is formed, which is then rolled out very finely. Cut out small circles of dough about 3 inches in diameter. Place the filling on half of each circle, then fold over in half-moon shapes. Paint with white of egg and cook for 15 minutes in a hot oven. Sprinkle with icing sugar.

If you want to delve more deeply into Spanish cookery there are two authoritative cookbooks, highly useful for American cooks. They are "The Art of Spanish Cooking" by Betty Wason, Doubleday and Co., and "Spanish Cooking" by Elizabeth Cass, published by André Deutsch, London.

The monasteries of Europe were the repositories for many culinary secrets which would have been otherwise lost due to wars and migrations.

The big soup that is virtually a whole meal can be a real star in a menu. Accompany it with a perfect salad, crusty bread, cheese and fruit, plus a robust wine.

Cosmopolitan in Portugal

The flavors of Portuguese dishes echo from Cape Cod to Japan

In writing the culinary history of the western world, most scholars are inclined to ignore Portugal, or else to assume that Spain and Portugal are alike. This is not true. Portuguese cooking, like the language and architecture, is rich, varied, florid, eclectic and cosmopolitan. And why shouldn't it be?

The Portuguese were almost the first of the world-ranging sea explorers. They were daring the Atlantic long before Columbus set sail. Vasco da Gama made the first European journey by sea to India in 1497-99, out of which grew the Portuguese colonial empire. Like the earlier Greeks, they were enormously curious and open-minded, so they borrowed many food practices to import back home. Among them were interesting ways with the cod *(bacalhau)*. The Portuguese pioneered in exploiting the Grand Banks of Newfoundland, where cod is caught in vast numbers.

The French term *à la portugaise* means a dish seasoned with tomato, garlic, olive oil, onion, and chopped parsley. Actually this flavor is characteristic of all Mediterranean cooking, while Portuguese food reminds you of the entire world. Because of the way they use fresh coriander you are reminded of China and India and Mexico. Their use of codfish reminds you of Boston. Their hard, crusty, yeasty bread reminds you of the sourdough of our own West Coast. Their deep-fried dish called *tempura,* using shrimp and vegetables, is the identical twin to Japan's *tempura,* but it is hard to know who taught whom. I am inclined to think it was Japan learning from the

Portuguese traders, for *tempura* is almost the only deep-fried recipe in all of Japanese cuisine.

PORTUGUESE PANCAKE

(from Gae Thwing)

2 pounds zucchini, diced
1 large onion, chopped
1 green pepper, chopped
1 garlic clove, minced
2-3 sprigs parsley, minced
3 celery tops, chopped
5 tablespoons olive oil
1 can tomato sauce (8 ounces)
1 teaspoon basil
1 teaspoon oregano
Salt and pepper to taste
5 eggs   ½ cup milk
½ cup grated sharp cheese
Salt, pepper, and paprika

Stir zucchini, onion, pepper, garlic, parsley, and celery tops into hot olive oil in a heavy frying pan; cover and cook over low heat, stirring frequently, until zucchini is lightly browned and wilted. Add tomato sauce and seasonings; mix thoroughly. Return to heat and simmer until mixture is moist but not soupy.

Beat eggs, add milk, salt and pepper. Pour over hot zucchini mixture. Cover and cook over low heat until eggs begin to set. Sprinkle with grated cheese and paprika. Slip under the broiler until lightly browned. Cut in wedges to serve. Serves 6 when used as a main dish. Serve with green salad and toasted French bread. (Fresh tomatoes or tomato juice may be used in place of tomato sauce.)

BACALHAU A GOMES DE SA

1 pound salt cod
3 medium onions, sliced
1 clove garlic
½ cup olive oil
3 potatoes, cooked and sliced
2 dozen olives, whole or sliced
2 hard-cooked eggs, sliced
½ cup finely chopped parsley

Soak codfish overnight in cold water. Drain, place flesh side up in pan, cover with fresh water and bring to a boil. Simmer until just tender(about 15 minutes.) Fry onions and garlic in hot olive oil until light brown. Flake the fish and add it to the pan, together with the rest of the ingredients. Stir with a fork until all is lightly browned. Serves 4.

BACALHAU A ECA DE QUEIROZ

Eca de Queiroz was a widely known 19th century Portuguese novelist and a gourmet too. In Lisbon there is a very select club named after him, where literary people meet. This is their recipe.

1 tablespoon butter
2 onions, chopped
1 cup cooked salt cod, shredded
6 eggs, well beaten
Salt and pepper

Fry onions in butter until soft and lightly browned. Add codfish and allow it to simmer for a minute or two. Add eggs and stir constantly with a fork until they are just set. Season to taste. Serves 4.

AMEIJOAS A BULHAO PATO
(Clams)

Bulhão Pato was a poet of the 19th century who is better known for inventing this recipe than for his poems.

4 dozen soft-shell clams in shell
1 bunch parsley
1 bunch fresh coriander
½ cup hot water
2 cloves garlic, crushed
Salt and pepper to taste
½ cup olive oil

Scrub clams thoroughly and rinse in cold running water until all trace of sand is removed. Place in pot. Add all the rest of the ingredients, cover, and cook slowly until shells open (about 20 minutes). Serves 4.

CAMAROES DA TI ANA DA POVOA
(Tomato shrimp)

Povoa do Varzim is a fishing town in the district of Oporto that dates back to the year 956. In a small hamlet nearby lived an old woman called Ti Aña (Aunt Ann), well known for the good dishes she used to prepare from the products of the sea. Here are two of her recipes which have come down to us from generation to generation.

2 cups peeled and mashed tomatoes
2 tablespoons chopped onion
2 or 3 eggs, well beaten
Salt and pepper to taste
1 cup cooked shrimp
½ cup soft bread crumbs
¼ cup grated hard cheese
2 tablespoons butter

Combine tomatoes, onion, and eggs, and season with salt and pepper. Pour into greased baking dish. Place shrimp on top. Top all with crumbs and cheese. Dot with butter. Bake in 425°F. oven until lightly browned (20 to 25 minutes). Serves 4.

LINGUADO RECHEADO A MODA DA TI ANA DA POVOA
(Stuffed sole)

1 large sole
½ cup chopped cooked bacon or ham
1 onion, chopped
1 tablespoon olive oil
1 tablespoon butter, melted
2 egg yolks, beaten
Salt and pepper
Bread crumbs
2 tablespoons port wine
1 tablespoon lemon juice
Potato chips or mashed potato

Skin sole and remove backbone. Fill opening with ham or bacon. Place fish in ovenproof dish with onion and olive oil. Pour butter over fish. Cover with egg yolks. Season, sprinkle with crumbs. Pour wine and lemon juice over all. Make border of potato chips or mashed potato and bake in 425°F. oven until brown. Serves 4.

PORTUGUESE FISH CHOWDER

¼ cup salt pork cubes (about ¼ inch square)
1 cup chopped onion
6 cups cold water   3 cups diced potatoes
1 teaspoon m.s.g.   1 teaspoon salt
¼ teaspoon pepper   ½ teaspoon saffron
1 teaspoon oregano   1 tablespoon vinegar
1½ to 2 pounds lean fish (haddock, flounder, or
whiting) cut into chunks

In deep, heavy kettle, fry out pork cubes slowly, turning occasionally, until only crisp pork bits remain. Remove these to use later. In the hot fat, fry onion slowly until soft and golden (do not brown). Add water, potatoes, m.s.g., remaining seasonings, and vinegar. Boil until potatoes are about half done. Add fish. Continue cooking gently until fish is tender. Add browned bits of pork. Makes 4 to 6 servings.

FRIED FISH, MOLHO CRU
(With raw sauce)

2 pounds cod, haddock, or flounder, cut in slices
2 teaspoons m.s.g.
Flour seasoned with salt and pepper
1 cup vinegar   1 bay leaf
¼ teaspoon saffron
½ cup minced onion   Fat for frying

Sprinkle m.s.g. over fish on all sides; let stand about 1 hour. Roll fish in seasoned flour, coating evenly. Pan-fry in heated fat, turning to brown nicely on both sides. Have ready a warm sauce made by combining the vinegar, bay leaf, saffron, and onion. Heat mixture but do not boil; keep warm. As each piece of fish is fried to tenderness, dip it in warm sauce; place on hot platter. When all are done, pour remaining sauce over all; serve at once. Makes 4 to 5 servings.

RABBIT FRICASSEE

1 domestic rabbit (about 3 pounds),
fresh or frozen
1½ teaspoons m.s.g.   1½ teaspoons salt
¼ teaspoon pepper   ¼ teaspoon saffron
¼ teaspoon oregano   Bacon fat for frying
1 large onion, chopped fine
1 tablespoon vinegar   ½ cup water

Cut rabbit in serving-size pieces. (If rabbit is fresh, wash pieces and dry on absorbent paper. If rabbit is frozen, allow to partially thaw.) Sprinkle m.s.g. evenly on rabbit pieces; cover and allow to stand in cool place several hours or overnight.

Mix together salt, pepper, saffron, and oregano, and rub into meat. Heat fat in deep, heavy skillet, to depth of about 1 inch. Fry rabbit slowly until rich, golden brown on all sides. Place onion in bottom of casserole; arrange rabbit on top of onion. Combine vinegar and water; pour over rabbit. Cover tightly; bake in slow oven (275°F.) about 2 hours, or until rabbit is very tender. Makes 6 servings.

PORTUGUESE KALE SOUP

1 cup dry beans (pea beans or navy beans)
3 quarts cold water
1 large onion, sliced
½ pound chorizo (garlic sausage)
1 tablespoon salt
1 pound kale, washed   1 teaspoon m.s.g.
¼ teaspoon pepper   1 tablespoon vinegar
2 cups cubed potatoes

Pick over and wash beans; soak overnight in the cold water, using kettle in which soup is to be made. In the morning, add to beans and water, onion, sausage (skinned and cut in pieces), m.s.g., salt, pepper, and vinegar. Bring to boil; reduce heat and cook gently 2 to 3 hours or until beans are almost tender. Add potatoes and about 1 cup additional water. Continue cooking until potatoes are tender. Serve in deep soup plates or bowls. Makes 4 to 6 servings.

This is not a soup to precede a meal! It is thick, hearty, and filling—really a complete meal, needing only a green salad for accompaniment, plus fresh, hot Portuguese bread—a meal to remember.

GRAO DE BICO
(Chick peas, Portuguese style)

½ pound chick peas
¼ pound linguisa (Portuguese sausage)
1 medium onion, chopped
½ teaspoon m.s.g.   1½ teaspoon salt
1 tablespoon vinegar

Soak peas overnight in cold water to cover. In the morning, drain beans and place in kettle; cover with fresh cold water. Add sausage, skinned and cut in pieces, onion, m.s.g., salt, and vinegar. Bring to boil; reduce heat to low and cook about 3 hours, or until beans are tender and practically dry. From this point on, beans may be served as is or may be baked. Transfer cooked beans to casserole or bean pot; add a little water; cover tightly and bake about 1 to 1½ hours in slow oven (250° to 300°F.). Makes 4 to 6 servings.

An ideal luncheon can be composed
by serving a variety of cold *hors d'oeuvre*
coupled with crusty bread and wine.
Many countries share this practice.

The Lavish Art
of Hors d'Oeuvre Variée

*Call them appetizers if you will, but the world's
many offerings can be stretched into a banquet*

Nearly every country in the world has a way of eating "a little something" just before tackling the main meal. Probably only an anthropologist could arrive at the reason. Perhaps it is to prolong the time spent on eating, always an enjoyable pastime. But when eaten in sufficient quantity and variety, they can become an entire meal.

The French word *hors d'oeuvre* means literally "apart from the main work," while the Italians have their *antipasto,* or "before the repast." Everyone knows the Swedish *smörgasbord* and the Danish *smørrebrod,* which translates as butterbread or open-face sandwiches. (See page 90.) The Netherlands has a groaning table akin to Sweden's and the Finns serve open sandwiches somewhat smaller than the Danes'. The Chinese and Japanese have their tantalizing pre-meal tid-bits, the Mexicans their *apperitivos,* the Brazilians their *entremesas,* the Greeks their *mezathakia.*

No matter the word, all are appetizers; but there has been a marked tendency, especially in the U. S. since World War II, to let the appetizers take over the whole meal. If they are numerous enough, offering many taste contrasts, this is quite enjoyable. For Americans this category of cookery is particularly useful for buffet parties; these are foods that "hold" well.

It would pay to sample the world's offerings of *hors d'oeuvre* and then work your favorites into your entertaining. In fact, you could make a career of gathering pre-meal recipes, which cookbooks, for the most part, pass over too lightly. Entrées and desserts have been, so far, the darlings of the food world. The French have made a full-fledged art of *hors d'oeuvre variée.* (There are 32 pages of tightly-packed, condensed recipes in *Larousse Gastronomique.*)

All the countries bordering on the Mediterranean Sea have their own versions of the cold dish that can be either an appetizer or the main course. All tend to use olive oil in more or less generous amounts. All tend to make such cold dishes the main part of the midday meal, particularly in hot weather.

But whether you call them *hors d'oeuvre, antipasto,* or whatever, it is essential that you know how to make a good *vinaigrette* dressing, which is a dressed-up, complex cousin of French dressing. Since it keeps almost indefinitely in the refrigerator, it can be made in quantity. *Vinaigrette* has an affinity for previously-cooked vegetables. It is best to add *vinaigrette* while the vegetables are still hot, then allow to cool to room temperature. All vegetables should marinate for at least half an hour, and they may be kept a week or more.

An old stand-by is cooked green beans in *vinaigrette.* Or try sliced celery root. Or an equal-part mixture of cooked broccoli, cauliflower, green beans, and little potatoes. Try a mix of string beans, carrots, broccoli, and diced eggplant.

bowl, sprinkle with salt, and put in refrigerator for at least 2 hours. After 2 hours, pour off water which has accumulated and press out any additional water, so that cucumbers are dry. Add sugar and stir. Combine sour cream and mayonnaise. Pour over cucumbers and toss lightly, adding half of dill. Place in refrigerator till needed.

Remove a circle from the stem ends of the tomatoes. Carefully scoop out pulp and turn upside down on paper towels so that any juice may drain. Stuff each tomato with cucumber mixture. Sprinkle remaining dill on top of each tomato and garnish with a slice of hard-cooked egg.

BALKAN VEGETABLE CASSEROLE

2 cups olive oil (approximately)
1 cup eggplant, unpeeled,
cut into 1-inch cubes
2 tomatoes, sliced ½-inch thick
1 cup zucchini, cut into ½-inch slices
1 cup green pepper, cut into 1-inch squares
1 large onion, sliced
and separated into rings
1 cup celery, cut into 1-inch slices
1 cup shredded cabbage
1 cup green beans, cut into 1-inch slices
1 cup carrots, cut into ¼-inch slices
2 potatoes, peeled and cut into ½-inch cubes
1 cup white seedless grapes
Salt and pepper
4 cloves garlic, sliced
2 cups chopped parsley
1 teaspoon oregano
1 teaspoon basil
½ teaspoon crumbled bay leaf
1 teaspoon sugar

Take your largest, most attractive baking dish. Pour a little olive oil into it. Make individual layers of all the vegetables and the grapes, seasoning each layer with salt, pepper, garlic, parsley, oregano, basil, bay leaf, and a little olive oil. Use the sugar on the layer of tomato. Make the top layer an assortment of all the vegetables and the grapes. Bake uncovered in a 350° F. oven for 1½ hours, or till oil is bubbling and vegetables are completely tender. Serve at room temperature. This will keep in the refrigerator for at least a week.

COOKED ITALIAN ANTIPASTO

⅔ cup olive oil
1 cup celery, cut into 1-inch pieces

1 cup fennel, diced
2 cups chopped onions
1 cup cauliflower pieces
1 cup small mushrooms
1 cup green pepper, cut into 1-inch pieces
4 cloves garlic, chopped
½ cup tomato purée
1 cup dry white wine
1 pound bay scallops
½ pound cleaned, shelled shrimp,
cut into halves
1 teaspoon dried basil
½ cup chopped parsley
Salt and pepper to taste
½ cup green olives
½ cup black olives
¼ cup capers   8 anchovies
4 hard-cooked eggs, quartered

In a heavy saucepan, heat oil till it almost smokes. Add celery, fennel, onions, cauliflower, mushrooms, green pepper, and garlic. Toss and continue to cook till vegetables begin to soften. Add tomato purée and white wine. When mixture begins to simmer, add scallops and shrimp. Simmer till seafood is cooked, no more than 8-10 minutes. Add basil, half of parsley, and salt and pepper to taste. Toss in olives and capers. Chill at least several hours. It will keep for 3 or 4 days.

Before serving, sprinkle with remaining parsley and garnish with anchovies and hard-cooked egg quarters.

GREEK STUFFED TOMATOES

8 small tomatoes
2 pounds fresh spinach
1 small onion, minced
1 clove garlic
¾ to 1 cup olive oil
½ cup pine nuts
1 teaspoon chopped capers
Salt and pepper
2 teaspoons m.s.g.
1 teaspoon sugar

Prepare tomatoes by removing a circle from the stem ends. Carefully scoop out pulp and turn tomatoes upside down on paper towels so that any juice may drain.

Wash spinach well. Place in a saucepan, cover and allow it to steam in its own liquid over a high heat. When it is wilted, drain well and squeeze out water. Chop fine.

Sauté minced onion and garlic in half cup of

VINAIGRETTE DRESSING

⅓ cup pimento, finely chopped
¼ cup scallions, finely chopped
¼ cup raw carrot, shredded or finely chopped
¼ cup capers
1 tablespoon sour gherkins, chopped
1 tablespoon sweet gherkins, chopped
1 small clove garlic,
very finely chopped or crushed
2 teaspoons salt
½ teaspoon fresh pepper, coarsely ground
½ teaspoon dried dill
½ teaspoon dried tarragon
1¾ cups olive oil
1⅛ cups wine vinegar

Place all but oil and vinegar in a 1-quart mason jar. Add oil and stir briefly. Add vinegar. Place lid on jar and shake vigorously for 2 or 3 minutes. Place in refrigerator until needed. Oil and vinegar will again separate in the jar, so shake well just before using the *vinaigrette*. Then add to each ¾ cup:

2 tablespoons fresh parsley, finely chopped
½ hard-cooked egg, finely chopped

Mix these in well and use on vegetables. Thinly sliced leftover meat such as boiled beef, roast pork, or veal is also delicious after it has been marinated an hour or two in a few spoonfuls of this *vinaigrette*. Delectable, too, is thinly sliced cooked sausage, such as knockwurst, or the Polish *kielbasa*.

ZUCCHINI PROVENCALE

2 cups olive oil
2 pounds unpeeled zucchini,
sliced ⅛ inch thick
12 anchovies   ¼ cup lemon juice
1 teaspoon freshly ground pepper
3 cups chopped parsley

In a skillet heat 1 cup of olive oil till it is smoking. Add enough zucchini slices to cover bottom of pan. Turn zucchini slices so that they brown lightly on both sides. Drain on paper towels. Repeat till all zucchini slices are cooked.

Place remaining olive oil in blender (or use a mortar and pestle). Add anchovies and lemon juice. Turn the blender on till all is reduced to a fine anchovy sauce. Add pepper.

Spoon a little of this anchovy sauce into an attractive serving casserole—it doesn't have to be heatproof. Sprinkle some parsley on top of the sauce. Arrange a layer of cooked zucchini on top. Spoon a little more sauce on top of the zucchini. Follow with a generous covering of parsley. Continue to make alternate layers of zucchini, anchovy sauce, and parsley till all the zucchini has been used. Allow this to mellow in the refrigerator at least a week. Serve at room temperature.

STUFFED PEPPERS, SICILIAN STYLE

8 small green peppers
4 cups tiny cubes of soft white bread
1¼ cups olive oil
2 cloves chopped garlic
8 chopped anchovies
¼ cup chopped parsley
¾ cup chopped ripe olives
3 tablespoons capers
3 tablespoons currants or chopped raisins
Salt and pepper to taste

Remove stems and seeds from peppers so that they may be stuffed. If they are large, cut them into halves. If bread is very fresh or of the very soft variety, place little cubes on a flat baking sheet and allow to dry out slightly in a 350° oven. Combine bread cubes with 1 cup olive oil and all remaining ingredients, tossing lightly.

Stuff the peppers, being careful not to pack the stuffing. Spoon a little more oil over each pepper. Bake in a 350°F. oven for 45 minutes. Serve at room temperature.

IMON BAYELDI

(an old Armenian recipe)

2 large eggplants or 4 small ones
1 cup olive oil
2 large onions, chopped
1 green pepper, chopped
4 cloves garlic, chopped
1 cup chopped celery
1 cup copped celery leaves
1 cup chopped parsley
½ cup tomato purée
¼ teaspoon crumbled bay leaf
½ teaspoon oregano
1 teaspoon dried mint
½ teaspoon sugar
Salt and pepper to taste

If eggplants are large, cut them into quarters. If they are small, cut them into halves. Brush cut sides with olive oil. Place in a 300°F. oven and bake till centers are soft and lightly browned.

While eggplants are baking, prepare the following stuffing: Sauté onions, green pepper, garlic, and chopped celery in olive oil till the vegetables are soft but not brown. Add chopped celery leaves and parsley. Stir till leaves are wilted, then add tomato purée and spices. Add sugar, then salt and pepper to taste. Cook a few more minutes. Set aside till needed.

When eggplants are tender, allow them to cool so that they may be handled. With a small knife, make an incision lengthwise, down the center of the cut side, being careful not to cut all the way through the eggplant. With your fingers, press soft pulp away from incision on two sides so that a good-sized hollow is formed. Using a spoon, fill the hollows with the prepared filling.

Arrange stuffed eggplants in a pan, close together. Sprinkle with additional olive oil if filling looks dry. Bake in a 350°F. oven 45 minutes, basting 2 or 3 times with the oil in the pan. Serve at room temperature.

The stuffed eggplants freeze very well. If time is a factor, this recipe may be speeded up. The eggplant is sliced ½-inch thick and, after it has been baked till tender, the slices are placed in a casserole, alternately with the stuffing, and baked as the individual servings are. This doesn't look as pretty, however.

MUSHROOMS STUFFED WITH TARAMA SALAD

1½ pounds medium-sized white mushrooms
1½ cups vinaigrette sauce
½ cup tarama (salted cod roe—available
by mail from Trinacria, 415 Third Ave., N.Y.)
or use ⅔ cup red caviar
Juice of 2 lemons   1 slice onion
2 slices white bread, crusts removed, soaked
in water till soft and then squeezed dry
1 to 1½ cups olive oil (approx.)
1 tablespoon chopped parsley
Pitted black olives

Remove stems from mushrooms so that they may be stuffed. Place the mushrooms in a bowl with *vinaigrette* sauce. Toss and allow to stand at room temperature for 6 hours or up to a week in the refrigerator.

Place *tarama* or red caviar in blender. Add lemon juice, slice of onion, and squeezed-out bread. Then add ¼ of the olive oil and turn blender on. Add more olive oil gradually, while blender is working. Use enough olive oil to make

a mixture which looks like a very thick, pink mayonnaise. Add chopped parsley.

After mushrooms have been kept in *vinaigrette*, remove them and drain well. Using a pastry bag, fill the hollow in each mushroom with *tarama* salad. Sprinkle with additional chopped parsley, and garnish with a small piece of black olive. Serve cold.

EGGPLANT WITH PESTO

Pesto, a deliciously pungent green sauce, will keep in your refrigerator for many weeks. It is a stand-by in much the same way that a good *vinaigrette* sauce is. *Pesto* may be used warm to dress noodles or spaghetti, or cold on vegetables, such as eggplant.

2 cups olive oil (approximately)
1 large eggplant, cubed
1 cup parsley   1 cup fresh basil
4 cloves garlic
½ cup pine nuts or walnuts

Heat 1 cup olive oil in a skillet till it smokes. Sauté eggplant cubes in olive oil, turning them frequently, till they are golden brown. Drain. Transfer eggplant to casserole. Bake in a 350°F. oven about 45 minutes, or till cubes are all very tender. Cool slightly.

While eggplant is baking, prepare *pesto:* Place remaining olive oil in blender. Add some of basil leaves and parsley. Turn blender on. As leaves are puréed, add more. Add garlic and nuts alternately. If necessary, use more oil so that all the leaves may be used. The end result will be a thick green sauce, of a consistency slightly thinner than mayonnaise. Keep in the refrigerator in a covered container.

When eggplant has cooled slightly, pour 1 cup of *pesto* on top and toss very gently so that eggplant cubes are not mashed or broken. Serve at room temperature.

STUFFED TOMATOES

4 cucumbers
2 tablespoons salt
1 cup sour cream   2 tablespoons sugar
½ cup mayonnaise
½ cup chopped dill
8 small tomatoes
2 hard-cooked eggs

Peel cucumbers. Cut in half, lengthwise. With a spoon, scoop out seeds, and slice thin. Place in bowl, sprinkle with salt, and put in refrigerator for at least 2 hours. After 2 hours, pour off water which has accumulated and press out any additional water, so that cucumbers are dry. Add sugar and stir. Combine sour cream and mayonnaise. Pour over cucumbers and toss lightly, adding half of dill. Place in refrigerator till needed.

Remove a circle from the stem ends of the tomatoes. Carefully scoop out pulp and turn upside down on paper towels so that any juice may drain. Stuff each tomato with cucumber mixture. Sprinkle remaining dill on top of each tomato and garnish with a slice of hard-cooked egg.

BALKAN VEGETABLE CASSEROLE

2 cups olive oil (approximately)
1 cup eggplant, unpeeled,
cut into 1-inch cubes
2 tomatoes, sliced ½-inch thick
1 cup zucchini, cut into ½-inch slices
1 cup green pepper, cut into 1-inch squares
1 large onion, sliced
and separated into rings
1 cup celery, cut into 1-inch slices
1 cup shredded cabbage
1 cup green beans, cut into 1-inch slices
1 cup carrots, cut into ¼-inch slices
2 potatoes, peeled and cut into ½-inch cubes
1 cup white seedless grapes
Salt and pepper
4 cloves garlic, sliced
2 cups chopped parsley
1 teaspoon oregano
1 teaspoon basil
½ teaspoon crumbled bay leaf
1 teaspoon sugar

Take your largest, most attractive baking dish. Pour a little olive oil into it. Make individual layers of all the vegetables and the grapes, seasoning each layer with salt, pepper, garlic, parsley, oregano, basil, bay leaf, and a little olive oil. Use the sugar on the layer of tomato. Make the top layer an assortment of all the vegetables and the grapes. Bake uncovered in a 350° F. oven for 1½ hours, or till oil is bubbling and vegetables are completely tender. Serve at room temperature. This will keep in the refrigerator for at least a week.

COOKED ITALIAN ANTIPASTO

⅔ cup olive oil
1 cup celery, cut into 1-inch pieces

1 cup fennel, diced
2 cups chopped onions
1 cup cauliflower pieces
1 cup small mushrooms
1 cup green pepper, cut into 1-inch pieces
4 cloves garlic, chopped
½ cup tomato purée
1 cup dry white wine
1 pound bay scallops
½ pound cleaned, shelled shrimp,
cut into halves
1 teaspoon dried basil
½ cup chopped parsley
Salt and pepper to taste
½ cup green olives
½ cup black olives
¼ cup capers   8 anchovies
4 hard-cooked eggs, quartered

In a heavy saucepan, heat oil till it almost smokes. Add celery, fennel, onions, cauliflower, mushrooms, green pepper, and garlic. Toss and continue to cook till vegetables begin to soften. Add tomato purée and white wine. When mixture begins to simmer, add scallops and shrimp. Simmer till seafood is cooked, no more than 8-10 minutes. Add basil, half of parsley, and salt and pepper to taste. Toss in olives and capers. Chill at least several hours. It will keep for 3 or 4 days.

Before serving, sprinkle with remaining parsley and garnish with anchovies and hard-cooked egg quarters.

GREEK STUFFED TOMATOES

8 small tomatoes
2 pounds fresh spinach
1 small onion, minced
1 clove garlic
¾ to 1 cup olive oil
½ cup pine nuts
1 teaspoon chopped capers
Salt and pepper
2 teaspoons m.s.g.
1 teaspoon sugar

Prepare tomatoes by removing a circle from the stem ends. Carefully scoop out pulp and turn tomatoes upside down on paper towels so that any juice may drain.

Wash spinach well. Place in a saucepan, cover and allow it to steam in its own liquid over a high heat. When it is wilted, drain well and squeeze out water. Chop fine.

Sauté minced onion and garlic in half cup of

olive oil. When vegetables are soft, add pine nuts and continue to sauté till pine nuts are lightly browned. Add to spinach along with capers and half of remaining olive oil. Toss so that ingredients are evenly distributed. Season with salt and pepper and 1 teaspoon m.s.g. Sprinkle the inside of each tomato with salt, pepper, a pinch of sugar, and m.s.g. Stuff tomatoes with spinach mixture, packing them firmly. Arrange tomatoes in baking pan. Spoon a little olive oil over each tomato. Bake in a 375° F. oven for 30 to 40 minutes, or till skins of tomatoes are wrinkled. Baste once or twice with pan juices and oil. Serve cold.

SPINACH, ROMAN STYLE

2 pounds fresh spinach
⅔ cup olive oil
8 scallions, sliced
4 cloves garlic, sliced
Salt and freshly ground pepper
Lemon wedges

Wash and trim spinach. Drain and wrap in towels so as much moisture as possible can be absorbed.

In a large, heavy skillet, heat olive oil till it is smoking. Toss in spinach. Immediately mix with two wooden spoons so that the wilted part is brought to the surface and the uncooked part comes in contact with the hot oil. As soon as all the spinach is wilted, remove from pan. If oil seems diluted with water, turn heat up high and let water cook away. Lower heat. Add sliced scallions and garlic. Sauté till soft. Pour over spinach. Season with salt and pepper and toss lightly. Serve at room temperature, with lemon wedges. Sometimes, hard-cooked egg slices are used as a garnish, reminiscent of America's "wilted" lettuce.

PEPPERS MEDITERRANEAN

8 frying peppers
2 medium-size tomatoes, cut into
halves and sliced thin
2 cloves garlic, sliced
2 medium-size onions, sliced thin
8 anchovies   M.s.g.
1 teaspoon oregano
Salt and pepper
1 cup olive oil (approximately)
½ cup chopped parsley

Cut frying peppers in half lengthwise. Remove stem and seeds. Place side by side, hollow sides up, on a flat baking sheet. Into each pepper place

Fresh caviar, the classic hors d'oeuvre, is traditionally served on toast or blinis, garnished with egg white, egg yolk, onion, lemon, and accompanied by champagne or vodka.

a slice of tomato, several slices of garlic, a slice of onion, and on top of all half a strip of anchovy. Sprinkle with m.s.g., oregano, pepper, and very lightly with salt. Spoon a little olive oil on top. Bake in a 400° F. oven for 30 to 40 minutes, or till peppers look wrinkled and other vegetables are lightly browned and soft. Garnish with parsley. Let cool to room temperature before serving.

World of Butter and Fat

*Thanks to variety in foodstuffs,
the more northerly lands have
contributed great inventiveness*

One of the most useful things
to be learned from the many European
cuisines is the art of blending
agreeably the many parts of a menu.

The Nature of European Cooking

*Why there are really two Europes,
and what's haute about haute cuisine*

Since even the most primitive peoples cooked their food, we must make it clear what we mean by a cuisine. It is a manner or system of cookery developed as a product of a particular civilization. Indeed, only a great civilization can produce a great cuisine. Said more pointedly, only a people with a well-developed culture ever seem to create food practices that other people admire. Also, before a great cuisine can flourish, a high percentage of the people must share in the way of life that such culture produces.

To be great a cuisine must have versatility—it must include many methods of preparation and many kinds of foodstuffs of high intrinsic quality. Great foodstuffs tend to beget great cookery. The *haute* (or high) *cuisine* is the greatest of the great. It is a system of cookery so universally admired for soundness, skill, and sophistication as to become a world standard.

In our country it is what we usually mean by "Continental" cuisine, because the *haute cuisine* best known to us and to the English on their island was developed on the continent of Europe, specifically at the courts of the Kings of France. Not all European cooking—not all French cook-

ing, for that matter—may be labeled *haute cuisine*. And the elements which comprise this modern standard of elegance developed not alone in France but in all parts of Europe out of influences originating all over the world.

The history of food and cookery in Europe presents an unbelievable crazy-quilt of migrating ideas. The maps of trade routes on pages 8-9 show the source, direction, and antiquity of some of the influences. Besides trading, wars and religious crusades surged back and forth, distributing seeds, spices, animals, fowls—and civilized tastes. The importation of spices from the East was "big business" as early as 500 A.D.. Viking, Moslem, and Magyar conquerors penetrated the continent well before the year 1000. Europeans such as Marco Polo were looking for an overland route to the sources of Asiatic foodstuffs as early as the 13th century. The same motivation sent those early explorers, the Portuguese and the Spanish, on maritime adventures which not only opened sea routes around Africa to the Orient but discovered the New World. Dozens of new foods were introduced and amalgamated into Continental cookery over the centuries. So if one wants to find any inner system or reason to European cuisines, certainly one has to look beyond national or political boundaries.

Climate and Cooking

One of the few valid criteria is climate. Nearly all foods are transportable to some extent. Those that are compact and will keep, such as spices, became an early staple of trade. Others moved with migrating peoples in the form of seeds or seedlings or a mated pair of animals. But in an unfavorable climate they would not flourish after transplanting. This circumstance divided culinary Europe into the "two Europes" of our classification scheme.

As mentioned earlier, the Mediterranean lands have mild, rainy winters and long, dry, hot summers. Such a climate is inhospitable to animal husbandry, that is, breeding herds on the scale required to make meat products a staple food of the people rather than a delicacy. But it is ideal for fig and olive trees and grapes, while the fish of the sea provide an alternative source of proteins.

North of this zone the climate changes, becoming better for the raising of meat animals and fowl. Even countries with difficult terrain and long, hard winters (like Switzerland) were able to base their cuisines largely on their cows, pigs, and chickens. The difference determined the kind of fat used in cooking; and this is crucial to the character of a cuisine.

Fats and oils are essential to nutrition, the amount required depending upon temperature and physical activity. They differ in flavor, but all are excellent bearers of flavor. They may be compared to a negative or positive electric charge in their effect upon cookery results.

Mediterranean Europe bases its cuisine upon olive oil, its most readily available source of palatable and digestible fats. Northern Europe, richer in animal husbandry, utilizes butter, cream, lard, goose and chicken fats, etc. Thanks to this diversity, the lands north of the Mediterranean climate have probably contributed the most to the cuisines of the western world, both in foodstuffs and inventiveness of cookery methods.

"French" but not French

The French in particular have been given the credit for developing the *haute cuisine* that is not olive-oil oriented. Certainly France had great and original chefs. But long before her culinary flowering in the 18th century, much development had already occurred in other lands. The great Carême did not try to conceal that he was a student of the writings of Athenaeus (*circa* 228 A.D.) and Apicius (30 B.C. to 40 A.D.), who documented the food of the Roman Empire.

My own feeling is that the key contribution of the French to gastronomy was in codifying and system-making. They were extremely alert, aware, sensitive to the intrinsic nature of any foodstuff and what happened to it in the cooking process. They could take the random findings of others, from everywhere, and fit them into an orderly system of cookery aiming at perfection. Certainly Escoffier's real contribution in his famous *"Le Guide Culinaire"* (published in 1902) is the clarity with which he arranged and explained all procedures.

Nevertheless, French eminence in cookery spread in all directions. Monarchs of nations as far away as Russia imported French chefs, as did the *grande luxe* hotels. So today the French strain pervades all of the butter-and-fat cuisines of Europe, no matter which country you are talking about. Differences show up mainly in the available foodstuffs, or in the richer, heavier diet needs of more northerly peoples.

There is much misunderstanding about the true nature of French cooking. When Americans patronize the famous *haute cuisine* restaurants of Paris, Saulieu, or Vienne, they get the erroneous idea that all Frenchmen dine in such superelegance every day. In actual fact the main French cuisine is bourgeois—meaning simple, uncomplicated but perfect in all its parts and preparation.

The utmost care and attention is given to procuring food. Menus change with the season, favoring foods that are in season over those that are not. The French have an acute sense of the nature of the material, which is always the mark of an artist. It was Frank Lloyd Wright who said, of architecture, "Do not violate the nature of the material." By following this precept in cookery, the French can make the simplest meal pure perfection, because they have rejected foods not at their prime *and* have handled the chosen foods with delicacy and skill.

All this takes a seeing eye, backed by knowledge and experience which the majority of the French population seems to share. Their critical and demanding shopping practices, the basis of their culinary art, help to maintain high standards in

Owning the classic tools of the world's cooking crafts is a good beginning for being a cosmopolitan cook. Fortunately they cost little: graters, whisks, sieves, food mills, steamers, peelers, slicers, crocks for terrines, molds for aspics.

French food markets and restaurants.

Having said this, one must add that historically the term "French cooking" for superior cuisine is a misnomer. The great chefs managed to incorporate the cookery of many cultures and to do it so successfully that only an anthropologist could trace the origins of their diversified practices. Today they are being challenged from other quarters. French cooking has become so rigid and formalized that the creativity which it once had seems almost to have died out.

Moving eastward from France into central Europe we find the unmistakable mark of the kettle cooking of the early nomads. (Hungarian goulash —everything in one pot—is an example of kettle cooking.) Foods that could be preserved became dominant: bacon, sauerkraut, sausage, goose fat, onions. Later these countries developed rigid class systems, so separate cuisines coexisted for the aristocrat, the gentry, the middle class, and the peasant. French *haute cuisine* prevailed in the upper levels of society, while other classes might be quite unfamiliar with it.

Other influences on central Europe included dough and potato dishes from the north. Rice, peas, cornmeal, and cheese stamp north Italian style or middle Europe. Cabbage, sour cream, fish roe, beet and sour soups show the influence of Russia. Stuffed cabbage recalls the stuffed vine leaves of Greece and Turkey.

The Balkan countries, on the land crossroads of Europe and Asia, were exposed to the cookery methods of many civilizations. Out of this welter emerged a highly improved and refined cuisine on which the Turkish culinary art exerted a profound influence, equal certainly to that of the French. (For definitive cookbooks on this varied Central European area, see "Viennese Cooking" by O. and A. Hess, Crown Publishers, Inc., and "Good Food from Hungary" by Kate Barlay, published by Frederick Muller, Ltd., London.)

So keep in mind that the French-named *haute cuisine* of Europe is really the peak of an edifice, built on a foundation of older civilizations and the cementing together of countless regional and provincial cookeries, fed by countless migrations and diffusions.

The following chapters discuss some of the methods that have reached a high degree of perfection in the World of Butter and Fat.

Butter & Fat/Two Europes 67

Striped bass Bonne Femme benefits by the extra touch of glazing. It is placed under the broiler until sauce bubbles.

The Misunderstood Classic Sauces

*They heighten and intensify, not mask
the taste of the food sauced*

The classic French sauces are not altogether understood by American cooks. We tend to think that a sauce changes the taste of the food it is put upon and that sauces are hard to make.

A French sauce in the classic tradition does not change the taste of food *because it is almost always based upon the same food with which it is to be used.* The heart of any sauce is the stock, which is made by boiling and reducing the meat or fish to a concentrated essence. This essence is then used as the liquid in combination with a thickening agent and other auxiliary or subordinated flavors such as mushrooms, tomatoes, herbs, shallots, or wine.

It is customary to use fish stock in fish sauces, chicken (or other fowl) stock for poultry sauces, veal or beef stock for all meat sauces. Assuming that you would rate the taste value of the main ingredient at 100 per cent, adding a sauce made out of the essence of that ingredient would raise

In filet of sole Dugléré the fish is rolled into turbans, sauced with tomato pulp, white wine, fish *velouté*, and cream.

the taste value to somewhere between 125 and 130 per cent.

In short, you should think of the classic French sauces as a way to *heighten* the taste of fish, fowl, or meat—to make them more themselves than they would be plain. But sauces also may bring out flavor nuances and overtones, thanks to the auxiliary flavors which add interest but do not dominate. And they are not difficult to make.

The explanations that follow come from Pierre Franey, formerly executive chef at New York's famous French restaurant, Le Pavillon.

How to Make the Classic Fish Sauces

Of the sauces in the entire repertoire of French cooking there are none more delicate than those for fish. There is a saying that it is *la sauce que fait le poisson.* This is not entirely true, of course,

since no sauce can disguise a fish lacking in freshness.

The culinary hobbyist should learn one thing first. The technique for making all these sauces is the same. A single sauce base, known as a fish *velouté,* serves for many sauces: *dieppoise, véronique, champagne, d'Antin, bonne femme, dugléré.* Any one of these may be used for any white-fleshed fish, whether it's halibut, pompano, sole, flounder, sea bass, or striped bass. Here then is the procedure for making fish sauces.

First we prepare a simple fish stock or, as it is known in French, a *fumet de poisson.* This is one of the easiest to make, since it only requires simmering fish bones and trimmings with vegetables and seasonings for one-half hour. It can be made with the heads (gills removed) and tails of the fish as well. This will make the sauce more gelatinous which is all to the good, for the gelatin adds body to it.

This stock is then used to create the *velouté,* a thick base that, as the name implies, is as smooth as velvet. The *velouté* can be frozen and kept for a year. Or it can be stored in mason jars and kept in the refrigerator for at least a month. The secret of a *velouté* is in the long cooking—about one hour—which does away with the raw taste of the flour. Any cook who has ever made a successful white sauce is capable of making a fish *velouté*, for it is nothing more than a simple white sauce made with fish stock rather than milk or another liquid.

The use of the *velouté* comes after the fish is cooked. A small quantity is added to the cooking liquid and thickens it to perfection. It is creamy and smooth. And the flavor is *vraiment exquise*. It can honestly be said that with a supply of *velouté* on hand a finished fish dish of a superb quality can be turned out by any home cook in half an hour.

There is one more trick of the trade used by French chefs. It is not essential, although commonly employed. That is glazing the fish before serving. To do this, a little beaten egg yolk or whipped cream is stirred into the sauce before pouring it over the fish. Then the sauce-covered fish is placed under the broiler for a brief moment until a golden brown glaze forms. It looks much more elegant and appetizing than the unglazed version.

In the recipes, glaze is included for striped bass *bonne femme*. You may add a glaze to *sole véronique* if you wish. However, filet of sole *dieppoise* should not be glazed.

Dry white wine employed in the fish recipes could be any of the excellent wines from Europe, or it can be a good quality domestic wine from California or New York.

FISH STOCK

(Fumet de poisson)

3 pounds fish bones
2 tablespoons butter
4 quarts water
1 teaspoon thyme
3 bay leaves
3 cloves garlic (unpeeled)
2 onions, coarsely chopped
10 peppercorns
3 carrots, coarsely chopped
1 bunch leeks (green part), tied
1 bunch celery (top part), tied
2 teaspoons salt

Wash fish bones in several changes of water. Put

butter into a large kettle and when melted over medium heat add fish bones and water. Cook, stirring, about 5 minutes. Add remaining ingredients, bring to a boil. Simmer 30 minutes and strain. This stock may be frozen and defrosted as needed. Makes about 3 quarts.

FISH VELOUTE

¾ cups butter
1½ cups flour
5 cups fish stock

In a large saucepan melt ¾ cup of butter and stir in slowly 1½ cups of flour. Stir over moderate heat with a wire whisk until mixture is blended and smooth. Add 5 cups of hot fish stock, stirring rapidly with wire whisk. When sauce is thick and smooth, cook about 1 hour, stirring occasionally. When finished, sauce should be as smooth as velvet. Makes 5 cups.

The following recipes all serve 6.

FILET OF SOLE DIEPPOISE

6 filets of sole
6 tablespoons sweet butter   Salt
Freshly ground black pepper
4 tablespoons shallots or onions, finely chopped
1 cup dry white wine
12 raw oysters with their liquor
Fish stock
12 raw shrimp, peeled and de-veined
1 cup fish velouté   1 cup heavy cream
1 tablespoon chives, finely chopped

Assemble all ingredients. Preheat the oven to 400°F.

Divide filets of sole lengthwise down the center line. Trim away and discard the tiny bone structure. Lightly score the skin side of each filet diagonally. Sprinkle sole with salt and pepper. Roll each filet like a jelly roll with the scored portion inside the roll. Secure the rolls or "turbans" with toothpicks.

Rub the bottom of a baking pan with 4 tablespoons of sweet butter and sprinkle lightly with salt and pepper. Scatter shallots over the bottom of pan. Arrange the turbans of sole in the pan and sprinkle with salt and pepper.

Pour wine over the fish. Drain oysters, reserving the liquor. Combine the oyster liquor with enough fish stock to make 1 cup and pour it over the fish. Scatter the oysters and raw shrimp over the fish. Cover the pan closely with aluminum foil and bring to a boil on top of the stove. Place the fish in the oven and bake for 20 minutes.

Remove from the oven and turn off heat. Transfer the fish to a warm serving platter or baking dish and cover with aluminum foil. Return it to the oven to keep warm.

Cook liquid from the baking pan over high heat until it is reduced by about one-third. It should be thickened slightly because of the reduction. Add fish *velouté* and heavy cream. Stir well with a wire whisk until smooth. Cook 5 minutes and remove the sauce from the heat. Add 2 tablespoons of cold butter, stir quickly into sauce.

Spoon the hot sauce over the fish. Sprinkle with chives. Serve piping hot.

FILET OF SOLE VERONIQUE

6 small filets of sole
6 tablespoons sweet butter   Salt
Freshly ground black pepper
4 tablespoons shallots or onions, finely chopped
¾ cup dry white wine
1 small can of white seedless grapes
1 cup fish velouté
½ cup fish stock
1 cup heavy cream
1 teaspoon lemon juice

Assemble all ingredients. Preheat the oven to 400°F.

Divide filets lengthwise down the center line. Trim away and discard the tiny bone structure. Rub the bottom of a baking pan with 4 tablespoons sweet butter and sprinkle lightly with salt and pepper. Scatter shallots over the bottom of pan. Arrange the filets of sole, each folded in half, in the pan. Sprinkle the fish lightly with salt and pepper.

Pour wine, ¼ cup of the liquid from a small can of white seedless grapes, and the fish stock over the fish. Sprinkle with drained grapes. Cover the pan closely with aluminum foil and bring to a boil on top of the stove. Place in the oven and bake 15 minutes.

Remove the fish from the oven and proceed as with *dieppoise* recipe above.

STRIPED BASS BONNE FEMME

1 5-pound striped bass, cleaned and boned
6 tablespoons sweet butter
Freshly ground black pepper   Salt
4 tablespoons shallots or onions, finely chopped
4 cups thinly sliced mushrooms
1 cup dry white wine   2 egg yolks
1 cup fish stock   3 cups velouté
2 cups heavy cream
3 tablespoons whipped cream
2 tablespoons chives, finely chopped
4 tablespoons parsley, finely chopped

Have butcher bone bass. Or this may be done in the home. Leave head and tail intact and trim off fins. Bone the fish by running a knife along its back down both sides of bone structure. Make incisions from behind the head almost to the tail. Use scissors to cut out bone. Remove the gill structure and carefully trim off any small bones inside of fish. Assemble all ingredients. Preheat the oven to 400°F.

Rub the bottom of a baking pan with 4 tablespoons of sweet butter and sprinkle lightly with salt and pepper. Scatter shallots over the bottom of the pan. Arrange the bass in the pan, leaving the boned sides exposed and the skin side down. Scatter mushrooms over and around the fish. Sprinkle with salt and pepper and 2 tablespoons of parsley. Pour wine and fish stock over the fish.

Cover the pan closely with aluminum foil and bring to a boil on top of the stove. Place the fish in the oven and bake 25 minutes. Remove from the oven and proceed with sauce as in recipes above. Before serving, however, beat egg yolks with 1 tablespoon of whipped cream. Fold this mixture and 2 more tablespoons of whipped cream into sauce. Sprinkle fish with chives and remaining parsley. Spoon the hot sauce over the fish.

Place the fish under the broiler until the sauce bubbles slightly and becomes lightly glazed. The fish should be placed about 2½ inches below the broiler flame. Serve piping hot. Serves 6.

Sauces for Chicken

Now let us consider the classic (and glorious) sauces for chicken. They start with two easily-made bases. Both can be stored in quantity for long periods in the refrigerator or freezer. Once a base is made, the finishing of the sauce itself is much easier than making a pie.

The usual base is a chicken *velouté*, an easily prepared cream sauce made with chicken stock.

The other foundation is a brown chicken base and, although it requires a longer list of ingredients, such as veal bones, chicken bones, vegetables, and seasonings, it can be made as easily as an old-fashioned vegetable soup. The chief requirement is a proper kettle, preferably of heavy metal with about six quarts capacity.

These bases serve two purposes: They add flavor to the finished sauces because they are concentrates of chicken flavors, and, equally important, they add texture and body.

The principles are easy to grasp. Notice that the special flavor of each sauce depends on just one or two delicate additions. The taste of the chicken is never covered up. It is always enhanced in some particular way. Here is how to make the stock and, out of it, the *velouté*.

BASIC CHICKEN STOCK

4 pounds chicken parts (wings or necks)
3 bay leaves
1 tablespoon thyme
3 cloves garlic
2 tablespoons crushed peppercorns
2 stalks celery, trimmed
2 leeks, trimmed, split down center and washed well
3 carrots, coarsely chopped
1 onion, peeled, stuck with 2 cloves
1 cup whole parsley leaves
4 quarts water
1½ tablespoons salt

Combine all ingredients in a large kettle. Bring to a boil and simmer over gentle heat for 1 hour. Do not cover. Skim the surface with a large spoon to remove foam as it rises to the top. Strain the stock through a fine mesh sieve lined with cheesecloth. This stock may be frozen in several containers and used as necessary. Or it may be stored in the refrigerator for a week or longer.

CHICKEN VELOUTE

¾ cup sweet butter (1½ sticks)
1½ cups flour
4 cups chicken stock

A chicken *velouté* is similar to a simple white sauce, but with long cooking to eliminate the raw taste of the flour. The *velouté* gives body and flavor to other sauces. While a wire whisk is not essential in making sauces, it is the best of utensils to prevent lumps. Like the other sauces in this chapter the *velouté* may be frozen and defrosted as needed and it will keep well in the refrigerator for several weeks.

The first step in making a *velouté* of chicken is to melt sweet butter in a large, open saucepan. Add 1½ cups of flour and stir, preferably with a wire whisk, until well blended. Add 1 quart of hot chicken stock and stir occasionally until the sauce is thick and smooth. Cook over medium heat for 1 hour.

BROWN CHICKEN BASE

3 pounds veal bones
2 pounds chicken bones or parts such as necks or wings
4 carrots, chopped
3 cloves garlic
4 cups coarsely chopped onions
1 tablespoon crushed peppercorns
3 bay leaves
1 tablespoon thyme
2 cups leeks, split down center, well washed, cut into 1-inch lengths
1¾ cups coarsely chopped celery tops
1½ cups quartered fresh mushrooms
9 quarts water
1 10½-ounce can tomato purée

Preheat oven to 475° F. Arrange veal bones and chicken on a large pan. Add seasonings and vegetables. Bake uncovered 45 minutes. Reduce heat if necessary to prevent burning. Transfer bones to a large kettle, add 1 quart water to pan. Cook over medium heat, stirring to dissolve any brown particles on bottom and sides of pan. Add liquid to bones in kettle along with remaining water and tomato purée. Cook over medium heat for 5 hours, stirring occasionally. Cool. Spoon into glass jars and seal tightly. The sauce will keep for several weeks in the refrigerator, or it may be frozen and defrosted as necessary.

POULET A L'ESTRAGON

1 3-pound chicken   Salt
Freshly ground black pepper
Fresh or dried tarragon (see below)
5 tablespoons sweet butter or chicken fat
Peanut oil
1 carrot, coarsely chopped
1 small onion, coarsely chopped
1 small stalk of celery, coarsely chopped
⅓ cup dry white wine
½ cup chicken velouté
½ cup heavy cream

Assemble ingredients. Preheat oven to 450° F. Sprinkle inside of chicken with salt and pepper and add 2 sprigs of fresh tarragon or 1 teaspoon of dried tarragon. Truss. Sprinkle chicken with salt and pepper, place it on its side in a small

In Poulet Washington, roast chicken is lifted to gourmet heights by addition of *velouté* sauce flavored with bourbon.

Here that hearty essence, brown chicken base, is combined with dry white wine to glorify the fowl in Poulet Beau Sejour

roasting pan and place around it the vegetables and 1 sprig of fresh or ½ teaspoon of dried tarragon. Roast the chicken 15 minutes and turn it on the other side. (Baste chicken as it roasts and if it starts to get too brown during roasting process reduce heat to 350° F. and cover lightly with aluminum foil.) Roast 15 minutes longer and turn breast side up. Roast 15 minutes longer. Transfer to a warm serving platter and keep warm. Place pan over high heat and add the wine. Deglaze by stirring to dissolve brown particles on bottom and along sides of pan. Cook until wine is almost totally reduced and add the *velouté* and cream. Cook 1 minute and strain into a sauce pan. Remove sauce from heat and stir in 1 teaspoon of freshly chopped tarragon or ½ teaspoon of dried. Stir in 2 tablespoons of cold butter and pour the sauce over the chicken. Serve immediately; 2 to 4 servings.

POULET WASHINGTON

2 3-pound chickens, trussed
Salt and black pepper
4 sprigs parsley
1 medium-size onion, and 1 small stalk of celery,
and 2 carrots, all coarsely chopped
3 cloves garlic, unpeeled
3 bay leaves   1 teaspoon thyme
7 tablespoons sweet butter or chicken fat
Peanut oil
¾ cup bourbon whiskey
1 cup chicken velouté
2 cups heavy cream
½ cup drained, whole kernel corn

Preheat oven to 450° F. Salt and pepper chickens. Scatter seasoning in baking pan, add chickens, side down. Dot with 5 tablespoons butter. Sprinkle lightly with oil. Roast 15 minutes, turn, roast 15 minutes more. Turn breast up and roast final 15 minutes. Baste. Transfer chickens to serving platter. Add ½ cup bourbon to roasting pan, and deglaze with bourbon. Stir to dissolve brown particles. Strain into saucepan. Add *velouté* and cream, stir till smooth. Bring to boil. Add corn. Season to taste. Remove from heat, stir in remaining butter and bourbon. Pour a little over chickens, serve remainder in a sauce boat. Serves 4 to 6.

POULET BEAU SEJOUR

1 3-pound broiler, cut up
5 tablespoons sweet butter

Freshly ground black pepper
Salt
4 cloves garlic, peeled
3 bay leaves
1 teaspoon thyme
½ cup dry white wine
1½ cups brown chicken base
1 teaspoon chopped fresh parsley

Assemble ingredients. Sprinkle chicken with salt and pepper. Brown in casserole or skillet on all sides in 3 tablespoons of butter. Add garlic, bay leaves and thyme. Cover and cook 10 minutes, turning occasionally. Transfer to hot serving platter. Add ½ cup dry white wine to cooking dish, and stir in all the dark particles around bottom and sides. Cover and cook over high heat for 5 minutes. Add brown chicken base and continue cooking over high heat, stirring with a wire whisk until blended and smooth. Remove the sauce from heat and stir in 2 tablespoons cold butter. This tends to thicken the sauce slightly. Pour the sauce over the chicken and garnish with chopped parsley. Serves 2 to 4.

POULET BONNE FEMME

¼ pound lean salt pork, cut into ¼-inch cubes
Water to cover
1 tablespoon sweet butter
8 small new potatoes, peeled
1 cup small mushrooms, preferably fresh
1 3-pound spring chicken
Salt   Freshly ground black pepper
3 tablespoons brown chicken base
Freshly chopped parsley

Preheat oven to 450°F. Place the salt pork in a small sauce pan and barely cover with water. Bring to a boil and simmer 3 minutes. Drain. Melt butter in a skillet and add salt pork. Cook pork bits until brown and, using a slotted spoon, transfer pork to a covered baking dish. (Preferably an oval cocotte.) Sprinkle the whole chicken with salt and pepper. Brown in the fat remaining in the skillet and transfer it to the baking dish, one side down. Add potatoes and mushrooms and cover. Bake 15 minutes on one side, turn, bake 15 minutes more, turn breast side up, and bake a final 15 minutes. Baste chicken occasionally. Remove it and potatoes to a warm serving platter and add brown chicken base to the pan. Pour a little of the sauce over the chicken. Sprinkle with chopped parsley. Serve the remaining sauce in a sauceboat.

POULET SAUTE
A LA BOURGUIGNONNE

¼ pound salt pork, cut into ¼-inch cubes
Water to cover
1½ tablespoons sweet butter
10 small onions, peeled
1 cup small whole or quartered mushrooms
1 3-pound chicken, cut into parts
Salt   Freshly ground black pepper
1 small clove garlic, peeled and crushed
½ cup dry red wine
½ cup brown chicken base
½ tablespoon flour

Assemble ingredients. Preheat oven to 350°F. Place salt pork in a sauce pan and barely cover with water. Bring to a boil and simmer 3 minutes. Drain. Melt 1 tablespoon of the butter in a large skillet and add salt pork, onions, and mushrooms. Cook, stirring frequently, until onions are golden brown. Using a slotted spoon, transfer the solid ingredients to an absorbent towel to drain. Sprinkle chicken with salt and pepper and brown it in the fat remaining in the skillet.

Add salt pork, onions, and mushrooms to the chicken and cover closely. Bake 30 minutes. Remove chicken parts to a warm serving platter and arrange vegetables around it. Pour off the fat remaining in the skillet and add the garlic, wine, and brown chicken base. Cook over a brisk flame until the liquid is reduced by half. Prepare a *beurre manié* by blending the remaining butter with flour. Add the *beurre manié* to the skillet, stirring with a wire whisk. Pour sauce over chicken and serve with buttered toast croutons rubbed with garlic. Serves 2 to 4.

SUPREMES DE VOLAILLE POLIGNAC

3 whole chicken breasts, halved
4 tablespoons sweet butter   Salt
Freshly ground black pepper
1 cup mushrooms, preferably fresh,
cut into thin matchlike strips (julienne)
1 black truffle similarly cut
⅔ cup chicken velouté
1 cup heavy cream

Have the 6 half chicken breasts skinned and boned but leave the main wing bone attached. Melt 2 tablespoons of the butter in a skillet and add chicken breasts. Cook over gentle heat about 3 minutes. Turn chicken breasts occasionally in the butter. Do not brown. Cover and cook 15 minutes. Uncover and sprinkle with salt and pepper. Add mushrooms and half the truffles. Cover and cook 15 minutes longer or until breasts are done. Transfer chicken to a warm serving platter and keep warm. Add the *velouté* and cream to the skillet and stir with a wire whisk until blended and smooth. Cook sauce on medium heat until it is reduced by about one-third. Remove sauce from heat and stir in 2 tablespoons of cold butter. Arrange chicken breasts in a circle and pour sauce over breasts. Sprinkle with remaining truffles and serve hot. Serves 6.

Work Magic With Brown Sauce

The most versatile sauces in classic cuisine are those made with a brown sauce derived from browned veal bones. A brown sauce is a veritable chameleon among sauces. Suitable in itself to complement any dish, it also may be altered to accommodate any cut of meat or poultry. Add a few mushrooms, and it glorifies game. Vary it with orange rind, and a simple roast duck can be a *tour de force*. Spark it with mustard, and veal kidneys can be made regal.

This method for making a genuine brown sauce is like that used in classic French cuisine. There are no secrets withheld, no compromises, and not one single ingredient is omitted. Not one condescending shortcut is utilized. This is the sauce which is the foundation for literally hundreds of sauces that you meet in *grand-luxe* restaurants.

The recipe below will provide enough basic brown sauce for 10 to 12 sauce recipes, each serving 6. I suggest the following applications (with recipes): *Sauce chasseur*, made with mushrooms and spices, used with game dishes; *sauce Robert* made with white wine for grilled pork or veal; *sauce charcutière* for grilled pork; *sauce Bercy* with white wine and herbs for broiled calves' liver, grilled dishes, or boiled tongue; an orange sauce for roast duck; mustard sauce for veal kidneys; *sauce marchand de vin* for roast meat dishes; truffle sauce for grilled beef, veal or chicken; and sauces made with madeira and port wines. The latter are for roasted and sautéed meat dishes.

All these sauces *and* their brown sauce base can be frozen and defrosted as necessary. Or you can store them tightly sealed in the refrigerator.

In pork chops Charcutière another variation of brown sauce gains piquancy from addition of white wine, mustard, gherkins.

BASIC BROWN SAUCE

5 pounds veal bones, cracked
1 large onion, quartered
2 stalks celery leaves,
coarsely chopped
5 small carrots,
peeled and quartered
½ teaspoon thyme
3 bay leaves
1 teaspoon crushed peppercorns
3 cloves garlic, unpeeled
1 tablespoon salt
½ cup flour
12 cups water
1 small can (about 1¼ cups) tomato purée
½ cup chopped leeks (green part)
3 sprigs parsley

1. Combine bones, onion, celery, carrots, thyme, bay leaves, peppercorns, garlic, and salt in open roasting pan. Bake 45 minutes in pre-heated 475°F. oven. Reduce heat if necessary to keep bones from burning. Add no liquid.
2. Sprinkle bones with flour. Using a two-pronged fork, stir bones around to distribute flour evenly. Bake 15 minutes or longer.

3. Transfer the ingredients to a large kettle.
4. Add 2 cups of water to roasting pan. Cook over moderate heat, stirring to dissolve brown particles that cling to bottom and sides of pan.
5. Pour liquid from roasting pan into kettle, add contents of a small can of tomato purée and the remaining 10 cups of water.
6. Add leeks and parsley. Bring to a rapid boil. Then simmer 2 hours. Add more liquid if necessary; skim often to remove fat and foam as they rise. Strain. Stock may be frozen, defrosted as wanted. Or it may be stored, tightly sealed, for several weeks in refrigerator. Yield: 2 quarts.

SAUCE MARCHAND DE VIN

This sauce may be made for roasted or grilled beef or game dishes using pan drippings, instead of separately in a saucepan. If you use drippings, the quantity of wine is reduced slightly.

⅓ cup finely chopped shallots
4 tablespoons cold butter
¾ cup plus 2 tablespoons dry red wine
1½ cups brown sauce

Cook the shallots in 2 tablespoons butter until they are golden brown. Add ¾ cup wine and cook until it is reduced by half. Add brown sauce and cook over high heat 8 to 10 minutes, stirring occasionally. Strain through a sieve and bring to a boil. Turn off heat and stir in 2 tablespoons cold butter. Add 2 tablespoons wine and serve hot. Yield: about 2 cups sauce.

ROAST BEEF MARCHAND DE VIN

Peanut oil
1 2-pound filet of beef, well trimmed of fat
Salt and pepper to taste
⅓ cup finely chopped shallots
1½ cups dry red wine   1½ cups brown sauce
4 tablespoons cold butter

Heat peanut oil to a depth of ⅛ inch in a large skillet with a heat-proof handle. Quickly sear the meat on all sides and sprinkle with salt and freshly ground black pepper.

Transfer skillet to a pre-heated 450°F. oven and bake 20 to 35 minutes, depending on doneness desired, basting meat occasionally as it cooks. Transfer meat to serving platter to keep it warm. Pour off and discard most of the cooking fat from the skillet.

Add shallots to the skillet. Cook and stir until they are golden brown. Add wine and cook until it is reduced to one-third of the original volume. Add the brown sauce and any juices that might have run out of the roast. Cook over high heat 8 to 10 minutes, stirring occasionally. Strain sauce into saucepan, scraping solids through the sieve with the bottom of a spoon. Bring to a boil, then turn off heat. Add butter which makes sauce smoother and thickens it slightly. Season to taste. Pour some sauce over beef, serving remainder in sauce-boat. Garnish platter. Serve immediately. Serves 4 to 6.

SAUCE ROBERT

⅓ cup finely chopped shallots
and onions combined
4 tablespoons cold butter
¾ cup dry white wine
1½ cups brown sauce
1 tablespoon prepared mustard, preferably Dijon

Cook shallots and onions in 2 tablespoons butter until golden brown. Add wine and cook until almost totally reduced. Add brown sauce and cook about 12 minutes. Turn off heat and stir in remaining cold butter. Add mustard and stir, but do not cook after mustard is added. Serve hot

with grilled pork and veal dishes. Yield: About 2 cups sauce.

SAUCE CHARCUTIERE

2 cups sauce Robert
3 small sour gherkins, julienne

Prepare sauce and add julienne gherkins along with mustard. Serve with grilled pork dishes.

PORK CHOPS CHARCUTIERE

6 lean pork chops
Salt and pepper   Peanut oil
⅓ cup finely chopped shallots
and onions combined
¾ cup dry white wine
1½ cups brown sauce
2 tablespoons cold butter
1 tablespoon Dijon mustard
3 small sour gherkins, julienne

Neatly trim, or have trimmed, 6 lean pork chops. Sprinkle them on all sides with salt and pepper. Lightly cover bottom of a skillet with peanut oil. Brown chops on all sides in the hot oil. Cook chops until done, about 20 minutes, depending on the size. Transfer to a warming dish.

Add shallots and onions to the skillet. Cook and stir for 2 minutes. Rinse the skillet by adding wine and stirring to dissolve brown particles in the skillet. Cook until the wine is almost totally reduced. Add brown sauce and cook about 12 minutes. Pour the sauce into a saucepan and bring to a boil. Turn off the heat and add the cold butter. Add mustard and stir. Sauce should not cook after this. Add gherkins, cut into thin, matchlike strips. Spoon a little sauce over chops. Serve remainder in sauceboat. Garnish platter with gherkins. Serves 6.

SAUCE CHASSEUR

½ cup chopped mushrooms
5 tablespoons cold butter
1 tablespoon finely chopped shallots
¾ cup dry white wine
½ cup tomato sauce
½ cup chopped, peeled and seeded tomato
¾ cup brown sauce
½ teaspoon each chopped fresh tarragon
and chervil (or half the amounts dried)

In a saucepan cook mushrooms in 2 tablespoons butter. When they start to wilt, add shallots. Cook, stirring occasionally, about 5 minutes or

Classic brown sauce laced with red wine makes a rich sauce for roast beef Marchand de Vin. Same sauce is used with game.

until the mushroom liquid nearly evaporates. Add wine and cook until reduced by half. Add tomato sauce, tomato, and brown sauce. Simmer 10 minutes and remove from heat. Stir in 3 tablespoons cold butter and add herbs. Serve immediately. For game dishes. Yield: About 2 cups of sauce.

SAUCE BERCY

⅓ cup finely chopped shallots
3 tablespoons cold butter
¾ cup plus 2 tablespoons dry white wine
1½ cups brown sauce
1 teaspoon each chopped fresh tarragon
and parsley (or half the amounts if dry)

Cook shallots in 1 tablespoon butter until golden brown. Add ¾ cup wine and cook until reduced by half. Add brown sauce and cook 10 minutes. Strain through sieve and bring to a boil. Turn off heat and stir in 2 tablespoons cold butter. Add 2 tablespoons wine and herbs. Serve hot. For

broiled calves' liver, grilled dishes, or boiled tongue. Yield: About 2 cups sauce.

CANARD A L'ORANGE

(Duck in orange sauce)

1 4- to 5-pound duck, dressed weight
Salt and pepper   2 tablespoons sugar
2 tablespoons white vinegar
1 orange   1 lemon
½ cup brown sauce
1 tablespoon red currant jelly
1 tablespoon orange liqueur (Cointreau,
Grand Marnier, or Triple Sec)

Preheat oven 375°F. Sprinkle inside of duck with salt and pepper. Place duck in oven and roast 15 to 20 minutes per pound, depending on doneness desired. Baste frequently with pan drippings and pour fat from pan as it accumulates. Reserve fat in glass cup.

Combine sugar and vinegar in saucepan. Cook over moderate heat until sugar caramelizes and becomes amber-colored. Do not overcook.

Using a swivel-bladed potato peeler, peel orange and lemon. With a sharp knife cut orange peel and half the lemon peel into thinnest possible strips. Discard remaining lemon peel. Combine slivers of orange and lemon peel in saucepan and cover with water. Bring to boil, remove from heat and let stand 3 minutes. Drain and reserve peel.

Extract juice from orange and combine with 1 tablespoon lemon juice. Reserve.

Pour off any fat remaining in roasting pan and add a little water. Swirl it around to dissolve any brown particles clinging to the bottom sides of the pan. Pour this mixture into the caramelized sugar and bring to boil. Cook over high heat 3 minutes. Add orange and lemon juice and brown sauce. Cook over high heat 10 minutes and add orange and lemon strips and jelly. Cook until jelly dissolves. Add liqueur. Spoon part of the sauce over the duck and serve remainder in sauce boat. The duck may be quartered before serving. Garnish platter with peeled orange slices and watercress. Yield: 4 servings.

ROGNONS DE VEAU A LA MOUTARDE
(Veal kidneys in mustard sauce)

2 veal kidneys
Salt and pepper to taste
Peanut oil
4 tablespoons cold butter
1 tablespoon finely chopped shallots
½ cup dry white wine
1 cup brown sauce
1 tablespoon prepared mustard,
preferably Dijon

Trim the kidneys, leaving a thin layer of fat around them. Split kidneys and trim away core in center. Slice thin and sprinkle with salt and pepper. Barely cover bottom of skillet with oil. Heat well and add kidneys. Cook quickly, shaking skillet. Do not overcook; kidneys should be browned but rare. Pour kidneys into sieve and let drain. Wipe skillet with paper towel and add 2 tablespoons butter. Add shallots and cook until golden brown. Add wine and cook until reduced by half. Add brown sauce and bring to a boil. Return kidneys to sauce and bring to a boil. Remove from heat and stir in remaining cold butter. Stir in mustard and serve immediately with hot, fluffy rice. Serves 2 to 3.

SAUCE PERIGUEUX
(Truffle sauce)

2 cups brown sauce
1-ounce can truffles
2 tablespoons cold butter

Heat brown sauce and add liquid from truffle can. Chop truffles and add to sauce. Bring to a boil and remove from heat. Stir in cold butter and serve hot with grilled beef, veal or chicken dishes. Yield: about 2 cups sauce.

SAUCE MADERE
(Madeira wine sauce)

⅓ cup finely chopped shallots
3 tablespoons cold butter
½ cup plus 3 tablespoons madeira
1½ cups brown sauce

Cook shallots in 1 tablespoon butter until golden brown. Add ½ cup madeira wine and reduce by half. Add brown sauce and cook 10 minutes. Strain sauce through sieve and bring to a boil. Turn off heat and stir in 2 tablespoons cold butter. Stir until butter dissolves and add 3 tablespoons madeira. Serve with roasted and sautéed meat dishes. Yield: About 1¾ cups sauce.

SAUCE AU PORTO
(Port wine sauce)

Prepare as for the *sauce madère* but substitute port wine for the madeira.

SAUCE BORDELAISE

This is one of the best-known of all French sauces, a derivative of sauce *marchand de vin*. The latter becomes *bordelaise* when rich, succulent poached slices of marrow are added.

½ cup sliced beef marrow (available
on request at most butcher shops)
Water to cover
Salt to taste
2 cups sauce marchand de vin (see above)

Place marrow slices in a saucepan and barely cover with water. Add salt to taste and bring to a boil. Cook, barely simmering, for 2 minutes. Add poached marrow to heated *marchand de vin* sauce and serve hot. Serve with roasted and sautéed meat dishes. Yield: about 2½ cups of sauce.

The Versatile Egg

and how the French work wonders with it

No area in the world has been as skillful and inventive in the use of eggs as the countries where butter is the dominant (or nearly dominant) cooking fat. France is generally given the credit for most of the sublime egg manipulations. It may very well be true, for in my opinion the best chicken in the world is grown in the town of Bresse. The first breakfast egg you eat on arrival in France is a startling experience—much as if you had never eaten an egg before. And there are French cookbooks that deal only in ways to cook eggs. So looking to French methods of egg cookery can do us nothing but good.

Omelets—the Single Most Useful Thing to Cook

Let us take the omelet. It can be the first, middle, or last course, or it can be almost the whole meal. It can even be a dramatic feature at a cocktail party, when it is small and is then called a "reception omelet."

The only thing necessary: it must be perfect, which means it requires skill and attention to technique. (The fact that its perfection is based on small details of manipulation is another reason I am inclined to credit France with its creation.)

The perfect omelet is golden in color, light in texture and voluptuous in outer appearance. Its center should be not quite liquid but creamy. Since a rolled omelet continues to cook even after it is on the serving plate, you should cook it only until it just sets, which could be called 95 percent done.

I learned to make omelets from Rudolph Stanish, a professional New York chef who makes 20,000 to 30,000 a year for big parties. He was willing to share his secrets of technique and know-how—down to the last fine point.

The eggs for fine omelet making should be very fresh. If you buy them in the market you may want to test their freshness at home. The easiest method is to place the egg in cold water just to cover. If it lies flat it is full and fresh. The fresher the egg the fuller it is. If it tilts slightly, it is good for baking or frying. If it sits up, it is not fit to eat.

The best way to keep an egg fresh is to store it in a cool place away from odors of strong-smelling fish or cheese. However, the eggs for the perfect omelet should be at room temperature. For best results remove the eggs from the refrigerator about one hour before using. Each omelet should have three eggs, though this may be too hearty for many. A two-egg omelet is perfectly acceptable, but a three-egg one will have enough thickness so that it may take a filling. One dozen large eggs thus will make four omelet entrées.

The Right Pan

A special pan should be kept solely for making omelets and *crêpes*. It may be of cast iron, stainless steel, or cast aluminum. Its sides should be curved and sloping and it should measure 8 to 10 inches across. Weight can vary according to preference. I use the Cordon Bleu omelet pan of heavy cast aluminum. (Available by mail from Thompson-Winchester Co., 165 Bridge St., Cambridge 4, Mass.)

When the pan is new, it should be cured by slowly heating a tablespoon of butter or oil in it. Sprinkle on a little salt and with a paper towel rub well on sides and bottom.

The pan should never be washed after it is thus cured. To clean away small egg particles that may remain, use a little salt and wipe out with a paper towel. If a cast aluminum pan is selected, before curing it polish the inside surface with a soaped steel wool pad till shiny. Dry it and give it the salt and butter treatment outlined above.

When using a new pan, be generous with the butter. The more the pan is used, the better it becomes. If you get in trouble and the omelet sticks, clean the pan by scouring it with salt and wipe it out with a paper towel.

THE STANISH
PLAIN BASIC OMELET

This recipe and all others here are for a main dish for one person. (But when meat, etc., is added, one omelet may serve two.) Break 3 fresh eggs in a bowl. In a cup place 2 tablespoons of water (or beer), ¼ teaspoon of salt, a scant ¼ teaspoon of Tabasco. Dissolve the salt. Beat eggs just enough to mix them. Do not overbeat as they will become liquid like water. The eggs should look stringy and make a sticky thread when you lift up the beater or whisk. Add the salt, water, and Tabasco, stirring into the eggs until just mixed. Place the omelet pan on medium heat. Let it get hot enough so that when you throw a few drops of water on the pan they bounce around, jump, and immediately disappear. If pan smokes, it is too hot. Take it off the heat and wave it in the air.

Put in 1 tablespoon of salted butter and grease well the sides and bottom of entire pan. Place in quickly ⅔ cup of the egg mixture, which is roughly three eggs, and with a fork flat on the pan make fast circular motions around the pan to raise the layers. (Stirring is to make many layers and for lightness and fluffiness.) While making the circular motion, shake the pan to and fro. Left hand goes back and forth, right hand goes circularly, till the egg sets and all the liquid has congealed. Then spread evenly over the bottom.

Pause briefly while the eggs set—but barely set—and look glistening. Only your eye can tell you this.

Position your left hand on handle so fingers and palm are up. Then up-tilt pan to a 45° angle and, with the fork closest to the handle, begin to roll the omelet to the opposite edge of the pan and out onto a hot dish. Eat immediately.

This is the purest version of the omelet. The entire operation should not take longer than one to 1¼ minutes. Make only one omelet at a time. Banish everything else from your mind, and concentrate on the eggs. Serve immediately.

SOME IMPORTANT POINTS

1. Always use salted butter.

2. Keep pan on medium heat with the heat readily adjustable.

3. Have all ingredients to be added readily available so you need not leave the stove.

In most cases leftover vegetables, rice, or seafoods marry to perfection embraced with pure egg and rolled into an omelet. It has been proven many times in our daily dining that food tastes better when given the second heat. Vegetables really come to life with a sprinkle of cheese before rolling the omelet. It then should be left to sit one moment before eating. Most vegetables are moist so they should be left to drain before adding them to the egg. Foods other than leftovers work just as well—from fresh herbs to caviar.

All omelet fillings should be very fine in texture (by chopping or whatever) before filling. Do not skimp when making the sauce—when a sauce is called for.

RICE OMELET

3 eggs
¼ teaspoon salt (at least)
¼ teaspoon Tabasco
½ cup cooked rice
1 tablespoon chopped flat leaf parsley
2 tablespoons butter
½ cup grated Parmesan cheese

Place the eggs in a bowl. Add the cooked rice, salt, and Tabasco. Have your omelet pan on medium so pan sides will be well heated.

Beat the eggs and other ingredients with a fork till just beaten through. Butter the pan. Add the egg mixture, proceeding as with the basic recipe. When the egg mixture appears set, spread evenly over the surface of the pan and sprinkle with rice, then with Parmesan cheese. Roll and eat while hot. Serve with Creole sauce or garnish with parsley.

CHICKEN LIVER OMELET

½ pound fresh chicken livers
3 tablespoons butter
2 tablespoons dry sherry
¼ teaspoon salt
3 eggs
1 tablespoon chopped parsley
¼ teaspoon Tabasco

Trim the livers of foreign matter. Cut in half. In a sauté pan (small size) add 2 tablespoons of butter. Place on medium heat and let butter slowly get light brown. Add the livers and stir them quickly until brown all over, or about 5 minutes. Heat the sherry in a flamer or small pot. Light and pour over the livers. Remove from fire and sprinkle with a little salt.

Take half of the heated liver (the total should be about 12 pieces) and chop the 6 pieces very fine. Set aside. Slice the remaining pieces and let set in the warm liquid. Beat the eggs in a bowl. Add salt, Tabasco, and the *chopped* livers. Put a generous tablespoon of butter in your hot omelet pan. Add the parsley and sauté a minute. Add the egg mixture, and again with the circular motion stir the omelet till it thickens. Roll out onto a hot dish. Place the *sliced* livers and sauce next to omelet. Garnish with watercress.

VEAL KIDNEY OMELET

1 veal kidney
4 tablespoons butter
1 tablespoon cornstarch
1 tablespoon chopped shallot
½ cup stock
3 tablespoons madeira
¼ teaspoon salt   3 eggs
1 tablespoon parsley
⅛ teaspoon Tabasco

Have the butcher skin the kidney and remove any foreign matter. Split into 2 parts lengthwise, then slice very thin. In a pan put 2 tablespoons of butter. On a medium heat make the butter quite brown but not black. Add the sliced kidney and mix till nicely brown, about 4 minutes. Remove from fire. Put kidney in a dish. In the pan make a sauce with 1 tablespoon of butter, 1 tablespoon of cornstarch. Mix over low flame. Add the chopped shallot and sauté for a minute. Remove pan from fire. Add ½ cup stock and the madeira wine. Over a low heat, stir till it thickens, then add the kidneys. Season with ¼ teaspoon salt. Keep warm but set it aside.

Make the 3-egg omelet using the remaining butter and seasoned with salt, Tabasco, and 1 tablespoon of chopped parsley. Turn onto a hot platter. Spoon the kidneys and their sauce around the omelet. Sprinkle with chopped parsley. Veal kidneys are really a garniture for the omelet and make a hearty main course dish for 1 or 2.

CHEDDAR CHEESE OMELET

3 eggs
1 tablespoon water
¼ teaspoon Tabasco (scant)
¼ teaspoon salt
1 tablespoon butter
1 teaspoon chopped marjoram
½ cup grated cheddar cheese

Place the eggs in a bowl. Add water, Tabasco, and salt. Have your pan on a medium heat. Omitting cheese, beat the eggs and other ingredients with a fork till just mixed. Butter the pan with a generous tablespoon of butter. It should bubble. Add the marjoram and sauté for a minute. Add the eggs. Proceed as with basic recipe till you spread the mixture over the pan. Make sure there are no holes. Now sprinkle on the cheese. Then roll and serve, for one or two portions.

OMELET WITH RED CAVIAR AND SOUR CREAM

3 eggs
¼ teaspoon salt (scant)
1 tablespoon butter
1 tablespoon chopped parsley
1 tablespoon red caviar
2 tablespoons sour cream

Make the basic omelet and serve onto a hot plate. Then cut an incision lengthwise (about 3 inches long). Spread it a little and neatly spoon in your mixture of red caviar and sour cream. Sprinkle with parsley and eat hot.

MOUSSELINE OMELET

3 eggs
1 tablespoon butter
3 tablespoons sugar
3 tablespoons apricot preserve

Separate the eggs. Beat the whites with one tablespoon of sugar till glossy and stiff. Using the same beater, beat the yolks with the remaining sugar till creamy and lemon colored. Combine both of these mixtures.

In hot omelet pan melt 1 tablespoon butter and pour in mixture. Spread over the entire surface of pan. When sides are brown and set, spoon the apricot preserve close to the handle with a spatula. Fold over (rather than rolling) and onto a hot oval dish. Dust with confectioners' sugar and eat hot. May be flamed with 3 tablespoons of Southern Comfort. Serve as a sweet for 2.

Soufflés—Small Miracles of Perfection

Another highly versatile category in Europe's egg cookery is the soufflé (which means puffed). Like the omelet, it may be a main course or a dessert. And it can be filled with many ingredients (seafood, cheese, meat, vegetables), or sweetened and flavored to become a beguiling dessert.

This fluffy mound of froth seems hard to make. Like the perfect omelet, it is all technique: meaning you cannot ignore any fine details, and you cannot grope your way to success.

Helen McCully, a long time food writer, has done a thorough research job to run down what these fine points are. Here are her findings:

Soufflés are not neurotic, as some think. Let us just say they tend to be nervous.

The secret of success lies in the egg whites. A soufflé is usually nothing more than a sauce *béchamel* (which we in America call white or cream sauce) combined with a flavoring, a purée, or other ingredients into which stiffly-beaten egg whites have been folded.

GUIDE FOR SUCCESSFUL SOUFFLES

1. *Egg whites.* When properly beaten, egg whites mount to seven or eight times their original volume, are smooth and glossy (the term often used is "wet"), free from granules (if granular or dry, much of the air has been lost), and firm enough to stand in peaks when the beater is lifted. Always add a pinch of salt to egg whites before you start beating.

2. *Temperature* of egg whites. Most authorities, including the Poultry and Egg National Board, recommend bringing the whites to room temperature, which means they should be out of the refrigerator at least half an hour. However, Elizabeth David, the distinguished English authority on French cooking, says: "I find the exact opposite to be the case. They come up much better if put in the refrigerator for 20 to 30 minutes previous to beating." Both seem to work.

3. *Extra egg whites.* French cooks always add extra egg whites (usually in the proportion of 1 egg white to 4 whole eggs). To give extra airiness, some chefs will add, with abandon, as many as three more. I think that soufflés will rise better with the addition of extra whites.

4. *The right beating bowl.* Any glass, porcelain, or stainless steel bowl may be used, although most French cooks prefer an unlined copper bowl, which for some chemical reason seems to help the egg whites to mount more smoothly.

5. *The beater.* The large balloon whisk, whip, *fouet* (call it what you will)—5 to 6 inches across—is preferred by professionals because, as they explain, you can keep the whole mass of egg whites in continual, air-circulating motion. Most cooks in the home depend on the electric or rotary beater, which may not yield quite the same volume but makes less rigorous demands on one's muscles. The whisk, or *fouet,* one of the most important of all French cooking tools, comes in many sizes. A smaller *fouet* would be used by a French cook to beat the basic soufflé sauce, to beat the egg yolks, and to incorporate the first batch of egg whites.

6. *Folding in* the egg whites. Once the basic sauce has been combined with the yolks, add about one-third of the stiffly beaten whites, whipping them in vigorously with a small whisk. This lightens the mixture and makes it much easier to incorporate the bulk of the egg whites. Scoop remaining whites on top and fold in with a rubber or flat wooden spatula. Folding is accomplished by cutting down from the top center of the mixture to the bottom of the saucepan, then drawing the spatula quickly toward you against the edge of the pan, up to the left, and out. This brings some of the soufflé mixture at the bottom up over the egg whites. Continue this movement while slowly rotating the saucepan, until the egg whites have been folded into the body of the soufflé. The whole process should not take more than a minute, and do not attempt to be too thorough. It is better to have a few unblended patches than to deflate the egg whites by overmixing.

The ability to make a soufflé should be in every cook's repertory because it has so many variations and many uses.

7. *The soufflé mold.* Although a soufflé may be baked in a fairly shallow (approximately 3 inches high) ovenproof dish or Pyrex, it is preferable and more attractive to use the straight-sided French porcelain soufflé mold, which is usually available in good stores and shops. The mold comes in three sizes: 1 quart, 1½ quarts, and 2 quarts.

8. *Preparing the mold.* The sides and bottom of the mold should be buttered heavily, then coated with grated cheese, bread crumbs, flour, or sugar (sometimes a combination of the last two), depending on the type of soufflé. To coat, spoon several tablespoons of the coating ingredient into bottom of buttered mold. Then, holding the mold in your hands, roll it around and around so that sides and bottom are evenly but lightly coated. Turn the mold upside down and give it a good tap to get rid of any surplus.

9. *Chilling the mold.* This professional chef's trick, which helps the soufflé not only to rise but to rise straight up, is recommended in all our recipes. Refrigerate the mold for at least 30 minutes while the soufflé is being prepared, or longer, if you like.

10. *Oven temperature and placement* of mold in oven. Oven temperatures vary in the recipes that follow from 325° F. to 425° F. All experts recommend placing mold on a rack at the middle level of a preheated oven, because this provides a more even distribution of the heat.

11. *When is the soufflé done?* This depends on the size of the soufflé. When it has risen 2 to 3 inches above the rim of the mold and has browned on top, it is approaching doneness, but there is no hard-and-fast rule. When the prescribed cooking time is up, it is safe to test by plunging a trussing needle, a thin wire, or a clean straw into the center of the soufflé. If the needle comes out dry—that is, without any batter clinging to it—the soufflé is cooked properly. For those who prefer a soft, creamy center, bake the soufflé a few minutes less than indicated in recipe. Here, only experience will tell you the precise timing.

FRENCH CHEESE SOUFFLE

*¾ cup grated Swiss or Parmesan cheese or a
combination of both
3 tablespoons butter
3 tablespoons flour
1 cup milk, heated
½ teaspoon salt*

*Dash of freshly ground pepper
Pinch of cayenne pepper
Pinch of nutmeg   4 egg yolks
5 egg whites, stiffly beaten with a pinch
of salt*

Butter a 1-quart soufflé mold generously, then coat with enough grated cheese to cover lightly. Chill well in refrigerator.

Melt butter in a saucepan, stir in the flour with a wooden spatula, and cook over a moderate heat until butter begins to foam, about 2 minutes. Do not brown. Take off the heat, stir in the hot milk and beat vigorously with a wire whisk. Beat in the seasonings. Put back over a moderate heat and cook, stirring constantly with a wire whisk, for about 1 minute. The sauce will be, and should be, very thick. Off the fire, add the egg yolks, one at a time, beating hard after each addition. Taste for seasoning. Then add about ⅓ of the stiffly beaten egg whites, beating them in well with the whisk. Stir in all but a tablespoon of the grated cheese, then fold in the remaining whites.

Pour the soufflé mixture into the prepared mold, smooth the surface with a spatula, and sprinkle remaining cheese over the top.

Place in a preheated 400° F. oven, turn down the heat immediately to 375° F., and bake 25 to 30 minutes. At this point, the soufflé will have a creamy center, which many people prefer. For those who like their soufflés firm, bake another 4 to 5 minutes.

CHEF DESBANS'S SOUFFLE A L'ORANGE
(Restaurant Le Perigord)

*1 cup milk   ¼ cup sugar
Grated rind of 1 orange
½ cup (1 stick) sweet butter
½ cup flour
3 egg yolks, well beaten
2 tablespoons orange curaçao
Red food coloring
4 egg whites, stiffly beaten*

Butter a 1-quart soufflé mold generously, then sprinkle bottom and sides with sugar. Dump out any excess. Chill.

Combine milk, sugar, and orange rind in a saucepan. Heat to the boiling point.

Melt butter over a low heat, then stir in flour smoothly and cook for a couple of minutes, whisking constantly. Add the hot milk mixture and simmer, still whisking constantly, for about 2 minutes or until sauce is very thick. Take off the heat. Add the egg yolks, whipping them in vigorously with a wire whisk, then the curaçao, and a few drops of red food coloring. Add about ⅓ of the stiffly beaten whites and whisk them into the batter until it is very smooth and creamy. Fold in remaining whites carefully with a spatula. Pour mixture into prepared mold and bake in a preheated 325°F. oven for 25 to 30 minutes. Serves 4. Serve with *sauce sabayon* (below).

SAUCE SABAYON

2 egg yolks
1 tablespoon orange curaçao
3 tablespoons orange juice
1 tablespoon sugar
Red food coloring

Beat the egg yolks in the top of a small double boiler, add all remaining ingredients, and cook over hot water, stirring constantly, until sauce has thickened to the right consistency. Take off the heat, stir in a few (very few) drops of red food coloring, and serve in a warm sauce bowl.

CHEF MILLIEN'S CHOCOLATE SOUFFLE

(The Colony Restaurant)

2 tablespoons butter
2 tablespoons flour
1 cup milk, heated
4 egg yolks
Pinch of salt
4 tablespoons sugar
½ teaspoon vanilla
1 ounce sweet chocolate
4 egg whites

Butter a 1-quart mold generously, then sprinkle bottom and sides lightly with sugar. Dump out any excess. Refrigerate while you prepare the soufflé.

Melt butter in a saucepan, stir in flour until smooth, and cook for a few minutes or until butter froths. Stir in hot milk and cook over moderate heat, stirring constantly, until sauce is thick. Take off the heat and add the egg yolks, one at a time, beating very hard after each addition. Then beat in salt, 2 tablespoons of the sugar, and the vanilla.

Meanwhile, melt the chocolate over hot, not boiling water. Stir thoroughly into batter.

Beat the egg whites until stiff but not dry, then beat in the remaining sugar gradually. Mix about ⅓ of the egg-white mixture into the batter very well, then fold in remaining mixture gently but thoroughly with a wooden spatula.

Pour batter into prepared mold and bake in a preheated 450° F. oven for 10 minutes; reduce heat to 350° F. and continue baking for 20 to 25 minutes. Serves 4. Serve with:

CREME CHANTILLY

Whip 1 cup chilled heavy cream until it forms little peaks when you hold up the beater. Then whip in sugar and vanilla to taste.

CHEF FRANCE'S COFFEE CUP SOUFFLES

(The Four Seasons Restaurant)

1½ tablespoons butter
¼ cup flour
1 cup milk, heated
4 egg yolks, well beaten
2 to 3 teaspoons instant powdered coffee
5 egg whites
½ cup sugar
Coffee ice cream

Butter 8 ramekins (6-ounce size) and sprinkle bottom and sides lightly with sugar. Dump out any excess. Chill in refrigerator while you prepare the soufflés.

Melt butter over a low heat, then stir in flour until smooth. Cook for a few minutes without browning. Add the hot milk and continue to cook over moderate heat, stirring constantly, until mixture is very thick or, as Chef France explains, "until the dough separates from the pan." When cool, thoroughly whip in the well-beaten egg yolks and the instant powdered coffee.

Beat egg whites until stiff but not dry, adding sugar gradually. Combine about ⅓ of the beaten whites with the first mixture, mixing in very well. Fold in remaining whites carefully with a spatula. Set 4 tablespoons of the soufflé mixture aside in a bowl (this becomes part of the sauce served with the soufflés).

Spoon remaining soufflé into the prepared molds the size of big coffee cups. Place in a preheated 425° oven for about 13 minutes for medium consistency; 15 minutes for firm.

SAUCE

Mix the 4 tablespoons of soufflé mixture with 4 tablespoons coffee ice cream. To serve, make a small incision in top of each soufflé with the tip

of a knife (this is done at the table) and spoon a bit of the sauce into it.

CHEF CHAUVERON'S SOUFFLE VANILLA
(Café Chauveron)

½ cup sugar   *½ cup flour*
5 egg yolks, well beaten
2 cups milk, heated
1 teaspoon vanilla extract
2 tablespoons Grand Marnier
1 tablespoon cognac
5 egg whites, stiffly beaten

Butter and lightly sugar bottom and sides of a 2-quart soufflé mold. Dump out excess and refrigerate.

Mix sugar and flour, then thoroughly stir in beaten egg yolks. Gradually stir hot milk into the egg mixture. Cook, stirring constantly, over a moderate heat until mixture is smooth and thick. Take off the heat, cool slightly, then stir in vanilla, Grand Marnier, and cognac. Beat about ⅓ of the egg whites vigorously into the mixture. Carefully fold in remaining egg whites with a wooden spatula. Pour into prepared mold and bake in a preheated 350° F. oven until well puffed and delicately brown on top, about 50 minutes. Serves 4 to 6, with this sauce:

To 1 cup whipped cream add 2 tablespoons Grand Marnier and ¼ teaspoon almond extract.

Quiche Lorraine— the Main Course Pie

Another egg classic, without as many variations as the omelet, is *quiche lorraine,* a cheese and egg pie supposedly invented in Alsace-Lorraine. But the Swiss also claim it, as do the Germans and the Belgians. Suffice to say you will meet it wherever cows, chickens, and pigs are plentiful; for cream, eggs, cheese and bacon are needed in most variations. It can be served as an hors d'oeuvre or as a main luncheon dish. Swiss Gruyère cheese (the processed variety that comes in wedges) seems to work better than any other type of cheese. Of the two recipes that follow, the Alsace version is the milder in taste.

Quiche Lorraine is a main course pie made of eggs, Gruyère, bacon, onion, and cream. If small, can be an appetizer.

QUICHE A LA SUISSE
(from Albert Stockli)

Beat 6 eggs with 16 ounces cream. Add ½ pound grated Gruyère cheese and 1 teaspoon salt. In 4 ounces butter, sauté until golden brown the following:

2 large onions, sliced very thin
¼ pound bacon, fried crisp
2 leeks, sliced very thin
1 teaspoon chopped chives
1 teaspoon fresh marjoram
1 teaspoon chopped parsley

Combine with egg mixture. Line pie tin with pie dough. Pour in mixture and bake at 375° to 400° F. until golden brown on top (about 25 to 35 minutes). Serves 8.

QUICHE LORRAINE FROM ALSACE
(à la Morrison Wood)

Unbaked pie crust shell
White of 1 egg
½ pound grated Gruyère cheese
1 tablespoon flour
6 slices bacon
1 cup minced onion
3 or 4 eggs   *Salt*
1 to 2 cups of rich milk or cream
Dash cayenne pepper

Make your favorite rich pie crust shell (9 inches), and brush the entire surface with white of egg after the shell is in the pie tin. This prevents any sogginess in the crust.

Combine the grated Gruyère cheese with flour, mixing well. Fry the bacon slices in a skillet until nicely crisp. Drain them on paper toweling, and cut in tiny pieces.

In the bacon fat sauté the minced onion until limp, then distribute the onion and the bacon pieces over the bottom of the unbaked pie shell. Cover the onion and bacon pieces with the mixture of grated cheese and flour.

Beat 3 eggs with 1 cup of rich milk (or 4 eggs with 2 cups of rich milk for a deeper tart), salt to taste, and add the dash of cayenne pepper. Pour this custard over the cheese.

Bake in oven (400° F.) for 10 minutes, then reduce the temperature to 350° F., and bake for 1 hour, or until a knife comes out clean from the custard. This recipe will serve 6 generously, or 8 scantily.

Danish open sandwiches can be appetizers
(if small) or can be the whole
meal if there is enough diversity in
the ingredients and tastes.

Cold Table of the North

*The Danish open sandwich matches—nay, outdoes
its Mediterranean cousins as a lusty appetizer*

The *hors d'oeuvre* of southern Europe is matched
and even excelled by Scandinavian ways with a
cold meal. They have exploited this area so fully
that Americans mistakenly tend to associate the
northern cuisines with their appetizers alone.
Certainly almost every element that goes into a
full menu is possible. Consider the gamut of
tastes offered with the traditional Danish open-
face sandwich *(smørrebrod):*

Salty: Caviar, anchovies, fish roe, corned beef,
salami.

Fish: Shrimp, herring, eel, tuna, anchovies,
sole.

Sour: Pickles, capers, lemons, rye bread,
pickled beets.

Smoky: Ham, smoked veal, smoked pork,
smoked salmon, smoked fish, smoked eel.

Fresh, raw: Tomato, cucumber, dill, parsley,
chives, radish, lemon.

Hot and peppery: Fresh horseradish, curry,
garden cress.

Sweetish: Sweet pickles, spiced apples, red
cabbage, prunes, cranberries, lingonberries.

Cheesy: Blue cheese, Samsoe, Camembert.

Oily: Anchovies, salmon, butter, mayonnaise.

Tart: Lingonberries, cranberries, red cabbage.

Bland: Potato, white bread.

Oniony: Onions, chives.

Meaty: Raw scraped beef, cold roast or
boiled beef, lamb, pork, duck, chicken, liver
paste.

Earthy: Mushrooms, truffles, beet.

Out of this kind of variety the Danes can turn
four or five pieces of *smørrebrod* into a complete
lunch, supper, or late evening meal, served and
eaten with knife and fork, in the same order as
the courses of a Scandinavian dinner—fish, meat
or poultry, salad, and cheese. Each course is
served on a fresh plate, with fresh utensils, to the
accompaniment of icy-cold *akvavit* and beer.

It is the prettiest, most effective way we know
to serve a complete cold meal that has the character, sustenance, and the charm of variety. If
you borrow the principles of the Danish *kaltbord,*
load a buffet with several kinds of bread, the best
butter, and a variety of makings. Then let the
guests engineer their own open sandwiches. You
might make a few "models" for them to emulate.

If you think that the "pretty picture" aspect of
smørrebrod, such as you see in the accompanying
photograph, requires tedious effort, you are
wrong. The secret is in following the Danish philosophy of garnishing and in mastering a few
small knacks of presentation. Remember the garnitures are never arbitrarily chosen for show.
Rather they are selected because they marry well
with the flavor of the main ingredient.

The effect comes of contrast; in creating combinations of textures and tastes—crisp-soft, as in
the cucumber pickle used to garnish the smooth-
ness of liver *pâté;* the saltiness of caviar or anchovy against the sweet blandness of fresh ground
steak; spicy-sweet-sour in the apple and prune
and spiced red cabbage which accompany the
richness of sliced roast duck. Visually there is the
contrast of color to intrigue the eye—the yellow
of scrambled egg and its dusting of green dill
against the coral-pink of smoked salmon; the red
and white of chopped radish and the golden
bloom of egg yolk against the gray-blue of cheese.

In the Danish lexicon, an open-face sandwich must never be skimpy; the contents must always completely cover the bread—as must the butter. But it must be trim, composed with care, to make the neatly-arranged combination count pictorially.

Over the years, one formula for presentation has become standard. A sandwich is most appealing when it is given the third dimension of height, when shrimps are piled and meat slices are rolled or otherwise arranged to give the food a rounded contour. Cheese goes on flat, then is given a build-up with a garnish. Since *smørrebrod* is knife-and-fork food, this "mounded" presentation is easy to eat.

The breads used are usually the square, dark, Danish whole-grain rye, sliced no more than 1/8-inch thick and occasionally found in our markets. Pumpernickel is an acceptable substitute, as is light rye. White crusty bread, similar to what we call French or Italian, is usually used under shrimp and smoked salmon. The chief requirement is that the bread be firm and closely textured, able to resist getting doughy or crumbly under a generous spreading of slightly salted butter.

In Denmark, salted or smoked fish (especially herring, which comes tinned in a score of different sauces) is frequently piled on buttered crisp bread such as Ry-King or Ry-Krisp. (Incidentally, put the Ry-Krisp in your toaster before serving. Makes a great improvement.)

Following these general principles, you can build up your own open-face sandwiches out of any ingredients you've a mind to:

FISH

Pickled herring pieces on crisp bread, usually made at the table by guests themselves, so that the bread does not become soggy. These are eaten with *akvavit*, as the very first course.

Tiny peeled shrimp, which come fresh in Denmark and in some parts of our West Coast, are everyone's favorite. (Most of us will have to settle for those in either tin or jar.) On a base of white bread, heap them "in a crowd," or arrange them meticulously in an orderly pyramid. Serve with a twisted lemon slice.

Smoked-salmon slices, rolled, topped with a wedge of solid scrambled egg, with or without a dusting of chopped dill. Scrambled egg is made of egg and butter only, cooked firm in a double boiler.

Smoked salmon garnished with chopped, stewed mushrooms.

Smoked salmon with raw egg yolk (a Danish taste worth acquiring). To keep egg yolk from slipping off, Danish housewives gently slide the yolk into an onion ring laid on top of the sandwich.

Lobster, boiled claw meat rising like little horns, garnished with lettuce and hard-cooked egg slices in an overlapping row.

Lobster salad with chopped lettuce in curry-flavored mayonnaise.

Smoked eel, thinly sliced, with scrambled-egg wedge and chopped radish.

Fried filet of white fish (sole or flounder), hot, with a standing twist of lemon slice and a dollop of tartare sauce.

Fried cod roe with tartare sauce.

Fried cod roe crisscrossed with strips of anchovies.

Pickled mussels with a dressing of tartare sauce.

Smoked mussels, garnished with grated horseradish and chopped lettuce mixed with oil and vinegar.

Smoked mussels with thin-sliced, vinegared cucumbers.

MEATS

Cold, thinly sliced, rolled or folded roast beef, with hot sautéed onions and hot fried egg on top.

Roast beef topped with potato salad, sprinkled with chopped chives.

Boiled breast of beef with chopped pickles, shredded fresh horseradish, and standing tomato slice.

Beef tartar—raw, scraped sirloin, centered with raw egg yolk, garnished with anchovies, capers, chopped raw onion, and shaved fresh horseradish. (Mushy, ground, vinegar-preserved horseradish is anathema. Fresh horseradish root is easily scraped with a swiveling potato peeler.)

Union Jack—scraped raw beef overlaid with two crisscrossed rows of tiny shrimp, topped with raw egg yolk.

Imperial—scraped beef overlaid with caviar. Perhaps also garnished with two oysters and a row of tiny boiled shrimp.

Liver paste, laid on buttered bread in rounded scoops, topped with sautéed mushrooms, garnished with a stick of meat jelly, a stand-up twist of beet slice and cucumber salad. (Whenever anything looks boring, a Danish friend tells us, just add a slice of beet. Cut it from one edge to

The Danes can get festive at the drop of a hat, and their food and table settings reflect this gay approach to life. This table is an uninhibited mix of things from many countries. Each of the place settings is equipped with glasses for aquavit, beer.

the center, and you can easily twist it into stand-up shape. The same trick goes for any circular garnish—lemon, orange, pickle, beet, tomato, cucumber.) Pickled-cucumber salad is simply made of very thinly-sliced cucumber, soaked overnight in heavy brine, wrung out completely dry, then covered with mild white vinegar, a little sugar, salt and pepper, and allowed to stand a few minutes more. Drain thoroughly before serving.

Hans Christian Andersen's favorite: Liver paste with truffles, topped with a layer of meat jelly, a crisscross of crisp bacon slices, garnished with tomato slices and shaved fresh horseradish.

Cold roast lamb with meat jelly, and cucumber salad dusted with chives or parsley.

Cold roast pork with meat jelly and smoked ham.

Cold roast pork with tomato slices and pickled cucumber.

Cold roast pork with a trim of pickled beet.

Cold roast lamb with a mound of cucumber salad.

This scene could be in any Scandinavian home, but the label on the beer, the china, and the furniture mark it as Danish.

Fried *frikadeller* (Danish meat balls), sliced, with a topping of spiced, cooked red cabbage, a wedge of meat jelly, and a twist of pickled beet slice.

Fried *frikadeller* with cucumber salad garnish.

Fried *frikadeller* with thin slices of veal and stick of meat jelly.

A whole cake of fried *frikadeller* similarly treated as above.

Ham with a generous slice of scrambled egg or a hot fried egg.

Ham with a wedge of Camembert cheese topped with raw egg yolk and chives.

Ham chopped with raw onion and centered with raw egg yolk.

Ham with vegetable salad (chopped beet, apple, and gherkins plus green peas, mixed with mayonnaise).

Bacon, crisply done, topped with hot fried egg or with creamed mushrooms.

Tongue with Italian salad (diced carrots, peas, and small white asparagus in mayonnaise).

Corned beef, heaped with potato salad and chives.

Salami, slices overlapped, one slice wrapped around a wedge of meat jelly.

Salami and meat jelly on rye bread, spread with seasoned lard.

Salami, topped with raw egg yolk, garnished with shaved horseradish and chopped chives.

Salami with scrambled or hot fried egg and chopped olives.

Chicken, thinly sliced, laid in overlapping layers, built up with cucumber salad.

Cold roast duck, sliced, heaped with spiced red cabbage, garnished with apple slices and a prune. This is a popular "leftover," since garnishes derive from the prune and apple stuffing of roast duck.

EGGS

Hot scrambled eggs, striped with flat anchovy filets, sprinkled with chopped chives, heaped on cold buttered toast.

Hot scrambled eggs on cold toast, topped with creamed fresh mushrooms.

Sliced hard-cooked eggs, garnished with twisted anchovy filets.

CHEESE

Blue cheese, centered with raw egg yolk, garnished with piles of chopped radish.

Blue cheese with a dollop of raspberry or strawberry jam.

Blue cheese with a drizzle of Cherry Heering.

Camembert topped with a row of anchovy fillets.

Camembert topped with rolls of salt veal, garnished with meat jelly.

Old Holsteiner cheese with currant jelly.

As a Danish *smørrebrod* artist, you would be a social outcast if you didn't keep on hand liver paste made at home, usually of calf or pig liver (see Sweden), *frikadeller* (meat balls of finely ground forcemeat, half veal, half pork—the test of a respectable cook), and meat jelly or aspic.

Authenticity in the matter of the open sandwich is not crucial in my eyes. The message is not that you *must* include smoked salmon or liver paste or *frikadeller* or meat aspic in your meals. It is rather that you get the principle of providing a palette of different flavors and textures, for which you can substitute any foods at hand.

As a guide to further investigation of this fascinating cold and garnished cookery, we suggest a cookbook, "Open Sandwiches and Cold Lunches: An Introduction to Danish Culinary Art," by Asta Bang and Edith Rode, published by Bonniers, 1957.

You could be ready on short order to produce a full meal if your basic "wardrobe" of ingredients contains the following, to be supplemented by whatever fresh foods you want to use:

ON THE PANTRY SHELF

Tiny Greenland shrimp

Mussels   Sardines   Tuna fish

Anchovies, both flat and
    caper-filled rolled filets

Salmon or cod roe

Herring tidbits (*gaffelbitar*)

Caviar, both red and black

Pâté de foie gras,
    or tinned liver paste

Pickled herring

Canned cranberries   Pickles

Mushrooms (canned and dried)

Tomato sauce   White asparagus

Preserved apple slices

Pickled gherkins   Capers

Red cabbage in jars

Beef consommé   Gelatin

IN THE REFRIGERATOR

Homemade liver paste, meat aspic

Cucumbers   Tomatoes

Radishes   Lemons

DELICATESSEN

Smoked Danish ham in tins,
    or Canadian bacon

Smoked turkey in tins   Smoked fish

Blue cheese or Roquefort

Samsoe cheese or Swiss

Smoked cheese   Salami

Liverwurst   Boiled tongue

Smoked Virginia ham

Corned brisket of beef

LEFTOVERS

These can be virtually anything from new boiled potatoes to roasted or boiled meats and poultry. Cold meats can be garnished with their dressings. Cooked vegetables can be turned into salads or used as trimmings.

Traditional *smörgasbord*, originating
in 17th century country parties,
always starts with herring served in many
delightful ways with bread,
butter, and a variety of garnishes.

Photographs courtesy Scandinavian Airlines System

The True Swedish Smörgasbord

*The cold (and hot) table where restraint
should be your best friend*

The *smörgasbord* of Sweden is a close kin to the other "cold table" offerings of Scandinavia, with fine points of difference. Some say it differs from its cousins mainly in the number of dishes based on salt herring. Certainly it offers more complexity, more prepared dishes and more hot dishes. Swedish *smörgasbord* should be thought of as a whole meal of six or seven courses, permitting as many trips back to the laden table.

An expert on the subject worth listening to is Tore Wretman, who owns and directs three of Stockholm's finest restaurants (the Riche, Stallmästergarden, *and* Operakällaren) *where smörgasbord is seriously featured and consequently enjoys international fame:*

The eating starts with bread and butter and salty, thirst-provoking things *plus* cheese. This means salt herring, fresh herring, Baltic herring, Swedish anchovies, caviar—all accompanied by piping hot boiled potatoes as a neutralizing accompaniment. From there on, the eater continues, making several visits to the long table for egg dishes, fish, cold cuts, meats, salads, hot dishes. One finishes up, perhaps, with a refreshing fruit salad. Relishes of various kinds which are always included in the *smörgasbord* are enjoyed whenever it suits you.

Among the herring dishes, the salt herring or *matjes* fillets with sour cream and chopped chives are paramount. Pickled herring comes next in rank, Swedish anchovies and other variations of cured or pickled herring and boiled eggs follow. Some kind of smoked fish should be included: smoked eel or salmon and also hot-smoked fish. In addition, jellied eel and boiled fish, served cold with mayonnaise. A fine selection of cold cuts, such as salami, liver pâté, smoked reindeer, sliced ham, pickled pig's feet, and head cheese is imperative.

Various kinds of salads are a fairly recent addition to the *smörgasbord*. Here the imagination has free play as to new and exotic combinations. Among the hot dishes, the following have top priority: Jansson's Temptation, herring au gratin, meatballs, and scrambled eggs. Many other dainty dishes may be offered, preferably those with a piquant flavor.

Finally, a little piece of advice how to fully enjoy the *smörgasbord*. Make as many visits to the table as you like, but do not overload your plate with too many different foods at the same time—it hardly stimulates the appetite and does not give full justice to the individual delicacies.

* * *

Following are some hand-picked recipes that were served on the *smörgasbord* table in the Swedish Pavilion at the New York World's Fair, catered by Scandinavian Airlines. You should think of them, however, as dishes which can be served individually without the complex, complete *smörgasbord* table. Quantities are for 8 to 10 persons except as indicated.

PICKLED HERRING
(Inlagd sill)

2 salted herrings
1 cup strong white vinegar
2 cups water   ½ cup sugar
15 whole allspice
¼ sliced carrot   4 sprigs fresh dill

Cut fillet of herring from backbone. Remove other bones and skin. Soak fillet in cold water 10-12 hours. Change water several times. Drain on absorbent paper. Slice crosswise. Arrange in narrow dish. (Or serve whole fillets on ice-block.) Mix marinade ingredients in saucepan. Boil and simmer a few minutes. Cool and strain. Pour marinade over herring. Garnish with sprigs of fresh dill and sliced, raw red onion. Cover with plastic film. Leave in refrigerator overnight.

HERRING SALAD

4 small herring fillets, soaked
1½ cups diced pickled beets
1½ cups diced boiled potatoes
⅓ cup diced pickles
½ cup diced apples
¼ cup finely chopped onion
Dressing:
4 tablespoons white vinegar
or liquid from pickled beets
2 tablespoons water
2 tablespoons sugar
Dash of white pepper
Garnish:
2 hard-boiled eggs, chopped parsley.

Cut herring filets in tiny pieces and mix with other ingredients. Prepare dressing and stir gently into salad. Pack into 5-cup mold, brushed lightly with salad oil. Chill in refrigerator for few hours. Unmold on serving platter and garnish with eggs and parsley.

KALL KOKT LAX PARISIENNE
(Cold poached salmon, Parisian style)

4 pounds salmon in one large piece
2 quarts water
½ cup strong white vinegar
1 sliced onion   1 sliced carrot
1 bay leaf   5 whole allspice
Salt, pepper, dill

Make a *court bouillon* with water and seasonings by combining all ingredients except the fish in a skillet or large saucepan. Bring to a boil; cover and let simmer 15 minutes. Place whole piece of salmon on a rack which may be set or suspended in the pan; this will enable you to remove the fish intact after cooking. Set rack with fish in the bouillon; cover and cook slowly, without boiling, 25 to 30 minutes. Remove fish carefully, skin, and allow to cool. Decorate with slices of tomato and hard-cooked eggs, shrimps, olives, mayonnaise, etc. Coat fish with an aspic based on fish stock (see chapter on *en gelée* cookery). Arrange on large platter with various vegetables.

BEEF TARTAR PATTY
(Rabiff)

¼ pound raw beef
1 tablespoon chopped pickled beets
1 tablespoon capers
2 tablespoons chopped onions
2 tablespoons chopped boiled potatoes
1 raw egg yolk

Scrape meat (top round or sirloin) or put through meat grinder 3 times. Arrange meat like steak or meat patty, and garnish with beets, capers, onions, and potatoes. Place raw egg yolk inside an onion ring on top of the meat patty. Duplicate the recipe for each person served. The same recipe can be converted to a hot dish by mixing ingredients, frying the patty quickly on both sides, and serving on a slice of white toast.

LIVER PASTE
(Leverpastej)

1 pound calf's or pig's liver
½ pound fat pork
6 to 8 Scandinavian anchovy fillets
1 onion, chopped
3 tablespoons flour
5 egg yolks
4 tablespoons butter melted
1 cup light or heavy cream
2 tablespoons sherry or cognac
½ teaspoon ginger
½ teaspoon marjoram
Salt and white pepper

Wash and dry liver. Remove membranes and tubes with sharp knife. Cut liver and pork in

Second course of a Swedish *smörgasbord* is also fish, but not herring. Usually included are a variety of smoked or boiled salmon, smoked eel, shrimp, lobster, and egg dishes.

small pieces and put through meat grinder 4 times. Add anchovies and onion, grind again. Make batter of cream, flour, melted butter, egg yolks, cognac, and spices. Add minced meat gradually, mixing well, and season with salt and white pepper. Butter loaf-pan and spoon in liver mixture. Cover with aluminum foil. Put in pan containing hot water; and bake in slow oven (300° F.) 1½ hours. Unmold when cold and serve with pickled beets or gherkins.

JANSSON'S TEMPTATION
(Jansson's Frestelse)

1 can Scandinavian anchovies
(about 20 fillets)
5 cups raw potatoes cut into strips
1 cup finely chopped onions
2 cups cream
Pepper, anchovy juice

Remove bones from anchovies. Butter baking dish and arrange alternate layers of potatoes, onions, and anchovy fillets, making certain the top layer consists of potatoes. Pour over juice from anchovy can and add half the cream. Sprinkle with butter and cover with aluminum foil. Bake in moderate oven (350° F.) for 20 minutes. Remove foil, add remainder of cream, and bake with foil covering for 20 minutes, or until potatoes are golden brown. Serves 10 or 12.

HERRING AU GRATIN

3 salted herrings
3 cups sliced onions
8 medium potatoes
2 tablespoons dry bread crumbs
½ cup butter

Cut fillet from backbone, remove other small bones and skin. Soak fillet in cold water for 10-12 hours, changing water from time to time so that herring will not be too salty. Drain fillets on absorbent paper. This amount serves 10 or 12.

Sauté onions lightly in butter. Wash and boil potatoes in jackets. Peel potatoes and cut thin slices. Butter baking dish and arrange onions, potatoes, and herring in alternate rows. Sprinkle with dry bread crumbs and dot with butter. Bake in hot oven (375° F.) about 20 minutes.

Third course in a Swedish "cold table" features cold sliced meats and sausages and meat pâté. Also much liked is beef tartar, raw ground beef garnished with a myriad things.

MEATBALLS
(Köttbullar)

½ pound each of beef, veal, and
pork, finely ground
2 medium onions,
chopped finely
3 slices fresh white bread
(crusts removed)
2 eggs
2-3 teaspoons salt
½ teaspoon ground white pepper
½ teaspoon ground allspice
1½ cups heavy cream
¼ cup water
½ cup butter

Fry onions in butter until golden brown. Soak bread in a little cream. Mix beef, veal, and pork in bowl. Add fried onions, bread, salt, pepper, allspice, and eggs. Add cream and water and mix until batter is smooth. Roll into 1-inch balls and fry in oil or margarine until evenly brown. Shake pan constantly to keep balls round.

The Swedes have many other recipes that are not part of the cold table. One especially should be added to the repertory of any household that dotes on hamburgers. It is a sort of hamburger patty with relishes inside instead of on the top.

BEEF A LA LINDSTROM

1¼ pounds of beef
chuck or round, ground
2 boiled potatoes, mashed
½ cup cream
2 egg yolks
2 pickled beets, diced
1-1½ tablespoons onion, chopped
2 tablespoons capers, chopped
Salt
White pepper or paprika
2-3 tablespoons butter

Mix ground meat and potatoes with egg yolks and cream gradually while stirring. Then add beets, onion, and capers carefully. Season, shape in meat patties. Brown quickly in butter on both sides in skillet. Place on hot platter and garnish with parsley. Serve with browned potatoes and pickled gherkins.

For a basic handbook on Swedish smörgasbord, I refer you to "The New Smörgasbord Cookbook" by Anna Olsson Coombs, published in 1958 by Hill and Wang, and now in paperback.

The French call it *pot-au-feu,* and it means pot on the fire. But in the pot are meat and vegetables cooked together so their tastes merge and enhance each other. Every country has such a dish.

The Hearty Peasant Dishes of Europe

With everything cooked together in one pot, they are almost a whole meal, savory and delicious

Already standard in our cooking is the one-dish meal revolving around the casserole, which is cooked in the oven. But the casserole has a twin, the hearty European peasant soup, cooked in a pot on the top of the stove. They are interchangeable in the menu. Often the soupy casserole and the big, meaty soup are very hard to tell apart if you want to be strict in your classification.

Meals based on hearty soups that are to be eaten as well as drunk have a long and colorful history. In the days before stoves, everything that was not roasted on a spit or baked in ashes was boiled in a pot. The results were a mélange of edibles, made up of everything at hand in the farm household.

Every nationality enjoys one or more traditional "big" soups. For instance, the *petite marmite* of the French, the *minestrone* of the Italians, the *olla podrida* of Spain. Many nations developed variations which became famous around the world, such as the *bouillabaisse* of Provence in France. You can distinguish three main types among them:

1. Soups that are based on meat stock, with meat that can be eaten along with the soup. The French *pot-au-feu* is the best example.

2. Vegetable soups, built on an oil or salt pork base, plus a mixture of chopped vegetables, such as onions, carrots, and celery browned in the pot. This type belongs to Mediterranean cookery. A good example is the Tuscan *minestrone.*

3. Fish soups that are complete main dishes. The best example is the Provençal *bouillabaisse.*

This soup also has Greek and Italian cousins.

These three were practically the only types of soup eaten until quite modern times. Then the idea arose that a meal should consist not of a single dish mingling many foods, but of a series of dishes aimed at the progressive satisfaction of the appetite. In the new set-up, soups became an introduction or overture to the meal, something to whet the appetite and at the same time give a hint as to what was coming as the main course.

In this evolution of the menu as we know it, the French *haute cuisine* developed two types of soups for the opening course: thin soups and thick soups. Thin soups are all based on stock or broth, which when clarified are called either bouillon or consommé. (Many use these terms interchangeably.) In French cookery stock is composed of meat or fowl juices and water. The *haute cuisine* did not recognize vegetable juice and water as a stock, although European peasant cooks do, and so do we Americans.

The thick soups created by the *haute cuisine* are divided into three classes: purées, which are self-explanatory, *veloutés* and *crèmes.*

Veloutés are based on white stock (made of chicken and veal) thickened with cream and egg yolks.

Crèmes are based on white stock, milk, and cream. They contain no egg yolks. Many soups are combinations of all three types. Actually the so-called thick soups should never be any thicker than thin cream, for they are designed to be the opening course of a dinner, not to be the main course themselves. If you use them in a soup-salad-dessert combination, all you will succeed in doing is to create a meal with a beginning and an end, but from which the middle appears to have dropped out.

If you want a big soup to be the main part of your meal, you can disregard these *haute cuisine* practices for the most part. But never discard the principles of making a good stock. If a hearty main course soup is to please us moderns, it must be based on a rich stock, whether it be meat, fowl, or fish, or a combination thereof. In addition, we do not want the solids in the soup to be cooked to death.

In old-fashioned recipes, the soup meat generally has most of the flavor cooked out into the stock. If you are making a meal of the soup, this leaves you with a "watered down" meat course. So if the solids are to be as delicious as the liquids, your course is quite clear. The flavor of the liquid must not be "stolen" from the flavor of the solids.

How to get rich stock without stealing it from the rest of the ingredients? There are several ways open to you:

1. The first obvious one is to make the stock yourself by buying soup meat and soup bones. But that is slow and time-consuming, though it will probably always be a good way to get what you want.

2. Use a canned stock. There are countless broths and bouillons made of beef, chicken, and fancy fowl. Some are dehydrated rather than canned; many restaurants, for example, use a Lipton product for this purpose. A number of chicken soups (without rice) make an ideal soup stock. And there are fancy ones made of pheasant and mallard duck, which can do wonders for turning ordinary ingredients into a super-gastronomic experience.

You need to experiment and try a number of brands in order to find the one with the richest stock. The proportion of the meat to the water is the essential thing. Or you can add a little raw meat, chopped to cook quickly, if you don't find a preserved stock rich enough to suit you.

3. Add a concentrate. We are not talking about a condensed soup here, but a real concentrate that boils down many gallons of broth into a small jar. The most commonly known are chicken and beef.

4. Mix two or more canned soups to fortify and enrich each other, making a stock to which you can add tasty solids.

The next step is adding garnishes, which is everything else that goes in. If you are using canned ingredients, the trick is to make the result taste as fresh as though the entire soup had been made in your own kitchen of raw materials. You should use the method of the great French chefs, who add vegetables to give a fresh taste to the soup. So use only those canned vegetables which do not lose or change their flavor in the canning process. Or use frozen vegetables (mixed ones work the best) which have a fresh flavor. Add fresh onion and fresh parsley, also a fresh herb bunch if you can.

There is an old French trick with vegetables that are to be added to casseroles and soups. Sauté them in butter first. It improves the flavor of the vegetables, helps enrich the stock.

Recipes for making old-fashioned big soups the old-fashioned way abound in every cookbook. But you can use modern, processed foods to accomplish the same, perhaps better, results. Successful soup making depends not so much on accurate measurements and specific ingredients as on the blending of flavors. Here is one of your greatest chances to become a truly creative cook, if you just master the one principle of using a rich stock to begin with.

In most provincial European restaurants there appears on the menu at least once a week a spectacular version of a boiled dinner. They call it *pot-au-feu*. Others would call it *poule au pot,* for in addition to the usual brisket of beef they also use a plump chicken. It is half soup, half entrée—in short, the main part of the meal.

When made in the orthodox fashion this dish requires many hours of cooking and tending. But with the aid of a large-size pressure cooker and a thermostatically controlled top-of-the-stove burner the cooking time can be cut in half and the pot-watching to practically nil. The quality of the dish is equal to or better than old-style.

POT-AU-FEU

Use equal quantities of beef and chicken. The chicken should be plump and fleshy, the fricassee type, and may be cut into pieces or left whole if your kettle is commodious. The same goes for the beef. Count on 1 pound of meat per person. To serve 8, use 4 pounds of lean beef and a 4-pound chicken. If you can get it, use a nice marrow bone cut into pieces and tied in cheesecloth to prevent the marrow from escaping into the broth.

Half fill the kettle with water. Add 2 tablespoons salt, 6 peppercorns, ½ bay leaf. Cook gently for 2 hours on top of the stove or about 20 minutes in a pressure cooker. Be sure that the pressure cooker is not more than ¾ full.

At this point the meats will be not quite cooked. This is what you want. Skim the surface carefully. Add 8 small carrots, 8 small leeks (only the white parts), 1 large onion stuck with 3 whole cloves, turnips if you like them, and potatoes if you so desire—1 small one for each person. Add also at this point a *bouquet garni,* which you can buy already put up in little bags at any specialty food shop. Allow to simmer, but only simmer (just under 210 degrees F.) for 1 hour. Never boil! Remove the fat from the surface. Correct the seasoning and serve.

Meat, vegetables, and broth may all be served together from the great kettle in soup plates or bowls. Or the soup may be served separately in cups, with or without thin slices of toasted French bread or rolls and a sprinkle of grated cheese. The meats and the vegetables are arranged on heated platters and served with coarse salt crystals, Dijon mustard or horseradish sauce, and gherkins or pickles.

Often a small head of cabbage is cooked along with the other vegetables, but since the flavor of cabbage is somewhat overpowering you might rather cook it separately and whole in a large pressure cooker. The curly green Savoy cabbage is most handsome.

POT-AU-FEU A LA CAMPAGNE

4 pounds short ribs or 6 ribs,
cut individually
3 tablespoons salt
Bouquet garni: a few sprigs parsley, 1 bay leaf,
pinch thyme, few celery tops
8 to 10 leeks   8 carrots
1 2-pound head cabbage
1 large onion, stuck with 2 cloves
3 large baking potatoes

Pour 7 quarts cold water into a very large kettle, add the meat, and bring to a boil slowly over low heat. Skim off any scum that rises to the surface. Add salt, *bouquet garni,* and cook slowly for 1½ hours, skimming several times.

To prepare the vegetables: Cut about half the green tops off the leeks, split the bulb in four, then wash very thoroughly. Tie together with a string; quarter the cabbage; scrape and wash the carrots. (If large, cut in two; if small, leave whole.)

Peel the onion and stick with 2 cloves; peel and wash the potatoes and cut into thirds.

At the end of the first cooking period, add all the vegetables except the potatoes, and cook slowly, skimming when necessary, for another 1½ hours. Then add the potatoes and cook ½ hour longer or until tender.

To serve, place the ribs in the center of a warm serving platter and surround with vegetables (the rich stock makes good soup, another day). Serves 6.

The usual accompaniments to this sturdy country dish are sour pickles, French bread, French mustard, and either a hot horseradish sauce or a cold one. And always, in France, a dish of coarse salt.

HOT HORSERADISH SAUCE

Make a cup of *Béchamel* (see chapter on sauces), add enough freshly grated horseradish to taste, and about 2 tablespoons of heavy cream.

COLD HORSERADISH SAUCE

Whip a cup or so of heavy cream and add enough freshly grated horseradish to suit your taste.

BEEF A LA BUCHERONNE

6 pounds cabbage
½ pound salt pork, cut into dice-size
2 onions, peeled and chopped
3 carrots, scraped and chopped
Salt and pepper
1 teaspoon monosodium glutamate
3 pounds of beef
6 juniper berries (available at drugstores)
½ cup chopped parsley
1 large bay leaf
½ teaspoon thyme
1½ cups red wine
1 large garlic sausage

With a long, sharp-pointed knife, remove core from cabbage. Cover with water. Bring to a boil. Lower heat and simmer for 3 minutes. Drain cabbage and chop it fine.

Put diced salt pork into a heavy pot. Cook over low heat till pieces of salt pork are almost crisp. Add cabbage, onions, and carrots. Season well with salt, pepper, and m.s.g. Place brisket on top of vegetables. Sprinkle with juniper berries, parsley, bay leaf, and thyme. Add wine. Cover tightly and cook over low heat about 2½ hours, or till meat is barely tender when pierced with a fork. Re-

move casing from sausage. Add sausage to pot. Skim surface and cook 30 minutes longer, or till meat is completely tender and sausage is hot.

To serve, mound vegetables in the center of a platter and surround by slices of beef alternating with sausage.

LA CHOUCROUTE GARNIE

This dish, the dream of gargantuan appetites, comes from Alsace, but it belongs to all of France, Germany, Belgium, Switzerland, and the Balkans. The burghers of Alsace eat it solidly at midday in a silence of devotion to food and digestion. Parisians eat it when they're roaring with hunger and animation. After the *Comédie,* any night, you can see actors and audience crowd across into the red plush Régence, and then you hear the waiters shout their orders of *"la choucroute"* into the kitchen.

The patrons eat it, the waiters eat it, everybody eats it. It has a compelling savor that makes people sit up, sniff and take notice. More than a dish, it is an institution.

It is a big pot of well-cooked, mild sauerkraut, with a wonderful variety of smoked meats buried in it. Nothing harsh or sour, since the pickling brine is washed out, leaving the *choucroute* itself only agreeably tart. When it's been braised in wine and juniper berries to a really melting texture, it becomes an intensely delicious amalgamation rather than simply sauerkraut.

Because sauerkraut is a perfect cooking medium, nothing else provides such a bed of constant gentle, moist heat. In it, smoked meats cook to their maximum of tenderness and savor. And as they cook, their richness slowly, slowly permeates the *choucroute,* giving it, in turn, an incomparable perfection.

It is perhaps the ideal party dish for the cooking hostess, as it not only heats up well, but is improved by reheating. In fact, fussy folk prefer not to serve a *choucroute* until the second day. Here are the ingredients:

Bacon: a good slab is essential. Use 2 two-inch pieces cut crosswise into 6 chunks but not through the rind.
Smoked pork: butt or shoulder, loin or spare ribs.
Baking ham: a thick slice.
Cooking sausages: several kinds, Alsatian and German types (not the spicy, hot Spanish ones).
Frankfurters: particularly good are the fat kind, called knockwurst.
Sauerkraut: raw, enough to cover all your meats.
Garnishes: 2 carrots, 2 small onions, cloves, juniper berries, peppercorns, lard, bacon rinds (optional).
Liquid: For every 2 pounds of solid sauerkraut (2 large cans, drained) use:

> *1 cup of meat stock*
> *½ cup of white wine*
> *1 jigger of gin (2 jiggers, if you haven't*
> *any juniper berries)*

If you use canned sauerkraut, you'll find that a No. 2½ can (1 lb., 11 oz.) yields just about 1 pound of drained sauerkraut. First of all, wash the kraut in several changes of cold water. Press out all the liquid (this is important) and fluff it out again before cooking.

Take a deep pot, big enough to hold everything with a couple of inches to spare at the top. Bacon rinds, if you have them, on the bottom, otherwise a little lard. Split 2 carrots, stick 2 small onions with cloves—they go in the bottom too. Now add the first round of sauerkraut, at least an inch thick. Press it down lightly and sprinkle with 6 juniper berries and 8 peppercorns coarsely ground.

Now the meats: First, figure out a rational way of placing them in layers in the *choucroute* (all except the bacon and knockwurst). Finish with a top layer of *choucroute,* at least an inch deep. And this again at least 2 inches below the top of the pot. Add the liquid as described above.

Now cover with a really tight-fitting lid. If you haven't one, improvise with a plate and put a weight on top. But tight it must be. Put into a slow oven or on top of the stove (over an asbestos) for no less than 3 and no more than 5 hours. And slow, this time, means really slow, slow, s-l-o-w. It is cooking perfectly when you can just hear, when you bend close, the merest whisper of simmering.

Never stir or at all disturb a *choucroute.* If it cooks slowly enough it won't burn; any slight caramelizing at the bottom only adds to the taste. Normally, you won't need to add any liquid. If accidental fast cooking or a loose lid makes it dry, simply add a few spoonfuls of wine-and-stock or just plain water. The finished *choucroute* should have no excess liquid, nothing that pours off.

You may test by tasting a thread of *choucroute*

Continentals can make a boiled dinner look as attractive as it tastes. Key is to cook vegetables separately, perfectly.

off the top. It is not enough for it to taste cooked; it is not done until the texture is absolutely melting.

Two and a half hours before you count on taking the *choucroute* off the fire, put in your slab of bacon. Excavate a place for it below the top, bed well down and cover so there's still a good top layer of *choucroute*. Again tightly cover and continue the same gentle simmering. Finally, half an hour before serving, bury the knockwursts around and on top of the bacon.

(If the *choucroute* is for the next day, hold the knockwursts until next day, too, adding them when the *choucroute* gets heated up for dinner. Same slow fire or slow oven. Count 45 minutes to an hour to reheat piping hot.)

To serve, take a big, handsome (hot) serving dish, make a great mound of *choucroute*, arrange the meats and sausages on top, and bear it in triumph to the table. No trouble about carving; everything will slice like butter. So do, indeed, carve at the table slices of meat, chunks of sausages. Let there be quantities of hot mealy boiled potatoes and some good mustard. They are both essential.

Beer, of course, is fine. Dry Alsatian or Swiss wine is also good—a Traminer from Alsace, or a Zinfandel from California.

A small casserole full of plain, ungarnished *choucroute* is one of the most useful things to have on hand. It is very fine with roast game birds like pheasant and partridge, and especially with turkey. (Try, for once, a roast turkey with sauerkraut and some hot lentils to absorb the juices.) It makes roast pork and pork chops more digestible. It lends itself to improvisation; it keeps for weeks in a cool place; freezes admirably. And it improves with every reheating.

It always wants a plain starch like boiled, baked or mashed potatoes, and is very good indeed with purée of split peas or lentils.

A small casserole of *choucroute* is made just like the big one. In the absence of meat, you use more fat. The *choucroute* still goes into the casserole in layers. Each layer gets its juniper and peppercorns, and now also a liberal dotting with lard (or fat from a roast of pork), and if possible, a thin slice or two of salt pork. And the top, too. Same proportion of liquid, same cooking time. Same slow cooking.

The key to the flavor of mock wild boar is in the many days of marinating and in using the Grand Veneur marinade.

And if you become addicted to bacon done in this way, which is entirely possible, there's nothing to prevent your making a small casserole of *choucroute,* and setting a square of bacon in it, just to have the bacon.

ROASTED MOCK WILD BOAR
(à la Paula Peck)

1 whole fresh ham (10 to 14 pounds)
2 tablespoons pepper
½ teaspoon thyme
1 tablespoon monosodium glutamate
1 teaspoon allspice
1 large bay leaf, crumbled
1 teaspoon caraway seeds, crushed
3 cloves garlic, mashed
4 tablespoons salt
½ teaspoon celery seed
½ teaspoon cinnamon
1 teaspoon grated orange rind

Ask butcher to remove rind from ham, leaving just a band of it around shank. Stick ham all over with a small knife to make slits. Combine next 11 ingredients, blending well. Rub ham with this spice mixture. Place in a large flat casserole. Pour over ham the following marinade, which has been cooled after cooking:

2 onions   1 carrot
2 stalks celery, including leaves
½ cup olive oil
1½ cups red wine
1 cup wine vinegar
⅓ cup cognac

Chop the onions, carrot, and celery. Sauté briefly in olive oil. Add wine and wine vinegar. Bring just to a boil. Let cool and add cognac. Let ham stand in marinade in the refrigerator at least 8 days or up to two weeks. Turn it twice a day.

To roast: Remove meat from marinade. Do not dry or attempt to remove bits of vegetable which cling to it. Place on a rack in a flat pan, fat side up. Place in a 300° F. oven to roast for 4½ to 5 hours, or until a meat thermometer registers 175° F. If ham should brown too quickly while roasting, cover with brown paper. Turn off oven heat and allow meat to rest in oven 20 minutes before carving. Finish making *Grand Veneur* sauce while meat is resting.

GRAND VENEUR SAUCE

Strained marinade from meat
2 cups red wine

2 cups beef gravy (canned if necessary)
1 cup stock
2 to 3 teaspoons currant jelly
Salt to taste
1 teaspoon freshly ground black pepper
1 teaspoon finely chopped scallions
2 tablespoons finely chopped parsley

Combine strained marinade, wine, and beef gravy in a saucepan. Allow to boil, over medium heat, till sauce is reduced by about half and is a little thicker than you would want it to be. (This part of the sauce can be made fairly early in the day—as soon as the meat has been taken out of the marinade.) It is thinned by the next steps:

Heat stock to boiling, pour it into the roasting pan after the meat and excess fat have been removed from it. With a wooden spoon, loosen all the brown crustiness sticking to the pan. Add to sauce. Add currant jelly and salt to taste, then pepper, scallions, and parsley. Simmer a few minutes. Taste and correct seasoning if necessary. When mock wild boar is being carved, add juices to sauce.

A good accompaniment to this roast and very peasanty is:

SAUTEED APPLES WITH RED CABBAGE

4 pounds hard, tart cooking apples
1½ cups butter
1 tablespoon sugar
Grated rind of 1 lemon
4 pounds red cabbage, coarsely shredded
⅔ cup dry red wine
Salt to taste

Peel and core apples. Chop coarsely. In a large skillet, melt 1 cup butter. Add apples. Sprinkle with sugar and lemon rind. Sauté apples over medium heat. Turn with a spatula occasionally so that they become lightly golden and soft, but not mushy.

While apples are cooking, melt remaining butter in a large heavy saucepan. Add shredded cabbage and stir to distribute butter through cabbage. Add wine. Cover pot tightly and cook till cabbage is tender and liquid has evaporated, about 10 minutes. If liquid has not evaporated, turn heat up high and cook uncovered a few more minutes.

Season cabbage with salt to taste. Combine sautéed apples with cabbage, tossing together lightly.

All of this may be prepared ahead of time,

placed in a casserole, and reheated in the oven at the time it is to be served.

POULET SAUTE A L'AIL

2 three-pound chickens
Salt   Pepper
3 tablespoons oil
4 tablespoons (½ stick) butter
2 heads garlic, unpeeled, separated
2 tablespoons finely chopped onions
3 ripe tomatoes, coarsely chopped
½ can (10½-ounce size) brown gravy
Few sprigs parsley, chopped
Few leaves tarragon, chopped; or
½ teaspoon dried tarragon

Have butcher cut the chicken into frying pieces. Salt and pepper lightly.

Heat the oil and butter in a heavy pan that can go in the oven, until very hot. Then brown the chicken pieces lightly on all sides. Add the unpeeled cloves of garlic and place the pan in a preheated 350° F. oven for 20 minutes, basting occasionally. Remove the chicken and garlic from the pan and keep warm.

Place the pan over medium heat, add the onion and tomatoes, cover, and simmer for 5 minutes. Stir in the gravy, bring to a boil, and boil for 15 more minutes. Put the chicken pieces and garlic back into the pan, add parsley and tarragon. Bring up to a boil once more, then serve. Serves 6.

FRICASSEE DE VEAU GRAND MERE

4 tablespoons butter, softened
2 pounds lean veal, cut in 2-inch cubes
1 onion, coarsely chopped
½ bay leaf
Dash thyme   Dash salt   Dash pepper
1 cup fresh, sliced mushrooms or 1 can
(4½-ounce size) mushrooms, drained
½ cup dry white wine
3 tablespoons flour
1 cup heavy cream   Juice of ½ lemon

Melt 1 tablespoon of the butter in a heavy pan, add the meat, onion, bay leaf, thyme, salt, pepper, and mushrooms (if fresh). Steam, covered, over a very low heat, stirring occasionally, 15 minutes. Do not allow meat to brown.

Add wine and enough water (approximately 3 cups) to cover the meat. Bring to a boil, then cook over a low heat until the meat is tender when pierced with the point of a knife.

Remove the meat from the pan with a slotted

spoon, place on a warm serving platter, and keep warm. Work the flour into the remaining butter to make a *beurre manié* and add to the broth, bit by bit, stirring constantly with a wire whisk. Cook for about 5 minutes. Stir in the cream and if you are using canned mushrooms, add them now. Bring to a boil, then add the lemon juice. Pour the sauce over the meat and serve with rice pilaf. Serves 4.

If you can't be sure when guests will arrive, plan to serve this:

CONTINENTAL BOILED DINNER

When this dish is made and served properly, it is one of the most attractive and delicious in the world. Fresh horseradish adds greatly to the flavor.

> *4 or 5 beef bones*
> *4 celery pieces, with leaves*
> *1 small bunch parsley*
> *1 large onion   Salt*
> *Monosodium glutamate*
> *6 beef consommé cubes*
> *3 pounds brisket of beef*
> *1 medium-size cabbage*
> *6 small zucchini*
> *6 to 9 small potatoes*
> *1 large turnip*
> *6 leeks, trimmed and cleaned*
> *1 can tiny carrots, drained*
> *Horseradish   Coarse salt*

Place beef bones in a deep, heavy pot. Cover with cold water. Add celery, parsley, onion, salt, m.s.g., and the consommé cubes. Cook, uncovered, over high heat, till liquid has slightly reduced. Taste, and add more seasoning if necessary. Add brisket to boiling liquid. When liquid begins to boil again, cover pot and lower heat so that liquid is barely simmering. Simmer slowly about 2½ to 3 hours, or until meat is tender when pierced with a fork. Turn off heat and allow meat to stand in broth till serving time.

Cut the cabbage into small, even wedges and the zucchini into 1-inch slices. Scrub the potatoes and cut away a strip of skin from around the middle of each. Cut the turnip into ¼-inch slices, then cut into fancy shapes with a cooky cutter. Place each cleaned, trimmed vegetable, including leeks and carrots, in a separate small pot. Add salt and m.s.g. Ladle about a cup of your beef broth over each vegetable. Cook over medium heat till each vegetable is tender. (The carrots already have been cooked, but re-cooking them in broth for a few minutes will give them extra flavor.) Turn off heat under vegetables as they are ready, and allow them to stand in broth.

To serve (and this is most important), slice meat evenly and arrange in the center of a large, hot platter. Arrange the hot vegetables around the meat, making separate bouquets of each kind. Serve with horseradish and coarse salt. The broth may be used as a first course, or served in bowls with the meat and vegetables.

WHAT TO ORDER
Menu-Hopping in Paris
SOUPS AND APPETIZERS
PATE EN CROUTE DU GATINAIS—a rich pâté made of chicken gizzard and liver plus veal and pork, blended with tarragon, sage, rosemary, eggs, and brandy
POTAGE AUX MARRONS—sieved chestnuts, with milk, egg yolk, and seasoning

FISH
TRUITE ROTEE POIVRE BOVILLI—baked trout, dressed with a sauce of wine, cream, egg yolks, and sorrel leaves
FILET DE SOLE, MARGUERY—poached fillets of sole which have been cooked in same dish with mussels, shrimps, and white wine.

MEAT
LE POULET EN CROUTE—sautéed and baked chicken done with onion, bacon, mushrooms, and red wine, covered with a flaky pastry
ROGNON SUR BRIOCHE—calves' kidney, sautéed and sauced with a blend of Armagnac, cream, shallot, white wine, lemon juice, and butter. Presented on a slice of sautéed brioche

VEGETABLES
LES PETITS POIS A LA FRANCAISE—tiny peas cooked with tiny new onions and lettuce hearts, parsley, and chives. Buttered after cooking.
POMMES DE TERRE SOUFFLEES—potatoes deep-fat fried, which process is interrupted toward the end, causing potatoes to puff up

DESSERTS
SOUPE AUX CERISES A LA PARISIENNE—Montmorency cherries briefly poached in red wine, flavored with sugar, orange rind, cinnamon, and red currant jelly. Served cool.
POMMES A LA DREUX—apples baked with sugar, cinnamon, and red wine.

The cook who wants to run the gamut of possibilities in wine cookery needs to keep on hand a fairly broad selection of wines and spirits. Most recipes call for small quantities, so your total investment is not extravagant per person.

Famous Dishes That Use Wine

Like the classic sauces, a touch of the right wine blends ingredients into something new

One characteristic that sets European cooking apart from American is the prevalent use of wine and spirits in recipes. Somehow the liquor adds character to what otherwise might be an undistinguished dish. Again, as with the classic sauces or even with garlic, a touch of wine seems to create something new by amalgamating or blending the flavors of the other ingredients.

There are no absolute rules in cooking with wine, except perhaps the basic one that the flavor should blend into the food rather than emerge strongly as a separate taste. As the result of experience over hundreds of years, preferred ways to accomplish this result have been adopted by home cooks and professional chefs alike.

In general, add red wine to beef. White wine marries well with chicken, veal, and pork. For sauces made with cream use only white wine. White, non-fatty seafoods call for white wines. Fatty fish, like mackerel or salmon, can take stronger alcohols in their sauces. The fortified and herbalized wines work well as basting for meats that are not delicate in taste; as for instance, roast mutton basted with port.

These pairings are not arrived at by color, but rather by strength of flavor and body. In short, use full-bodied wines with foods having a full-bodied flavor, and light wines with foods of delicate flavor. There are exceptions: *coq au vin,* for instance, is a chicken dish with red wine.

One other point should be remembered: the presence of vinegar in a food precludes the use of a dry wine, unless the wine is high in acidity or high in bitterness. (This does not apply to the acids of fresh fruit, which do go agreeably with dry wines.) Heavily peppered or highly spiced foods are not compatible, either. In Europe salads are served *after* the meat course, for by then the most important wine has probably been consumed. When dressed with wine vinegar or lemon juice, salads are a little kinder to the wine, but few salads can be considered a real adjunct to its enjoyment.

Here are some classic dishes using various wines, fortified wines, and spirits.

JAMBON PERSILLE

(Ham in parsley aspic)

One of the great classics of the Burgundy country is a jellied *pâté* of ham so liberally bestrewn with parsley that the pink ham appears to be cushioned in gleaming new grass. By tradition it is the Easter dish of the Dijon region, but even in stark autumn or deep winter it carries the look and taste of a spring day.

Any good canned ham may be used, but you can be sure of getting the true taste of this great Burgundian dish if you use one of the fine French hams from Lyon. Weighing about 10 pounds, they can be found at good gourmet shops.

You will need canned ham, white table wine, chicken or veal stock or bouillon, parsley, tarragon, bay leaf, thyme, shallots or white onions, garlic, pepper corns, and gelatin.

Cut off a piece of ham weighing 2 pounds. Add the aspic and any juices that are in the can and put into a kettle with a half bottle dry white table wine, like Chablis or Pinot Chardonnay of California, which is its close kin. Also add 2 cups chicken or veal stock or bouillon, a small handful of parsley, 1 tablespoon dry tarragon leaves or 3 tablespoons fresh tarragon, 2 bay leaves, 1 tea-

spoon thyme, 3 shallots or tiny white onions, 1 clove garlic crushed, a few peppercorns. Bring slowly to a boil and simmer about 20 minutes.

Remove ham from the stock and chop or dice it coarsely, meat and fat together. Press gently into the bottom of a glass bowl or earthenware jar (*terrine*). Strain the stock through a fine sieve, then add 2 envelopes pure gelatin which has been soaked in ¼ cup of water for 5 minutes, then dissolved in warm broth. Cool to lukewarm, remove all the fat from the surface, pour a small amount of the stock over the ham and allow to set in the refrigerator. When remaining stock is completely cool add a full cup of finely-chopped parsley. Pour over the ham and allow to jell in the refrigerator.

The dish may be unmolded, if you like, but generally it is served in slices cut directly from the bowl. Serve with crusty French bread or rolls and sweet whipped butter and, of course, a glass of white or red Burgundy.

TERRINE A LA MAISON

In every restaurant and *charcuterie* and in almost every household in France you will find a *pâté maison,* a crock filled with a richly aromatic combination of meats and livers. All sorts of bits and pieces are used, leftover meats, choice morsels of game or poultry. A great deal of improvisation is possible. Following is a sort of basic pattern.

You will need freshly ground lean pork (or fresh sausage, if it is not too vividly seasoned); liver (chicken, calves', beef, or pork); cognac or brandy, dry madeira or sherry wine; garlic; parsley; shallot or small white onion; ginger, clove, cinnamon, nutmeg; sliced bacon; pepper; Tabasco.

Use 2 pounds each of fresh lean pork and liver. The meat should be ground quite fine, two or three times. The liver need not be ground quite so fine and can easily be reduced to the proper consistency in your electric blender.

Place in the blender 2 tablespoons cognac or brandy, 2 tablespoons dry madeira or sherry, 2 cloves garlic, 4 good sprays of parsley, 1 shallot or small white onion, ½ teaspoon clove, ¼ teaspoon cinnamon, ¼ teaspoon nutmeg. Add diced livers and blend a cupful at a time. Season with 1 tablespoon salt and ½ teaspoon freshly ground pepper, perhaps adding just a suspicion of Tabasco or cayenne pepper. Mix the ground pork with the blended liver.

Line a casserole or *terrine* with strips of crisp

bacon, fill with the meat mixture and bake uncovered in a moderate oven, 350°F., for about 1¼ hours. Cool the *pâté* under a weight so that it will become firm and fine-textured. To do this lay a piece of waxed paper or aluminum foil over the *pâté* and on top of the entire surface set a board weighted with a heavy object. Chill in the refrigerator for several hours.

At serving time, bring the *terrine* to the table, slice and serve with crusty French bread or rolls and a glass of wine. This makes a perfect first course for any meal, and with a bit of lettuce and sliced tomatoes it is an excellent luncheon dish.

BOEUF BOURGUIGNONNE
(Beef stew of Burgundy)

As in all traditional dishes, there is an astonishing lack of unanimity in recipes for this most famous of beef stews. The essential ingredients must include red wine, beef, of course, and no other meat. The meat must be browned in salt pork and never in butter or other shortening except perhaps a little lard. Small white onions go into this stew and mushrooms may be added but no other vegetables—no carrots, no celery, no potatoes.

The wine must be a good robust red. "The better the wine the better the dish." Many recipes use some water along with the wine but this is a practice frowned upon. Heating the wine beforehand is a refinement which speeds up the cooking.

You will need chuck beef, salt pork, small white onions, flour, peppercorns, garlic, orange peel, *bouquet garni* (bay leaves, thyme, nutmeg or mace, parsley, marjoram or oregano), red table wine, mushrooms, and salt.

To make 8 or 10 servings, have 4 pounds of lean chuck beef cut into two-inch cubes. Get ½ pound salt pork and have it sliced about ¼ inch thick and then cut into 1-inch squares. Place these bits of salt pork into a heavy pan or Dutch oven, preferably of cast iron, and brown until crisp. Remove the pork, leaving the fat, and in this same fat sauté 24 small, whole white onions and let them take on a lovely brown. Remove onions from the fat and in that same fat brown the pieces of meat. The pan should be commodious enough to allow the pieces of meat to stand side by side and brown evenly on all sides. From time to time stir with a wooden spoon.

Then put the pieces of salt pork back. Sprinkle them, if you like, with a tablespoon of flour.

Many cooks use 2 or 3 tablespoons; however, the best cooks use little or none. Sprinkle liberally with freshly ground peppercorns. Add 1 or 2 cloves garlic crushed, a piece of orange peel or about ½ teaspoon of dried orange peel (which now comes conveniently in a jar). Then add the *bouquet garni*. This, too, you can buy already tied up in cheese cloth. Or you may use instead 2 small bay leaves, a sprig of thyme, a little sliver of nutmeg or mace, 4 sprigs of parsley, and ½ teaspoon of marjoram or oregano.

Heat ½ bottle of dry red table wine and pour over the meat. There should be barely enough wine to cover the meat. Cover tightly and cook over very low heat or in a slow oven 250° to 300°F. about 3 hours. If you think it necessary, add a little more hot liquid, preferably wine or stock—water only if you must.

Fifteen or 20 minutes before serving time, add the browned onions to the stew and in the very center, place a cupful of tiny button mushrooms which have been browned in butter. One should treat this stew as respectfully as a soufflé. Don't peek too often. Don't let the glorious vapors escape.

At serving time, sprinkle generously with finely-chopped fresh parsley. Add pieces of bread lightly browned in butter. Serve accompanied by vegetables if you like, but always by crusty French bread for dipping up the sauce, and red wine, preferably a Burgundy.

CANETON A L'ORANGE
(Duck in wine and oranges)

Of all the fowl, duck is the one which seems to call most vociferously for a rich, full-bodied wine. As you might expect, duck appears often on the Burgundy bill of fare. Duck with onion, with green olives or, most popular of all, duck with oranges! The orange flavor in the sauce does not quarrel with the wine.

You will need duck, butter, salt, pepper, *quatre épices* (equal parts of cinnamon, clove, nutmeg, and ginger), lemon, oranges, red wine vinegar, sugar, Cointreau, and brandy.

You may roast the duck in the usual way—unstuffed, please. But since the duck is a devil to carve, try roasting it quartered, or cut into even smaller serving pieces if you like. Rub each piece, skin and flesh side, with butter. Sprinkle with salt and pepper, and with the French combination of four spices. Place the pieces of duck well separated, skin side up, on the rack above a deepish pan that will catch the drippings. Roast in a moderate oven 350°F. until done, basting from time to time. If you want an especially crisp crust, turn the oven up high the last 5 minutes.

While the duck is cooking, peel the colorful outer skin (known as the zest) from 1 lemon and 2 navel oranges, leaving all the bitter white part. Cut these peels into thin strips and drop into boiling water for 1 minute, then drain. Juice the lemon and oranges. Cook this juice separately to reduce it one quarter.

In a small frying pan place 3 tablespoons red wine vinegar, add 4 lumps sugar, and cook until it begins to caramelize. Add the cooked-down lemon and orange juice and then add the slivers of peel.

Arrange the duck on a heated platter and keep hot. Carefully remove the fat from the roasting pan and stir into the remaining rich brown juices 2 or 3 tablespoons of Cointreau and brandy—equal parts of each. Add to this the caramelized juices and simmer, never boiling, for about 5 minutes.

At serving time garnish the duck with thin orange slices or sections. Pass the sauce separately. Serves 4 to 6.

Cooking with Madeira

There are wines so negative, or so delicate, that their flavor disappears in cooking. There are others so aggressive that they drown out all other flavors. Madeira has the ability to add its own characteristic flavor without overpowering others. Perhaps it is at home in the kitchen because having already been through a heating process of its own, it takes kindly to heat. Madeira is especially good with variety meats.

ROGNONS DE VEAU, DUC DE CLARENCE

(Veal kidneys in madeira sauce)

2 veal kidneys   2 tablespoons butter
1 carrot, diced
8 small white onions
½ cup chopped parsley
2 cups sliced mushrooms
Salt and pepper   ½ teaspoon thyme
1 small bay leaf   1 cup madeira
½ cup brown meat gravy
(canned may be used)

Trim fat and core from kidneys. Slice ½ inch thick. Cover with cold water. Place over a medium flame and bring just to a boil. Remove from heat and drain kidneys.

Melt butter in a heavy pot. Add carrots, onions and a little parsley. Cook over low heat till vegetables are soft on the outside. Stir in sliced kidneys and mushrooms. Season with salt, pepper, thyme, and bay leaf. Add ¾ cup madeira. Cover pot tightly and place in a 350°F. oven for an hour and a half, or until kidneys are tender.

Remove lid from pot. Skim off fat, if any. Liquid in the pot should barely cover kidneys. If there is too much, reduce it over a high heat (after removing kidneys) till it has cooked down. Stir in meat gravy. When mixture begins to bubble again, add remaining madeira. Arrange on serving plate, sprinkle with chopped parsley and serve. Serves 4.

CELERI ZINO

(Celery hearts, Portuguese style)

3 green onions, minced
1 clove garlic, minced
2 tablespoons olive oil
3 cups celery hearts, cut
in 1-inch pieces
Salt and pepper
¼ cup chicken stock
¼ cup madeira
2 egg yolks
1 teaspoon chopped
fresh dill

Sauté green onions and garlic in olive oil till soft and golden. Add celery, salt and pepper to taste, and chicken stock. Simmer, covered, about 15 minutes, or till celery is just tender. Stir egg yolks and madeira together. Add some of hot pan liquid to yolk mixture. Then stir yolk mixture into celery. Continue to cook over a low flame, stirring constantly but gently, until the sauce thickens. Sprinkle with chopped dill. Serves 4.

POIRE DELICE

(Baked pears in madeira)

6 ripe whole pears
⅔ cup sugar
1¼ cups madeira
1 lemon (juice and grated rind)

Peel pears and place whole in a baking dish

which can be covered. Combine sugar, 1 cup
madeira, lemon juice and rind. Pour over pears.
Cover dish. Bake in a 375°F. oven till pears are
soft, about half an hour. Baste pears occasionally
with liquid in dish. When they are soft, remove
from oven and cool. When cold, add remaining
madeira. Serve chilled.

BOEUF A LA PORTO NOVO

(Beef scallops with madeira)

*4 half-inch slices of French bread sautéed in
butter until golden
⅔ cup cooked beef marrow
1½ pounds fillet of beef,
sliced ¼ inch thick
2 tablespoons butter
2 tablespoons olive oil
¼ cup finely chopped shallots or green onions
1 cup sliced mushrooms
1 cup madeira
½ cup beef gravy (canned may be used)
¼ cup finely chopped parsley
2 tablespoons chopped truffles (optional)
Salt and pepper*

To obtain marrow, have butcher crack marrow
bones lengthwise, so that marrow may be easily
removed with the point of a small knife. Poach
marrow in a little stock for 10 minutes, or till
it is soft and quivery. Drain marrow, keep it
warm.

Spread sautéed bread with cooked marrow and
place on baking sheet to keep warm while dish is
being made.

Melt butter and olive oil. When hot, add beef
scallops. Turn heat very high. Sauté quickly, first
one side, then the other. These cook very fast and
should be at least pink when they are served, so
be careful not to overcook them. Remove to a
plate and keep warm.

Add to pan finely chopped shallots and mushrooms. When they are soft, in just a minute or
two, add ¾ cup madeira. Turn heat high and
reduce liquid till only a third of the original
amount remains. Stir in beef gravy. When sauce
bubbles, add remaining madeira. Season with
salt and pepper. Pour over sautéed beef. Mix
thoroughly so that beef and sauce blend well
together.

Place bread slices on a warm serving plate or
on individual plates. Spoon beef in madeira sauce
on top. Sprinkle with finely chopped truffles, if
available, and with chopped parsley. Serves 4.

OIGNONS SAUTE, CAMARA DE LOBOS

(Madeira onion rings)

*4 large onions, sliced ¼ inch thick
and separated into rings
4 tablespoons butter
⅔ cup madeira
1 tablespoon chopped parsley
Salt and pepper*

Melt butter in a heavy skillet. Toss onions in hot
butter, but do not sauté long enough to make
onions soft. Add ½ cup madeira. Cover pan.
Raise heat and let onions cook over a medium
flame until they are tender. Remove cover and
let the wine reduce to a glaze in the pan. Stir in
remaining madeira and chopped parsley. Serve
with grilled steak. Serves 4.

RIS DE VEAU
AVEC SAUCE MADERE BLANC

(Sweetbreads with white madeira sauce)

*1½ pounds blanched and
trimmed sweetbreads
¼ cup butter
½ pound mushrooms
¼ cup chopped shallots
⅔ cup madeira
½ cup heavy cream
4 egg yolks
¼ cup chopped parsley*

Cut sweetbreads crosswise into scallops. Melt
butter in skillet. Sauté sweetbreads on both sides
lightly until lightly browned. Remove to heated
platter and keep warm. Add shallots and mushrooms to skillet. Sauté briefly. Add ½ cup madeira. Raise heat. Use wooden spoon to blend pan
drippings. Allow liquid to reduce to one-half
original amount. Stir cream and egg yolks together with a fork. Stir 2 tablespoons of hot
sauce into egg mixture. Remove sauce from stove.
Stir in egg mixture. Replace over very low heat
and stir until sauce thickens. Add sautéed sweetbreads and chopped parsley. Stir together. Transfer to heated platter and serve. Serves 4.

DRESSING FOR DUCK, GOOSE,
OR SUCKLING PIG

Start with 2 or 3 pounds of dried fruit (pitted
prunes, apricots, apples, pears, peaches, raisins,

White wine is particularly sympathetic to cookery of all
seafoods and particularly shellfish, which is much enhanced.

currants). Place in a clean crock. Add enough madeira to cover. Let stand for at least a week. More madeira should be added periodically, since the fruits absorb large quantities of it.

Sauté several sliced onions in butter until soft and golden. Add enough fruit to the sautéed onions to make an amount which will fill the cavity of the bird or pig you are roasting. Any fruit left over can be returned to the crock with more madeira. This mixture also makes a delicious relish to be served with any meat or fowl.

CHAMPIGNONS A LA MADERE
(Mushrooms in madeira)

2 pounds mushrooms
¼ cup chopped shallots
¼ pound butter
¼ cup madeira
⅔ cup heavy cream
¼ cup chopped parsley

If mushrooms are small, simply trim off stems and leave whole. If they are large, trim off stems and slice mushrooms ¼-inch thick.

Melt butter in a skillet. Add chopped shallots and mushrooms. Sauté over high heat until mushrooms change color, stirring or shaking pan. This will take less than 5 minutes. Place 2 tablespoons of madeira aside. Pour remaining madeira and heavy cream into mushrooms. Keeping heat very high, continue to cook until liquid has reduced to the point where it has the consistency of a medium cream sauce. No other thickening is necessary. Stir in remaining madeira and chopped parsley and serve. Serves 4.

FRAMBOISES
EN GELEE MADERE
(Raspberries in madeira jelly)

2 packages frozen raspberries,
completely thawed
⅔ cup madeira
1 envelope gelatin
1 cup heavy cream

Drain frozen raspberries. Reserve 1 cup of raspberry juice.

Stir gelatin into ¼ cup raspberry juice. Heat remaining juice until it is boiling. Add gelatin mixture. Stir until gelatin is completely dissolved. Cool. Add madeira. Refrigerate until mixture begins to set but is still liquid.

While gelatin mixture is chilling, beat cream till it is stiff. When gelatin mixture is ready, com-

bine it with whipped cream, beating the two together with a rotary egg beater until they are just blended. Replace in refrigerator for 15 minutes, or till mixture has regained some degree of stiffness. Fold in drained raspberries. Chill thoroughly before serving with additional whipped cream if desired. Serves 6. *Note:* This dessert may be chilled in an oiled mold and unmolded before serving.

APRICOT D'APHRODITE
(Apricot whip with madeira)

½ pound dried apricots
¾ cup sugar
⅔ cup madeira
2 egg whites
1 cup heavy cream
¼ cup blanched, sliced toasted almonds

Soak apricots overnight in water to cover. In the morning, place them in a saucepan. Add half of sugar and additional water, if necessary. It should just about cover the fruit. Bring to a boil and simmer till apricots are tender. Drain apricots. Reduce any remaining liquid as much as possible. Do not let it burn, however. Add to cooked apricots. Cool. Purée fruit in blender with ½ cup madeira.

Beat egg whites till they are stiff. Gradually beat in remaining sugar a little at a time. Continue to beat whites till sugar is dissolved.

Beat cream until it is stiff. Fold stiffly beaten egg whites and half of whipped cream into apricot purée. Pour into serving dish. Sprinkle with almonds. Chill well before serving. Beat remaining madeira into remaining whipped cream for topping. Serves 6.

Cooking with Vermouth

The vermouth type of wine—that is, fortified and resinated for scent and flavor—may be traced back to the Egyptians, Phoenicians, and Greeks, who had a high respect for its medicinal qualities and used it as a specific for almost everything from heartache to migraine.

The spiced wines of Hippocrates, circa 400 B.C., seem to have been a type of grog livened with herbs and spices. Later, Romans Cicero and Pliny infused the dry white wine of the Campagna hills with dittany and absinthe blossoms.

Seafaring men from the city-states of Genoa and Pisa brought back cardamon, myrrh, cloves, rhubarb, ginger, sandalwood, nutmegs, and rare seeds from Mediterranean ports. The addition of these new seeds, flowers, nuts, and herbs gave such character to fortified wines that the name *wehrmuth* (German, meaning war spirit) was adopted and an industry was born.

Understandably, the formula for manufacturing each individual vermouth is secret, but the possible listings of ingredients are as poetic as if culled from Shakespeare's sonnets. There is lemon balm, berries of juniper, valerian, blue gentian, lungwort, flower of camomile, coriander, wild mountain flags, cinnamon, orange, sage, yarrow, thyme, and currants for the distinctive flavor. There is (limited by law) a little caramel which contributes to the color and aging process, and a "stick" of brandy or alcohol for a happy marrying of herbal blend.

For cooking, vermouth has its practical as well as poetic side. Dried herbs—basil, mint, chives, rosemary, chervil, parsley, tarragon, and oregano —when soaked a little in dry white vermouth are hard to tell from freshly picked crops. Veal, which has a tendency to dry during cooking, is sweeter and more delicately moist it vermouth is used in preparation. A sauce gains authority in a subtle way when fortified wine lends its strength. Sole, shrimps, and scallops are improved by vermouth and a little fennel, added with a not-too-heavy hand.

VEAL CHOPS NONPAREIL

Ask your butcher for 6 veal chops cut 2 inches thick. Brown them in 2 tablespoons of butter and 2 tablespoons of corn oil. Pour over 1 cup of dry white vermouth; cover with a tight lid. Steam slowly for 20 minutes. Add ½ cup more of vermouth, ½ cup hot water, salt, pepper, and a pinch of basil leaves. Re-cover and cook slowly another 20 minutes. Arrange chops flat in serving casserole which can go to the table. Thin 1 can of condensed or frozen cream of mushroom soup with liquid from chops; mix well and pour over casserole. Sprinkle with Parmesan cheese and place under broiler for 5 or 6 minutes. Serves 6.

FISH KEBABS

Marinate 1 pound scallops and 1 pound cooked shrimp (parboiled 1 minute) for 2 or 3 hours in salt, pepper, pinch of fennel, and 1 cup dry white vermouth. Alternating with 1-inch pieces of bacon, thread shrimp and scallops on skewers for 4 people. Broil over charcoal 10 minutes, turning once and basting twice with marinade.

Serve immediately when done. Broiled separately, to spear with toothpicks, these are a delicious cocktail bite.

MAILA UMBRIACCA
(Drunken pork chops)

Trim 6 thick pork chops of most of their fat. Render fat in frying pan. Discard brown bits of fat and quickly brown the chops on both sides. Arrange in flat casserole atop a half-inch bed of uncooked rice. In remaining fat, plus 2 tablespoons of butter, sauté 1 large white onion finely chopped; when done, add ¼ cup chopped celery, 1 can (No. 2 size) tomatoes put through a sieve, salt, pepper, and 1 cup of red vermouth. Pour the sauce over the casserole of chops and rice. Place a ring of green pepper on each chop. Seal with foil or cover with a very tight lid and bake for 1 hour in 350° F. oven. This dish must go directly to the table when the cover is removed to prevent the rice from losing its fluffiness. Serves 6.

HAPSBURG POTTED CHEESE

Put a package of Liederkranz cheese in a pot with a tight lid. Cover with dry white vermouth, seal, and keep in the refrigerator two days. Pour off vermouth. Mix cheese with 3 tablespoons of room-temperature whipped butter and 3 tablespoons of fresh dry white vermouth. Chill and serve with hot, toasted water crackers.

VENETIAN DUCK WITH BLACK OLIVES

Roast 2 young ducks cut in quarters and placed skin side up in an open casserole for 30 minutes

at 425° F. Meanwhile chop gizzards, livers, 25 pitted black olives, and 2 white onions until they are all a fine mince. Pour off duck fat; brown mince mix in 2 tablespoons of fat, and add salt, pepper, 1 can consommé, ½ the same can filled with red vermouth, and 1 can of hot water. Cook sauce 15 or 20 minutes until it thickens slightly. Pour over duck and return to oven tightly covered to bake 1 hour longer. Turn duck in sauce at least once. Serves 8.

FILET OF SOLE PROVENCAL

Curl each of 12 filets of sole around a large cooked shrimp. Arrange side by side in casserole. Half cover them with dry white vermouth. Pop the casserole into a 350° F. oven, tightly covered with foil. Cook 10 minutes. Remove casserole from oven and quickly drain off vermouth to a small saucepan. Add 2 tablespoons of butter, 1 cup thick whipping cream, salt, pepper, a pinch of fennel, a few chopped cooked mushrooms. Without letting sauce boil, whip in (with a fork) 2 beaten egg yolks. Pour thickened sauce over sole; return to cook under broiler 5 minutes only. Serve immediately. Serves 4.

FRESH FRUIT DESSERT

Marinate whole peeled figs, mandarins, peach halves, or sliced fresh pineapple for 3 hours in enough sweet white vermouth to half cover the fruit in the bowl. Remove bowl from refrigerator 2 or 3 times to turn fruit in vermouth. Pour over enough stiffly whipped, unsweetened cream to cover fruit. Turn once with a silver spoon to blend vermouth and cream. Return to the refrigerator for an hour. Grate fresh nutmeg over the bowl. Bring to the table with chilled glass bowls or plates.

Cooking with Sherry

There are some great cooks who say that if they could have only one wine or spirit to use in the practice of their art, they would settle for sherry. The famous wine of Jerez, Spain, has been called the prince of catalysts. In some mysterious way, it points up the flavors of other ingredients, seems to meld them into a unity while at the same time emphasizing their individuality.

In almost all other cases when wine is used in cooking, the special character of that wine disappears into the amalgamated character of the dish. The alcohol also is dissipated by the heat. This is not true with sherry, for foods are not usually cooked in sherry. Generally it is added afterward. So even the alcohol is retained.

When sherry is used as a finishing touch, its aromas are as important as its taste. And when you think of aroma, you must think of *oloroso*. In Spanish, they are one and the same word. So it is the *oloroso* sherry you reach for—the Bristol Milk or Bristol Cream—that is put in at the last minute to smooth a sauce, to heighten aroma, to add sparkle to the dish.

Though Spanish in origin, sherry has been adopted by the cooks of the whole world. It is widely used in French sauces, extremely popular in England, a primary requisite in Sweden and Denmark. Because there is such a wide range of sherries, it is sad that recipes rarely specify the type. It does make a difference.

In seafoods or with sausages, a *fino* is much the best. If you want to be even more precise you would use a *manzanilla* with the seafood and an *amontillado* for the sausages.

Everybody knows that sherry is the ultimate seasoning for many soups. But which sherry for what soup? For beef consommé, an *amontillado* or a dry *oloroso*. For chicken consommé, a *fino*. For a shrimp bisque, a *fino*, preferably a *manzanilla*. For cream of chicken soup, blackbean soup, a dry *amontillado*. For the sweeter cream soups like tomato, cream of green pea, mushroom or corn bisque, one of the mellower *amontillados*, or one of the drier *olorosos*.

When sherry is used in the actual cooking, a dry one is best, as a general rule. Unless the dish has a sweet flavor, you will probably find a *fino* most appropriate.

Olorosos, which include all the cream sherries, can be used for ham and other spicy meats, in sauces with a hint of sweetness, and for desserts.

Many of the brown sauces and cream sauces taste best when enhanced with the nutty zest of an *amontillado*. To thin sauces and to round out pan gravies always use a *fino*.

The sherry that you use to cook or to flavor the dish is the one to serve along with that dish. But sherry-flavored foods do not quarrel with other wines, whether white, red, or rosé. Choose whichever seems appropriate.

DESSERTS WITH SHERRY

Add 1 or 2 tablespoons of *oloroso* sherry to a custard sauce. Serve over cut-up fresh fruit, like sliced bananas, orange sections, strawberries or raspberries. To keep the fruit from softening unduly, it is a good idea to add the wine at the table.

When you make old-fashioned shortcake (with biscuits), or new-fashioned shortcake (with sponge layers), sprinkle the fruits with sherry at least an hour or so ahead of time. Generally no sugar is needed.

PEACH MELBA

The classic recipe for peach Melba, as given in Escoffier, requires that the peaches be poached in a vanilla-flavored syrup: "Put them in a timbale upon a layer of vanilla ice cream, and coat them with a purée of fresh raspberries well flavored with sherry."

SHIRRED EGGS JEREZ
WITH ROSEMARY

Melt a teaspoon of butter in an egg shirrer or an individual baking dish. Add 2 tablespoons of *fino* sherry. Break 1 or 2 eggs into a cup, and carefully slip them into the shirrer. Sprinkle with salt, pepper, and a bit of rosemary rubbed between the fingers to release the bouquet. Arrange the shirrers on a cookie sheet and bake in a moderate oven, 350° F., until the white is firm, about 6 minutes. If you want the yolks to be veiled, cover the shirrers with a lid or aluminum foil.

QUICK SHRIMP NEWBURG

A can of quick-frozen shrimp bisque and a package of frozen shrimp attain enchantment in this extra-quick, very fine Newburg. Empty both bisque and shrimp into a pan; add thin cream or top milk (¼ of the soup can). Thaw slowly over very low heat. Then add 1 teaspoon lemon juice; cook 2 or 3 minutes. Slightly beat 2 egg yolks with 2 tablespoons *fino* sherry, and gradually stir soup into the egg yolks. (Don't try to do it the other way or it might curdle.) Taste and season with a bit of salt if needed, a few grains of nutmeg and a drop of Tabasco sauce. Serve from a chafing dish, over rice or toast. Six servings.

LIGHT-AS-AIR SABAYON

This is a modern version of the famed Italian *zabaglione* which is served as a sauce, as a pudding, or sometimes even as a beverage, rather like egg-nog. The original Italian recipe calls for Marsala wine, but many people believe that sherry is even better. Use an *oloroso*. If it is sweet and rich, use less sugar.

Classic recipes use only the egg yolks, but try using the whites too. It's lighter, more delicate and much more economical. Made with the blender it's practically failproof. Fast, too.

Place in the glass container of the blender 8 egg yolks, ¾ cup superfine sugar, ½ cup *oloroso* sherry. Blend about 2 minutes or until very light, pale and foamy. At this point it will be at least double in bulk. Place in the top of a double-boiler, over but not in or touching the water, and heat while stirring constantly until it begins to thicken. It will take 2 or 3 minutes. Fold in 8 egg whites, beaten until stiff, with a speck of salt. Serve warm or chilled in champagne glasses. Some people like to add a spot of cinnamon. Makes 6 generous servings.

Cooking with Cognac and Champagne

Under the French trademarking system, cognac is not just any brandy but specifically a distillate of wines from the Cognac region. Similarly, champagne specifies the sparkling wine of Champagne, in northern France. Although widely imitated, often with considerable success, the originals each have a distinctive bouquet which is sought in any recipes that call for them.

European cooks always keep a bottle of good cognac on the kitchen shelf. Like salt, it brings out the flavor; also it may often be ignited for a colorful *flambé* effect. Champagne is reserved for the ultimate in creative *haute cuisine*.

ONION SOUP WITH COGNAC

Put 4 sliced onions in a saucepan in which 4 tablespoons butter are bubbling; sprinkle 1 teaspoon sugar over the onions. In about 10 minutes when they are golden, not browned, remove from heat. Cut 1 pound French bread in ⅓-inch slices and toast them. Butter these croutons generously and cover each with a slice of Swiss cheese. Place the onions in a large fireproof earthenware dish and pour over them 6 cups of hot beef bouillon, ½ cup cognac. Add salt and pepper and prepared bread. Place in a preheated moderately hot oven for 20 minutes. Serve piping hot and pass grated

Parmesan cheese. This is an onion soup with a distinct difference, an excellent one to start a meal.

JUGGED HARE

Wipe the hare with a moist cloth and disjoint it (or you might use quick-frozen cut-up rabbit). Marinate for 24 hours in this mixture: A bottle of excellent dry red wine (the better the wine the better the sauce), ½ cup olive oil, 1 teaspoon salt, ½ teaspoon pepper. Turn the pieces twice before removing from their bath the next day. Save the marinade. Dry each piece thoroughly. Brown them in 6 tablespoons butter.

In a covered saucepan cook very slowly 1 sliced onion in a tablespoon butter. Put 4 tablespoons butter in a Dutch oven. When it bubbles, add 1 tablespoon flour; stir until golden brown. Add the browned pieces of hare, the cooked onions, ½ tablespoon fat, a bouquet of several stalks of parsley, thyme, basil, celery, 2 bay leaves, 3 cloves, 3 shallots, and a blade of mace. Cover the pot and allow hare to stew in its own juice for 15 minutes over very low flame. Bring to a boil and add the marinade which you have taken the precaution to heat. Cook gently for ¾ of an hour and then add 1½ cups of cognac. The hare, depending upon its age and size, will require about 1 hour further cooking. It should be served surrounded by toasted croutons covered with:

SOUBISE SAUCE FOR HARE

Make 1 cup thick Béchamel sauce to which has been added 2 tablespoons onion juice, 2 tablespoons very rich veal or chicken bouillon, 2 tablespoons heavy cream, salt, pepper, and a pinch of nutmeg. Brown the croutons lightly in the oven or under the broiler.

FRIED SPRING CHICKEN

Wipe 2 broilers with a moist cloth, dry them, and rub with half a lemon, (this will keep them white). Disjoint them. Keep backs and wings to make a bouillon. Cover the pieces of chicken with 1 beaten egg to which has been added 1 tablespoon olive oil, 1 teaspoon salt, ¼ teaspoon pepper, and a pinch of nutmeg. Cover each piece completely with fine dry bread crumbs.

In a heavy frying pan heat ¼ cup butter and add ¼ cup olive oil. Lightly brown the pieces of the chicken, being careful not to disturb the egg and crumb coating. Add 1 cup lighted cognac.

Lower the flame and cover the pan. Shake the pan frequently so chicken will not scorch. In ½ hour it will be ready to serve with:

OYSTER SAUCE FOR CHICKEN

Slice 3 truffles and put aside. Chop another truffle very fine with 3 stalks parsley, 1 shallot, and 1 green onion. Pound through a fine sieve. Mix with ½ cup soft but not melted butter. Add ½ teaspoon salt and ⅛ teaspoon pepper and put aside.

Allow 2 dozen oysters to come just to the boil in their juice. Drain and keep the juice. Paint a saucepan with the truffle-butter mixture. Place half of the sliced truffles on the bottom of the saucepan. Dot with ⅓ of the remaining truffle-butter mixture. Then add a layer of all the oysters, dot with truffle-butter, add the rest of the sliced truffles, and top with all the remaining truffle-butter. Cover and keep hot but do not allow to boil. Skim excess butter and add oyster juice, ⅓ cup cognac, and ¼ cup chicken bouillon. Bring slowly to a boil. Remove chicken from frying pan to preheated serving dish. Add a little of the hot sauce to pan and stir to thoroughly mix. Add to sauce, heat well and pour over chicken. Serve at once.

ROAST CHICKEN WITH OLIVES

This is a 1691 recipe. Entirely cover the breast of a fine roasting chicken with a large thin slice of fat back of pork (rind removed), or use bacon. Tie securely but not too tightly in place. Put the chicken in a roasting pan or better still on a spit. In the dripping pan put ½ cup butter and ½ cup chicken bouillon with which the chicken will be basted.

In a saucepan place 3 stalks of parsley, 1 diced green onion, 2 tablespoons lard, and 1 tablespoon flour. When the lard commences to bubble add the contents of the dripping pan, bring to a boil and add ½ cup hot chicken bouillon, ½ cup cognac, 1 laurel leaf, a twig of thyme, 1 tablespoon olive oil, 12 pitted and finely chopped olives, and 1 crushed, boned anchovy. Cover and simmer for 15 minutes. Then add little by little another ½ cup hot chicken bouillon.

When the chicken is done place on a preheated shallow serving dish. Strain the sauce and reheat. Pour a little of it into the pan (if the chickens have not been cooked on the spit), and stir to release any of the juice adhering to the pan. Add this to the sauce and skim the sauce. Pour sauce over chicken.

Surround by green tips of asparagus lightly cooked and sprinkled with 2 chopped hard-cooked eggs mixed with fine bread crumbs browned in butter.

BOEUF AU COGNAC
(à la Alice B. Toklas)

Marinate 5 pounds top round of beef for 24 hours in 1 bottle good dry white wine and 1 cup good cognac, turning the meat several times. The next day remove meat from its bath and dry thoroughly. You will do the larding; your butcher can't do it for you. First soak the strips of fat back of pork for 4 or 5 hours in cognac. Place each strip in the larding needle after pressing into it a mixture of finely chopped parsley, powdered basil, salt, pepper, a good pinch of cloves, mace, and thyme all well mixed, rubbed into the fat. Push the larding needle into the meat with the grain of the meat at 8 or 9 evenly separated places. Allow the lardons to extend ¾ inch beyond the meat on either end. (Larding needles of various sizes may be secured at Bazar Français, 666 Avenue of the Americas, New York City.)

Rub into the meat 1 tablespoon salt, 1 teaspoon pepper, ½ teaspoon ginger, and ¼ teaspoon mace. Put 4 tablespoons butter in a heavy enameled pot and brown the meat gently on all sides. Pour ½ cup lighted cognac over it. Remove meat and line the pot with a piece of fat back of pork, about ¾ inches, rind included. Place the meat on it and pour over the marinade, brought to a boil with 1 cup beef bouillon, ½ pound sliced carrots, 2 large sliced onions, a bouquet of parsley, thyme, and laurel leaf, and a calf's foot washed in hot water and thoroughly scraped. Cover and bring to a quick boil. Reduce heat and simmer for 4½ hours.

Remove meat and carrots to preheated shallow serving dish. Skim sauce and strain over meat. (If you haven't a calf's foot handy, use 2 envelopes of Knox gelatin to give the needed gelatinous texture to the sauce.)

This is a succulent dish and is equally delicious cold, in which case the juice must be clarified.

TURKEY LEGS REVIVED

This recipe is dated 1797. Put 2 roasted turkey legs (second joints and drumsticks) in a saucepan with ¾ cup cognac, ¾ cup beef bouillon, ½ teaspoon salt, ¼ teaspoon pepper, a bouquet of 1 stalk parsley, ½ clove garlic, 1 green onion, and 2 cloves. Cover and cook over medium flame until the liquid is completely absorbed.

While turkey is cooking, prepare this garnish:

STEWED SWEETBREAD

Soak a sweetbread for 1 hour in cold water. Place in saucepan, cover with cold water, add 1 teaspoon salt, cover saucepan and bring to a boil. The sweetbread will be cooked in 20 minutes. Remove from pan and allow cold water to run over it until it is tepid. Then remove tubes and skin and cut sweetbread in cubes.

Put 4 tablespoons butter in a saucepan. When it bubbles add cubed sweetbread, ½ pound sliced mushrooms, 1 chopped green onion, and 1 tablespoon lemon juice. Stir with a wooden spoon, sprinkle 1 tablespoon parsley over this, and gradually add ½ cup hot beef bouillon and ½ cup hot cognac. Simmer for 15 minutes, stirring with the wooden spoon. Pour over turkey legs and serve.

SWEET POTATOES AND ORANGES AU COGNAC

Boil 6 sweet potatoes in their jackets until they are not quite tender. Peel, slice, put a layer in a buttered oven-proof dish, dot with butter, sprinkle with brown sugar, cover with a layer of thinly sliced unpeeled oranges from which seeds and the white center have been removed. Continue in this manner until the 6 potatoes and 2 large oranges, ½ cup brown sugar, and ⅓ cup butter have been used. Pour over the contents of the dish ½ cup cognac. Sprinkle with brown sugar and dot with butter. Bake about ½ hour or until well browned in medium oven. Serve hot with pork roasted or grilled.

SHELL FISH IN CHAMPAGNE
(à la Alice B. Toklas)

Use about equal quantities of lobster, crab, and shrimps—say a 2-pound lobster, and 1½ pounds shrimps. Make a *court bouillon* using 2 carrots, 2 onions, 1 bay leaf, sprig of thyme, several stalks of parsley, several whole black peppers, and enough water to float the lobster. Cook flavorings a few minutes, add lobster, and simmer 25 minutes or until done.

Prepare the crab in the same way. Boil shrimps in water just long enough to have them turn pink. Cut the lobster in half lengthwise, crack the claws, and remove all meat. Put the meat aside. From the shell remove and discard sack. Scrape everything else from shell and put aside.

Shell shrimps and remove black vein from back. Cut the lobster and crab meat in neat slices and mix with shrimps.

Strain through a sieve, or put into your blender everything that was scraped from the lobster and crab shells. Melt ⅓ cup butter in a saucepan over medium heat, add 1 finely chopped onion, and 2 finely chopped shallots. Cook for 10 minutes but do not allow to brown. Add lobster, crab meat, shrimps, and ½ teaspoon salt. To strained or blended scrapings of the shells add the yolks of 3 eggs and 1 tablespoon flour. Stir until perfectly smooth. Add 6 tablespoons heavy cream.

Pour into saucepan 2 cups champagne, bring to boil; reduce heat and add scrapings, egg and cream mixture, and the shellfish. Do not allow to boil but turn constantly in the same direction until sauce is hot and has thickened. Serve at once.

CHICKEN IN CHAMPAGNE
(à la Alice B. Toklas)

Rub a fine big chicken on all sides with half a lemon, to keep the flesh white. Then rub in ½ teaspoon salt. Melt ¼ cup butter in a casserole with a tight-fitting cover. Place the chicken in the casserole and heat it on all sides, but without browning. Reduce heat, cover. After 15 minutes, raise heat and add 1½ cups dry champagne. Cover, lower heat and cook gently for 45 minutes or till done.

During this time, boil 4 large artichokes for about 30 minutes, depending upon their size. When a leaf can be removed easily, take from heat, drain, and remove leaves, leaving the hearts. (The leaves can be scraped later and used in an omelette.) Also, boil in salted water ¾ pound green asparagus tips. Do not overboil, but when sufficiently tender, drain. Boil 1 pound very small new potatoes, add to casserole. After the juice boils up again, place the fowl in a preheated serving dish surrounded by the artichoke hearts, asparagus, and new potatoes.

Understanding the principles and developing the skills to present attractive dishes is a most gratifying activity.

These are Swedish pancakes (called *plättar*) to be served as a dessert topped with lingonberry sauce or your favorite jam or preserve. Sour cream is also a tasty garnish.

International Travelers:

The Universal Pancake

It knows no international boundaries, but can be anything from a hoecake to a crêpe Suzette

Certain types of foods are found everywhere, because the ingredients for making them are available everywhere. One of the most ubiquitous types is the pancake. Nearly every civilization has one or more versions. Every type of cereal that can be ground into flour has been rolled or patted into pancakes.

To prove the universality of the principle, Poppy Cannon once made a world survey of all the different forms the pancake could take. Her list, on page 130, makes you realize that foreign cuisines are as much alike as unlike.

Pancakes are so useful and versatile in enlarging your menu repertoire that it pays to master a few classic ones, from several countries. First, we'd better try to define:

What exactly is a pancake? A dough, a batter cooked in a pan or on a griddle, most often on top of the stove, though it could be done in the oven, and generally served straight-away and hot.

When and where does the pancake belong? At any hour of the day, from early breakfast through lunch, tea time, dinner, and far-after-midnight snack. Even in the highest realms of *haute cuisine* it has its place, in one form or another, in any course of the meal.

Hors-d'oeuvre range from *pannequets* to Chinese egg rolls. For the soup course, Celestine *crêpes,* cut into ribbons to garnish consommé. The fish may be served *en chemise* (wrapped in a crisp pancake). Or it might be fish in a New-

burg sauce topped, Finnish fashion, with the thinnest pancake rondelles. With roast beef comes Yorkshire pudding—a baked pancake, no more, no less! Or, it could be a Swedish meat pancake casserole, with well-sauced meat between layers of pancakes baked in the oven and served like a pie in wedges. Perhaps a pancake-topped meat loaf with layers of zucchini, green beans, and potato, which in certain Hungarian provinces is known (somewhat inconsistently) as *moussaka.*

Poultry? In rolled chicken pancakes browned with crumbs and cheese. Or *canelloni* in the North Italian style, where the covering is a *crêpe* instead of a noodle or pasta dough.

Vegetables? Potato pancakes, green corn cakes often called corn oysters, or West Indian fritter cakes. Or spinach pancakes from Rumania.

Even the salad may be served upon or enclosed in a pancake, like the Mexican tacos—a tortilla filled with spicy meat and beans, shredded lettuce and tomatoes.

As for dessert, possibilities are endless, ranging all the way from a hot hoecake with sorghum, in a Tennessee mountain cottage, to *crêpes Suzette,* flambéed with cognac and cordials in Paris.

Like ancient Gaul, the pancake world is divided into three parts, but each part is a host of things most difficult to organize. Highly individual, each pancake has many names and nicknames, many twins, brothers, cousins, and kin.

The first might be called the Primitive School

though it includes a number of extremely elegant trifles like the lacy French *galettes* and the Swedish cream *munk*. Flour or meal plus liquid and a little fat are the basic ingredients. Essentially this is the unleavened bread of the Bible. Ordinarily it's cooked on a hot stone or griddle but sometimes in an oven.

Without the addition of fat and when the dough is rolled out thin (instead of patted) and cooked in hot water, it becomes a *pasta*. When more fat is added and the cooking is done in an oven we have a pie crust.

The second group is the Egg Cakes. There an egg, or many eggs, whole or separated, are added to the basic flour, together with liquid and fat. Rolled, folded, filled, sauced, glazed, gratinéed, cut into strips, torn into bits as in the *Kaiser-schmarren* of Austria, these are the most numerous, the most varied, the most versatile, and probably the most exquisite and delicate.

In this group the pancake may lose almost all its flour and come marvelously close to the omelet and soufflé. Dropped into deep fat, it becomes a fritter. Baked, the same batter is a popover, which explains why a packaged popover mix is so useful in the preparation of a dozen continental pancakes, ranging all the way from Swedish *plättar* to Polish *nalesniki*.

In the third pancake group are the "Risen" Cakes where some form of leavening—either yeast, baking powder, soda, or even new fallen snow—is added to the mixture to make it light and puffy. All our American griddle cakes belong in this category, including our popular pancake mixes. Crumpets belong here, too, and so do English muffins. Steamed, they are dumplings. Baked, they are rolls, or sometimes muffins, or gems. Shaped into loaves, they become bread.

In some curious way, the pancake in many regions has taken on almost mystical significance. In many Anglo-Saxon areas the first three pancakes were often reserved for the unseen deities. In later centuries there was a rhyme:

> The first is for Peter,
> The second for Paul,
> And the third for the One
> Who rules us all.

When the eating of milk and eggs as well as flesh foods was forbidden to Christians during Lent, pancakes were the delicacies of the Fat Tuesday before the long fast. All the bits and pieces of food in the household could be used. Later they became a convenient and heartening adjunct to meatless meals in Lent or other times.

Tricks and Thermostats

The techniques of pancakes are many and varied. They can be as simple as making mud pies, or they may call for the utmost skill and dexterity, as witness the Shrove Tuesday pancake-tossing contests that have been popular in many parts of England through the centuries. Actually, pancake-tossers have won fame, at least locally, in Egypt ever since ancient days. Their counterpart today might be the Italian pizza baker who causes bread discs 15 to 18 inches in diameter to fly and turn in the air with what looks like the greatest of ease.

Recently, pancake techniques have been revolutionized by an American innovation—the thermostatically-controlled griddle and frying pan and the thermostatically controlled surface unit on stoves. Now we can all be pancake experts. No longer need we be able to judge by "look and sniff" or by the way a drop of water dances on the griddle. No longer must we exercise almost psychic control over the heat of the fire. The first pancake is no more a sacrifice, nor the last one a burnt offering.

To Better the Butter

As a general rule, pancakes are cooked at about 370° F., although one of the world's acknowledged pancake experts, Lester Highet, owner of the Pancake House of Portland, Oregon, has his griddles set at 380°F. His higher temperature does give a crisper product but there is the danger of burning the butter, a danger which he obviates by returning to a method devised in India, where traditionally the cooks clarify the butter of buffalo milk in order to make "ghee."

Clarifying butter is no particular chore. Simply melt it slowly, skim off the froth, or pass through a fine cheesecloth. Freed of its milk solids, butter does not burn so readily. It is a wonder-thing to have on hand, not only for pancake making but also for pastries. Vegetable shortening and salad oils may be used, but they don't impart the same flavor. Margarine? Not in this case, please. Subjected to high heat, it gives an off-taste.

The Pan's the Thing

With pancakes, equipment is often as important as ingredients. Special cakes demand special pans.

The Primitive School is mostly griddle-baked, though some, like hush-puppies and curd cakes, may be dropped into shallow fat in a frying pan.

Griddles must be properly seasoned, the pores impregnated with fat, if they are of the old-fashioned type; or else treated with silicones so that they will not stick. The metal should be one that will hold the heat. Even heat is what you want and no "hot spots." Good, old cast iron still has many devotees. So do the old-time soapstone griddles which you can still buy at The Vermont Country Store, Weston, Vermont. The newer metals too, magnesium, aluminum, and stainless steel—many teflon-treated—combine all the virtues with ease of handling and quick cleanability.

For the Egg Type there exists a battery of special pans. You could, if you are skilled enough, make a perfect *crêpe* or *blintz* or the tiniest of Swedish *plättar* with an ordinary frying pan or even on a griddle. But the most expert dote upon their pans. The best *crêpe* pan should have shallow sloping sides, the handle set at a proper angle for convenient grasping.

At the Pancake House they have a long row of electric frying pans with the sides cut down to half-inch height for the making of large Swedish pancakes. Their German *pfannküchen*, on the other hand, are baked in aluminum frying pans with sides about 2½ inches high and slightly rounded. Every few weeks the silicone coating is renewed, for the pancake must take the shape of the pan, yet draw away from its edges.

Swedish *skivers,* antecedent of the muffin, no doubt, and perhaps the dumpling, are dependent upon a particular pan like that pictured on page 130. *Munks* and Dutch *poffertjes* use much the same utensil, though the Dutch version is slightly more rounded beneath. You could, if you like, use a set of iron gem pans.

Turners are as specialized as pans: use big ones for big cakes, and slender, flexible models for thin, small *crêpes*. Use a fork for turning *skivers*. Note the perforated hoe also on page 130 for turning a cake of large proportions like the hoe-cakes of our ancestors. These were not cooked on a hoe as some people claim, but have this name because a sawed-off hoe was kept near the chimneyplace for turning them.

Mixing and Baking

The mixing and beating of different pancakes vary widely. The Primitive school is the least fussy. The Egg Type, from time immemorial, has been correctly stirred only in one direction. While the blender works well, the electric mixer does not appear suitable. The expert, Lester Highet, does not approve of the rotary beater either, but considers the wire whisk the best possible utensil. If this type of batter should have lumps appear in it, it must be strained. But a griddle cake mixture for the "Risen" pancake is not harmed by lumps if it is leavened with baking powder. Over-mixing, then, is a mistake. For yeast-leavened cakes, however, much beating and handling makes for tenderness.

Despite the diversity of pancakes there are a few very simple rules which seem to apply in many, if not all cases

First: The thinner the batter, the thinner the cake.

Second: To assure even cooking place all the batter for each cake on the pan at once.

Third: Cook until the pancake begins to look a little dry or is covered with tiny holes. The edges at this time should begin to draw away from the pan and crinkle slightly. Certain pancakes intended for filling, like *blintzes* and Chinese egg rolls, are cooked only on one side.

Fourth: Never turn a pancake more than once or it will become heavy and sodden.

Would that we could include here recipes for all 76 pancakes listed on the next page! However, we can offer bibliographical clues. Literally dozens of old-fashioned cakes can be found in Sheila Hibbens' "American Regional Cookery" (Little, Brown & Co.), and also in "America Cooks" by the Browns (Doubleday). André Simon's "Encyclopaedia of Gastronomy" (William Collins Sons & Co.) contains a drove of English, Welsh, Scottish, and Continental specialties, modern and archaic, too.

"The Wise Encyclopedia of Cookery" (Wm. H. Wise and Co.) has griddle cake recipes and variations galore. In the "New Fannie Farmer Boston Cooking-School Cook Book" (Little, Brown & Co.) you will find all the basic techniques and several imaginative variations.

Irma Rombauer's always-to-the-rescue "Joy of Cooking" (Bobbs-Merrill Co.) is especially helpful in the German, Austrian, and Viennese categories. Or use "Contemporary French Cooking" by Waverley Root and Richard de Rochemont.

For tortilla making, look in the section of this book on the World of Corn and Beans.

German Pfannküchen

Pancakes of the World and Their Pans

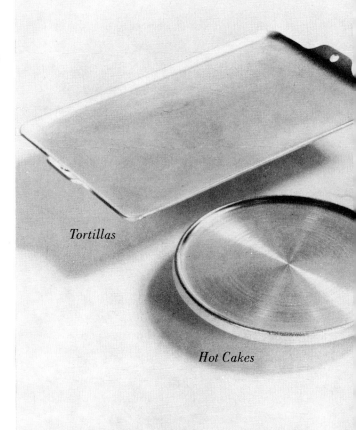

Tortillas

Hot Cakes

Potato Pancakes

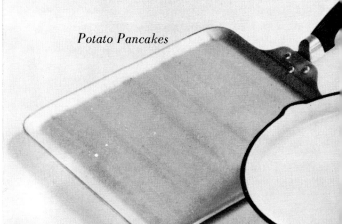

THE PRIMITIVE
(Meal plus liquid)

Any grain from finest wheat to corn, oats, barley, peas, lentils, buckwheat, or cassava is mixed with water, beer, milk, or cream.

Ashcake
Cassava bread
Chapati
Chinese doily
Corn dodger or finger pone
Corn dollar or corn cake
Cracklin' bread
Curd cake
Galette
Hoecake
Hush puppy
Indian meal slapjack
Ireland potato cake
Jamaica lace cake
Oatcake
Poppadum
Raspados
Rhode Island jonny cake
 (no "h" here)
Roti
Scratch back
Swedish cream munk
Tortilla

Swedish Skivers

Swedish Plättar

Crêpes Suzette

THE EGG TYPE
(Meal plus liquid plus egg)

These might be called European pancakes, except that they were known among the Chinese, Persians, and the ancient Aryans.

Alsatian eierküchen
Batty cake
Blintzes
Celestine pancake
Chinese egg or spring roll
Crêpes Suzette
Danish beer pancake
Elderberry flower pancake
German pfannküchen
Green-corn oysters
Hungarian palacsinta
Indonesian baked meat rissoles
Kaiserschmärren
Lacy panty-cake
Malpoa
Marvels
Matzos pancake
New Netherlands izer-cooky
North Italian cannelloni
Pannequets
Polish nalesniki
Pork cake
Raw potato pancake
Rolled chicken pancake
  au gratin
Salzburger nöckerl
Sirniki
Swedish pancake casserole
Swedish plättar
Toad-in-the-hole

THE "RISEN"
(Meal plus liquid plus leavening)

To flour or crushed meal and liquid there came to be added—early in history—the magic of leaven: yeast, soda, baking powder.

Bannocks
Blini
Bockings
Boxty-on-the-pan
Chinese "thousand flour"
  bread
Crumpets
Dutch pfofferjes
Egyptian katief
English muffin
Flannel cake
Flapjack
Griddle, girdle,
  or drop scones or scots
Karnatsi
Mexican buñuelos
New England fire cake
Oblaty
Old-fashioned buckwheat cake
Stack cake
Singing Hinny
Snow pancake
Sour dough hot cake
Swedish skiver
Trinidad bake
Welsh crempop
West Indian fritter cake

Rolled Pancakes

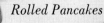

Blini

West Indian Fritter Cake

Salzburger Nöckerl

Portrait of an Imperial Sandwich:
half steak tartar and half fresh
caviar, garnished with capers
and egg. Accompany with icy vodka
and beer. Native to Russia and the
Scandinavian countries.

"Caviare to the General"

*All about the greatest international traveler
among foods: where to get it, how to serve it*

Unlike the universal pancake, which is universal because grain flours are indigenous everywhere, other foods are encountered throughout the world precisely because they are *not* grown locally. They reward traders profitably for whatever pains and dangers it may take to bring them from distant places of origin. Spices, as we have seen, dominated the East-West trade of the ancient world. In modern times, caviar is an outstanding example of the international traveler among foods.

Why, you may wonder? Isn't caviar merely fish eggs, and don't fish have eggs in all waters? Yes, but in a few places the waters (and the fish) are more beneficent to flavor. So some fish roe has gained an acceptance of remarkable stature. The roe of the Caspian sturgeon has spread from a relatively remote Russian sea to captivate literally the world.

Caspian sea caviars are considered the best, have the greatest gourmet standing, and therefore cost the most in the international marts of trade. Shakespeare's often misquoted phrase, "caviare to the general," meant "too sophisticated to be appreciated by the ordinary person." This Caspian or true "Russian caviar" is found only at the finest restaurants and food purveyors.

I could wish for you that your first meeting with caviar would be to meet it fresh, unsalted, and to eat it straight—plain. But this means going abroad, in the direction of the landlocked Caspian Sea. All that comes to the U.S. has to be cured with salt. You can order it fresh, only lightly salted, shipped in sawdust and real ice, by air parcel post or express at a cost of around $44 for 14 ounces, plus shipping charges. If the fresh costs too much you can get a good imported caviar for as little as 79¢ an ounce, vacuum-packed. It comes from the same Caspian Sea catches of sturgeon as the fresh, and is quite acceptable for garnishing.

Of the 65 tons of caviar consumed by Americans last year, only 25 per cent was fresh caviar. Seventy-five per cent was vacuum-packed. These statistics are not only proof of our opulence, but of the spreading popularity of a food which two decades ago was eaten mostly by the so-called "elite."

According to the Food and Drug Administration, red caviar is not caviar technically, but salmon roe. Only the dark caviar, the egg of the sturgeon, can be accurately labeled caviar. There are three kinds, coming from three species of sturgeon. The most valuable is the giant grain gray *beluga. Osetra* is the next largest in size and slightly cheaper. The smallest grain, *sevruga,* is

BLINIS: Using black caviar as filling, turn old-fashioned buckwheat pancakes into those famous tangy blinis that make gourmets smack their lips. Garnish with sour cream.

AVOCADOS: Their mild creaminess begs for salty red caviar. Fill avocado halves with jellied consommé, top with two tablespoons caviar and a good dollop of sour cream.

seldom seen in this country as fresh caviar. Taste, not cost, should decide your preference.

In buying caviar you will find that different packers use different designations for their processing. (See our explanation of the terms below.) Check the container you buy to see whether or not it needs refrigeration.

Any person learning to like caviar, like one learning to like oysters or olives, acquires the taste faster if the caviar is used as a garnish for familiar foods. Try it natural pressed. This caviar is made from very ripe roe, too soft to be prepared as grain caviar; but it has an excellent flavor because a roe becomes sweeter as it ripens, like a peach or a banana. Also since the grains are pressed, very little salt is needed as no deterioration can occur between the grains.

Some caviar lovers who have indulged their

taste abroad insist that the borax-treated berries they get in Europe taste much sweeter. Our Food and Drug Administration forbids entry of borax-preserved food.

However, I once conducted a test at the gourmet restaurant, "The Four Seasons," sampling and comparing eight lightly-salted American brands with the European variety — a borax-treated tin contributed by a friend who had just brought it home from abroad. We concluded that an imported Iranian *beluga malossol* (meaning lightly salted) was crisper, fresher, and sweeter-tasting than the European offering.

Once opened, any caviar loses freshness fast, so it should not be held for long. Recap what's left, using a layer of wax paper under the cap to keep out air, and turn it on its side every day to allow oil to seep through the grains. After dipping into

RED CAVIAR: Use it to season fresh oysters, as in this sea-food platter as served at "The Forum of the Twelve Caesars." Caviar adds a much more pungent taste to any bland food.

FISH ROLLS: Caviar, used to season smoked fish, heightens its ocean-salt taste. For a colorful dish, roll black caviar in slices of smoked salmon, red caviar in sturgeon slices.

a tin or jar, level the grains with a knife blade so there'll be no holes for oil or juice to run into and draw moisture off the other eggs.

Fresh caviar, so special it travels at great expense under constant refrigeration, deserves to have its unique taste enjoyed for itself alone. Some connoisseurs call it a crime to confuse the flavor with anything—except possibly a few drops of lemon juice and toasted white bread without butter. But many knowledgeable gourmets consider the use of shredded whites and yolks of eggs and finely chopped onions to be quite permissible.

Connoisseurs also feel strongly about the choice of beverages to drink with caviar. Some choose the driest champagne, like a Dom Pérignon or a Bollinger. If it is to be vodka, try a martini made with vodka.

Other devotees favor a good Moselle or Rhine wine, such as *Bernkastler Doktor,* or a *Schloss Johannisberger.* These are the choices of Albert Stockli, formerly Chef Director of "The Four Seasons," who created the recipes given below.

To make these dishes, you can use natural pressed caviar, or any good grade of vacuum-packed, or even one of the commonly-used caviar staples. Staples are the so-called "caviars," such as whitefish (domestic) or lump-fish (Icelandic), both of which are black; or salmon caviar, which is red. Sometimes you can get genuine domestic sturgeon caviar, mildly salted and of excellent quality, which comes from northern Canadian lakes and our own Great Lakes.

Where the recipes call for red caviar, the better the color of it, the better the quality. Don't stop with the recipes given here. Draw upon your pantry stock of caviar for dozens of other recipes you'll be able to invent yourself.

For example, make your mayonnaise for a sea food salad tastier by mixing in 1 ounce of red caviar, lemon juice to taste, and a stalk of finely-minced scallion.

To make a party dip, mix 1 cup heavy sour cream with ½ cup red caviar, juice of lemon, ¼ cup minced scallions. Heap mixture in shallow silver bowl, top with fresh black cracked pepper, and surround with thin Swedish crackers.

Give artichoke hearts, either canned or frozen, the richness of caviar's flavor. Cut in half, scoop out a little hollow, stuff with a mixture of caviar and cream cheese.

To stuff hard-boiled eggs, simply remove the yolks, mix them well with French dressing and red caviar, and put back in the cavities. And nothing is better than bland celery when stuffed with a mixture of cream cheese and red caviar.

One of the world's great vehicles for caviar is the Russian buckwheat pancake called *blini*—hot, tender as a baby's ear, bland, and totally receptive to the pungent saltiness of caviar and the tartness of sour cream.

There are many schools of thought about how the *blini* should be made. The most prevalent leans to the yeast recipe that produces a light, fluffy pancake on which the crispy grains of caviar ride. The opposite point of view votes for the crisp, almost crunchy pancake which, by contrast, lets the grains of caviar seem tender and delicate.

I will take sides about caviars, but not about the *blinis*. Here are recipes for both types.

YEAST BLINIS WITH CAVIAR

(*à la* Ambrose Heath)

Dissolve 1 to 2 ounces of yeast in a cup of tepid water, then gradually stir in 6 ounces of buckwheat flour, 3 ounces of ordinary white flour, and a pinch of salt. Add 2 egg yolks, beat well, cover with a cloth, and leave to double its bulk. Now stir in 3 ounces of melted butter, another egg yolk, and a half pint of cooled, scalded milk. Just before frying, add 2 stiffly beaten egg whites.

Bake the pancakes on a griddle till golden-brown on each side. Make pancakes whatever size you want. Stack them covered with a moistened cloth in a 150° F. oven, while you are getting ready to serve. Then serve either as individual finger food for the cocktail hour or stacked four or five deep (with sour cream and caviar heaped on each pancake) as a first course or as a main course for luncheon, married to a green salad.

CRISP, THIN BLINIS WITH CAVIAR

(as presented by "The Four Seasons")

1 cup milk
1 cup flour
½ cup water
5 egg yolks
1 egg   Pinch salt
3 ounces melted butter
½ pound toasted buckwheat groats (Wolff's Medium Brown Roasted Buckwheat Groats)
Peanut oil to grease skillet

Mix ingredients well. Use a *blini* pan (or any 5-inch, cast-iron skillet), lightly greased. Pour in a thin layer of batter, pressing later with a spatula to make as thin as possible. Brown on one side, then brown the other side.

This recipe makes 24 *blinis,* which can be prepared in advance, put on a cookie sheet, and reheated in the oven just before serving.

To serve, spoon a generous tablespoon of caviar on top of each *blini,* stacking from 1 to 6 on a plate. Top each stack with heavy sour cream, and another big dollop of caviar. They can also be served like individual wafers. Use segments of lemon. Optional, but nice, is a garnish made by mixing minced red radishes and black truffles.

SMOKED STURGEON AND SALMON ROLLS STUFFED WITH CAVIAR

(as presented by "The Four Seasons")

12 slices smoked sturgeon
12 slices smoked salmon
2 jars red caviar (8 oz.)
2 jars black caviar (8 oz.)
10 small red radishes, chopped fine
4 or 5 truffles, chopped fine (½-oz. can)
1 lemon, cut in four segments

If you buy the smoked fish from a delicatessen, have it sliced thin. If you use canned sturgeon, get the ready-sliced Vita brand (a 1-pound can has approximately 12 slices). For your salmon needs, there's also a Vita brand ready-sliced smoked lox salmon, 6 slices to a vacuum-packed plastic package.

Fill each of the 12 sturgeon slices with 1 tablespoon red caviar and each salmon slice with 1 tablespoon of black caviar. Roll each, fasten with toothpick, and arrange in contrasting pairs on serving plate. Garnish with chopped radishes

mixed with chopped truffles. Accompany with
lemon segments.

TAMARA SALATA
(Red caviar dip)

Nobody knows how many millenia ago the fisher-
folk of Greece began to rub fish roe and onion
in a wooden bowl with a wooden pestle, gave it
body with the soft crumb pulled from the inside
of crusty loaves softened in water, sharpened it
with the juice of lemons (which many Greeks believe were the original Golden Apples of Hes-
perides), and then made it unguent with olive oil
added drop by patient drop, and sometimes with
an egg yolk.

This is *tamara salata,* one of the most popular
of Greek delicacies. You will find it in every
restaurant, in every home, the type of seasoning
varying according to family tradition. In the
great barn-like market in Athens glistening gray-
pink mounds of the roe are at almost every stall.
In America, wherever there are many Greek
families, you can buy this inexpensive, strongly
flavored, pressed red caviar. The regular delicatessen red caviar put up in a jar by Vita or
Romanoff makes a more delicate and prettier
spread.

Place in your blender the juice of 2 lemons
(about 6 tablespoons), one-third of an 8-ounce
jar of red caviar, 1 medium-size onion cut into
½-inch pieces. Blend about 1 minute until all
particles have disappeared. Then add 2 cups
white bread, crusts removed. First dip bread
quickly in water, squeeze dry, break it into
pieces and place in the blender. Blend about 30
seconds. Remove the lid and while the blender
is still running at low speed, gradually add 1 to
2 cups of olive oil. Blend until oil disappears. If
a stronger-flavored, saltier spread is desired, use
only 1 cup of bread. Serve in a shallow bowl
lined with lettuce and garnished with black or
red Greek olives.

SEAFOOD PLATTER A LA FORUM

The New York restaurant, "Forum of the Twelve
Caesars," uses red caviar in place of cocktail
sauce for oysters on the half-shell. Garnish each
oyster with 1 teaspoon red caviar (about 2 ounces
for 2 dozen). Sprinkle fresh grated horseradish on
caviar. Serve with lemon wedges, on iced platter with sliced cooked lobster, crabmeat, shrimps,
or other seafoods and their seasonings.

WHERE TO ORDER
FRESH CAVIAR

If you are unable to buy fresh caviar in
your local stores, you can order it from the
following sources. They will ship it in ice
by parcel post, special delivery, within 300
miles of New York; by air parcel post or
air express to any other point in the country. Fresh *beluga* costs approximately $44
per 14-ounce Russian pound, fresh *osetra*
approximately $39, and natural pressed
approximately $14, plus shipping charges.
Smaller quantities in proportion.

CHARLES AND COMPANY, 340 Madison Avenue, New York, N. Y. 10017: Fresh Iranian
beluga, 14 ounces. Fresh Iranian *osetra,* 14
ounces. Natural pressed caviar, 8 ounces.

ELLEN GREY, 712 Madison Avenue, New
York, N. Y. 10021: Fresh Iranian *beluga,*
14 ounces, 7 ounces, 3½ ounces. Natural
pressed caviar, 14 ounces.

A DICTIONARY
OF CAVIARS

Fresh caviar means choice, firm, not-too-
ripe whole eggs of three sturgeon species,
yielding roe of three sizes: *beluga* (giant
grain), *osetra* (medium-size), *sevruga*
(smallest). Low in salt, it must be iced.

Pressed caviar: When sturgeon eggs are
too ripe to be preserved whole, they are
pressed. This type needs refrigeration when
bought from a keg or in lightly-sterilized
jars, but not when vacuum-packed for
pantry shelf.

Special pressed or "sandwich caviar," less
ripe than the type above, is as densely
pressed but thinned by returning some of
the drained oil. It is packed in vacuum-
sealed jars.

Vacuum-packed caviar: More heavily
salted than fresh caviar, the vacuum-packed
uses less ripe grades. It is given long shelf
life by in-the-jar sterilizing. It includes
both of the pressed caviars, the whole-grain
Caspian Sea caviars, and the whole-grain
Great Lakes and Canadian caviars. The
vacuum-packed group also includes the
whole-grain varieties of so-called "caviars"
such as the roe of red salmon, lumpfish,
and whitefish.

Yogurt can be an ideal dessert if garnished with brown sugar, crumbled ginger snaps, powdered cinnamon, and minced preserved ginger. This is the way it's served in Sweden.

Yogurt, That Smooth Emigré

Another food that knows no national boundaries, it's the Balkans' gift to world cuisine

Although virtually unknown in the United States until the present century, yogurt is one of the oldest and most prevalent foods of the western world. A curdled milk product made with lactic ferments of a particular kind, it changes name with the country. It is *matzoon* to Armenians, *laban* to the Arabs, *koumis* in Mongolian lands (compare Russian *kumyss*), or *mâst* in Iran and the Middle East. In all countries today, the tanginess and voluptuous texture of yogurt have made it a delicious adjunct of fine cookery.

Originally yogurt was a primitive people's way of preserving milk. They simply left it out in a warm place to turn to curd. The kind of milk used, and the type of organism that fermented it, would vary from one region to another. A goat's-milk yogurt helped sustain Abraham for a goodly 175 years. From the milk of the mare and the yak came the yogurt that nourished Genghis Khan and other conquerors from the Mongolian plains. In our own time, Bulgarian peasants were reputed to live 100 years or longer because they ate yogurt three times a day.

In 1908 a Russian bacteriologist, Dr. Elie Metchnikoff, came to believe it was their cultured milk that made the Bulgarians so long-lived, so resistant to disease. By putting yogurt organisms under the microscope, he discovered a vein of truth under the mountain of folklore. He isolated two beneficial bacteria cultures that ferment and flavor yogurt: the *lactobacillus bulgaricus* and the *streptococcus lactis.*

Modern yogurt is a culture, in milk, of these same bacterial strains. Although isolated less than 60 years ago, they must date back into antiquity when first turned to the production of food for man. They are what distinguish yogurt in taste and texture from ordinary sour milk, which is fermented by wild bacteria picked up at random from the surrounding air. The culture has been kept alive through countless generations by adding a little yogurt containing the specific organisms to a fresh batch of milk.

It is sometimes called "the almost perfect food," since it is practically predigested milk. The body converts it into absorbable form in less than 45 minutes, compared to several hours for the digestion of milk. Yet it retains the same food values as the fresh milk it is made from. Used in recipes in place of sour cream, it adds a similar zesty flavor with fewer calories. Yogurt also may be used in many dishes instead of milk, a boon for those who find the non-cultured kind hard to digest.

How to Make Yogurt

You may buy yogurt commercially in most places. Or you can make it yourself, using as a "starter" either some previously made yogurt or a liquid or dried culture obtainable from various laboratories.

Boil up 1 quart of fresh milk (once only) and let cool to lukewarm. In a cup dissolve 2 or 3 tablespoons of yogurt in some of the warm milk. Add this to the rest of the milk, mix well, and pour into glasses or crockery. Cover with wax paper with a plate on top. Then cover all (top and sides) with 3 or 4 dishtowels to keep the incubating culture at an even temperature (about 77° F.). Keeping it uniformly warm is the only real problem in making yogurt.

Let it stand overnight in the kitchen, away from drafts, and possibly over the pilot light of the stove or in a warming oven. It takes from 8 to 18 hours to thicken to the consistency of custard. When the yogurt is ready, store in a refrigerator. It will keep about a week, and you can use some of it as a starter for a new batch.

It is better to make yogurt every couple of days in order to keep the culture going and to assure a fresh taste. Eventually you may find the culture losing potency, when you will have to revive it by crossbreeding with a culture from a new source. Exchanging yogurt starters is a neighborly practice among Armenians and other Near Eastern groups in our large cities.

In cookery, yogurt offers cool taste contrast to highly spiced dishes, for example as a garnish to curry. It may be substituted for sour cream even in such classics as *blinis*, beef Stroganoff, and borscht. It makes a delicious addition to dressings for fruit, salads, vegetables and meats, mousse of tongue, lamb or beef *en gelée*, and jellied fish. A natural blender of spices, yogurt makes a good meat marinade (especially for lamb), improves hot or cold soups, and can be a dessert. Somehow yogurt brings unrelated flavors together without intruding its own.

Cucumbers and yogurt are a favorite culinary kinship, as in the following recipes:

IRANIAN YOGURT SOUP

3 cups yogurt
1 cucumber, peeled and puréed
½ cup raisins
¾ cup water
Salt and pepper to taste
2 tablespoons chopped chives
(fresh, frozen, or dried)
1 hard-boiled egg, sliced in rounds

Beat yogurt in a bowl. Add puréed cucumbers (a brief whirl in the blender at low speed), and raisins. Mix well. Add water slowly, stirring constantly. Season with salt, pepper, and chives. Stir again. Chill, and just before serving garnish with egg slices. Serves 4 to 6.

YUGOSLAVIAN CUCUMBER SALAD

2 cucumbers, peeled and sliced into thin rounds
Salt   1 onion, finely sliced
⅔ cup yogurt
Pepper   Paprika

Sprinkle cucumber slices with salt, let stand a few minutes and drain. Mix with yogurt and onion slices. Sprinkle with pepper, and garnish with paprika, making a pattern on the top of the salad with it. Serve chilled. Serves 4 to 6.

EGYPTIAN YOGURT SALAD

1 cup yogurt
1 garlic clove, put through
garlic press or minced
Fresh mint leaves, chopped
2 cucumbers, peeled and sliced in thin rounds
Salt and pepper to taste
3 red radishes, sliced

Mix yogurt and garlic. Stir in chopped mint leaves. Add cucumber slices, salt, and pepper to mixture. Garnish sides of serving dish with radish slices. Serves 4 to 6.

RAITA ALU
(Potatoes in yogurt)

Raita alu is freshly boiled potato cubes chilled in a deliciously flavored yogurt dressing. It can be variously seasoned—with chili powder instead of curry powder, for instance. Also, try the same dressing with hot baked potatoes, gashed as you do for inserting butter or sour cream. Or use it with other vegetables, salads, and cold meats. It's that versatile!

2 large potatoes
(boiled in jackets)
1 pint yogurt
Pinch of salt
1½ teaspoons caraway seeds
1 teaspoon curry powder
1 tablespoon chives, chopped

When potatoes are cool, skin and cut into cubes. Make a dressing of yogurt, seasoned with salt, caraway seeds, and curry powder. Gently stir it in with potato cubes and let chill for a few hours before serving. Garnish with chives. Serves 4 to 6.

LAMB KEBAB

2 pounds leg of lamb steak (or top sirloin of beef), cut in 1½-inch cubes

1½ pints yogurt
1½ teaspoons powdered ginger
Salt and pepper to taste
6 small tomatoes, unpeeled
10 small white onions, peeled
Butter
Lemon wedges

Put meat cubes into a marinade made of yogurt, ½ teaspoon ginger, salt, and pepper, and soak for about an hour. Sprinkle remainder of ginger over vegetables. Spear the meat and each vegetable on separate skewers, so each can be broiled to the required degree of doneness. Baste lamb with butter and remainder of the marinade. Serve meat, onions, and tomatoes hot, with rice and lemon wedges. Serves 6.

KHORRMA

1½ pounds well-marbled top sirloin
of beef, cut into small cubes
½ cup yogurt
¾ teaspoon salt
1 tablespoon vegetable oil
1 onion, finely chopped
1 green pepper, finely chopped
4 garlic cloves, minced
2 tomatoes, peeled and chopped
2 tablespoons curry powder
1 teaspoon turmeric
1 slice green ginger, minced
(optional)
½ teaspoon chili powder
1 tablespoon grated unsweetened coconut
1 teaspoon garam masala
(a spice-and-herb blend; optional)

Soak meat cubes in yogurt for a minimum of 2 hours—the longer the better. Add ½ teaspoon salt and simmer meat and yogurt in an uncovered saucepan over moderately low heat until meat is tender, stirring occasionally. Reserve. Fry the onion and green pepper in oil and gradually add remainder of salt, garlic, and tomatoes. After 1 minute of frying this mixture, add curry powder, turmeric, ginger, chili powder, coconut, and *garam masala*. Continue frying about 3 minutes, and add mixture to meat. Mix well, and simmer (with saucepan covered) for 15 minutes.

Serve with rice and individual dishes of chilled yogurt for cooling the spicy hotness of the dish. Add, as desired, such garnishes as chutney, raisins, cashew nuts, and grated (packaged if you can't get fresh) unsweetened coconut. Serves 4 to 6.

BULGARIAN MOUSSAKA

This casserole of eggplant and lamb emerges from the oven looking as puffy, deliciously browned, and glamorous as a soufflé—thanks to its unusual topping of yogurt cooked with egg yolks and flour to a custard-like consistency.

2 large eggplants, peeled and
sliced into rounds ¼ inch thick
2 teaspoons salt
2 onions, finely chopped
1 green pepper, finely chopped
3 garlic cloves, minced
2 tablespoons olive oil
1½ pounds lamb steak, ground
Pinch of freshly ground pepper
2 teaspoons paprika
¼ cup flour for dipping (approximate)
½ pint yogurt
4 egg yolks
½ cup sifted flour (for topping)

Sprinkle 1 teaspoon salt over eggplant slices and let stand for 1 hour. Drain and set aside. Using a big iron skillet, fry onions, green pepper, garlic in oil, then add meat, separating into particles with fork, and brown well. Season with remainder of salt, pepper, and paprika. Remove mixture from skillet and set aside. Dip eggplant slices in flour. Using any oil remaining in skillet, brown eggplant slices on both sides, adding more oil sparingly if necessary.

Using a serving casserole, arrange alternate layers of eggplant slices and meat mixture, and bake covered at 350°F. for about one hour. In a bowl, mix together yogurt, egg yolks, and flour for topping, spoon over contents of casserole, and bake for another 15 minutes. Then uncovering casserole, pass it briefly under the broiler to get a rich brownness on the custard-like topping. Served with a crisp salad, this casserole makes a meal, glamorous enough for a party luncheon. Serves 4.

GINGER YOGURT

1 cup yogurt
6 tablespoons ginger marmalade (or chopped
crystallized ginger)
4 teaspoons brown sugar
1 teaspoon lemon juice

Beat yogurt, marmalade, sugar, and lemon juice together in a bowl. Pour into custard cups and chill. Serve with lady fingers or crisp vanilla-flavored cookies. Serves 4.

World of Corn and Beans

The intermingling of European with American Indian and African food ways has produced a cuisine of stature in our own Hemisphere

A portrait of the basic foodstuffs
of Spanish-oriented Latin America:
beans, corn and rice plus that
enormous family called capsicum
(and erroneously called pepper).

Great Cuisines of *Las Americas*

*Discover the piquant gastronomy
of our neighbor nations to the south*

The cook or traveler in search of new sensations in cuisine need not look much further than just beyond the southern borders of the United States.

In the Latin countries of the Americas you will see one of the most remarkable cultural mixes in history. You will taste a blend of Old World food habits with native products and ideas, both antique and modern, that is equally remarkable.

Our title for this section is a simplification that applies best to the nearby Caribbean region, Mexico, Central America, and the northern (warmer) parts of South America. To the pillars of the *Latino* way with food, corn and beans, one may add rice, tomatoes, garlic, and of course the many varieties of *chillis*. Notice that all but the rice and garlic are of native American origin. In other parts of the continent, in Argentina, Chile, or southern Brazil, European and Mediterranean food ways remain somewhat less altered.

No area of the world reveals so dramatically the non-nationalist character of the cooking art. Countless ethnic groups have accommodated themselves to each other for four centuries. It follows that Latin American cuisine would be a many-layered thing. Built on a base of native culture (meaning Indian), it is thickly overlaid with influences brought by diverse colonizers and immigrants. These influences have been affected in turn by such factors as proximity to the sea, latitude and altitude, rainfall, urban development, and contact with the rest of the modern world (including the United States).

For instance, Argentina's population is racially Spanish, Italian, German, French, plus native Argentine—but the cooking is about 60 per cent Italian. Nevertheless, 90 per cent of the fat used is lard or butter rather than olive oil.

Chileans are a similar racial mix, but the cuisine is a broader representation of Europe. They have added a magnificent handling of the splendid seafoods which abound in Chilean waters.

Peru is predominantly mestizo, which is to say a mixture of Spanish and Indian, typical of the populations on the west coast of Latin America, north to Mexico. In these mestizo countries a new culture is coming into being, under modern as well as colonial and aboriginal influences. Their common denominators in food are corn, the many legumes, bread, rice (in coastal areas), cassava or manioc flour (in the tropical and subtropical regions), plus many types of fresh peppers, which boost the daily vitamin intake.

Brazil is different again. It was colonized by the Portuguese, and wherever the Portuguese went—to Africa, to China, to Japan, or the New World—they intermarried with the native peoples. (The homeland Portuguese themselves in the 16th century had a mixed racial background —descended from the Phoenicians, the Vandals, the Huns, the Visigoths, the Mohammedan Moors.) In the 17th century, Negro slaves were imported to work the flourishing plantations of Brazil. Then between 1874 and 1939 a wave of

immigration brought Italians, Spaniards, Germans, Japanese, Austrians, Turks, and Poles.

The present population is predominantly a mixture of European Caucasian, Negro, and American Indian racial stocks. Just as they all speak Portuguese, their cuisine is mainly Iberian, but multi-flavored with African and American Indian ways. The Brazilian upper classes are emotionally, intellectually, and gastronomically oriented to France (whereas the rest of South America is oriented primarily to Spain). The lower classes base their diet on manioc flour, black beans, rice, dried beef *(charque),* and coffee. Guava and quince paste, with a piece of cheese, are standard desserts. The upper classes switch back and forth from these native dishes to the standard European.

Among our leading experts on Latin American cuisine are the executives of Restaurant Associates, who created and operate the New York restaurant called La Fonda del Sol. They did several years of research from Mexico to Patagonia. Their purpose: to reproduce in New York the authentic flavors of the best dishes from 14 countries. In each country they retained local food experts to lead them to the typical and to the best. I respect them mightily, for the food they serve at La Fonda del Sol is as good as (sometimes even better than) you can get as a tourist in Latin America.

All the recipes in this section are as tested at La Fonda del Sol. The ingredients, which may be hard to find unless you live in a town with Mexican, Cuban, Puerto Rican, or other Spanish ethnic groups, may be ordered by mail (see page 201).

The Discovery of Corn

In English as spoken in England, the word "corn" means any grain, in that country usually wheat. When the invading Spaniards arrived in the lands of the Incas, Aztecs, and Mayas, they found the natives eating foods made of a coarse-kernel "corn" called *zea mays.* This was maize, the Indian corn (grain), or in American English, simply corn. Nine of the original Indian corn dishes are still eaten today:

ESQUITE—salted, toasted kernels of corn.

ROSCAS—popcorn balls made with brown sugar syrup.

SOPITAS DE ELOTE—corn soup.

ATOLE—maize gruel flavored various ways.

GORDITAS—cornmeal cakes fried in fat.

PINOLE—powdered corn, sweetened and flavored, to which water is added. It is often carried by men who have long distances to travel.

TAMALES—cakes of cornmeal, rolled in a corn husk and steamed.

POZOLE—a rich stew made with corn kernels or hominy, usually with meat.

TORTILLA—a thin pancake made with a special corn flour *(masa),* ground fresh every day.

These foods must have seemed very strange to the Spaniards. For the traditional diet of Spain was founded upon wheat bread, rice, olive oil, garlic, and wine. The Mexican-Guatemalan-Peruvian diet today is basically corn, chilli, and *pulque* (the fermented sap of the maguey plant).

Whatever the Spaniards brought, they found much more. They found many varieties of beans and peas, potatoes, sweet potatoes, chillis, tomatoes, chocolate and vanilla, turkeys and ducks. They found fruits such as papaya and the avocado (a native of Guatemala).

The cross-pollenization of the food ways of Spain and Indian South America that started in the 16th century has been going on in Europe ever since. It is even beginning to make an invasion of the Asiatic world.

The French in Mexico

Next on the list of sizable contributions, after Spain, was that made by France. French philosophy influenced the Mexican revolution as much as it did that of the United States. Then came the 19th century and the attempt of Napoleon III to set Maximilian on the throne of Mexico. For five years battles raged, until the misguided Maximilian was shot in 1867. But many French remained.

To that invasion may be attributed the vast variety of breads found in most Mexican towns today. In Mexico City you can choose among more than 60 different kinds of bread made into every size and shape, sweetened and unsweetened, chewy and soft. Most notable may be the *cuerno,* a half-moon shaped roll made of flaky puff paste like the *croissant,* a favorite in France.

To guide you through this new world of interesting dishes and exotic flavors, the following section lists the key foodstuffs in alphabetical order of their menu names, with recipes interpolated where appropriate.

How a Mexican family would set their table in the patio for lunch or dinner. Bowls would hold *guacamole* or *seviche*.

A Dictionary With Recipes of Latin American Delicacies

ACHIOTE or ANNATTO, the seed of the annatto tree used to impart a gold red color, as well as a delicate flavor and a fragrance similar to paprika. Easy to find in Spanish shops and markets.

ANISE, a seed with a licorice-like flavor, much used in Spain, has been adopted by Mexico. When using anise seeds, it's well to grind or blend them to release the oil. Anise flavoring extract or anisette liqueur may be substituted. (Do not confuse with star anise of China.)

BUNUELOS, thin, crunchy, fried dessert pancakes, are made as follows for 15 persons:

BUNUELOS

4 cups sifted flour
2 tablespoons sugar
1 teaspoon baking powder
2 teaspoons salt
2 beaten eggs   ¾ cups milk
¼ cup melted butter
Oil for deep frying

Mix all dry ingredients together. Beat eggs and milk together and stir in dry ingredients. Add melted butter and mix well until the dough does not stick to the fingers. Divide into 15 pieces and let stand about 15 minutes. Roll each piece into a ball and roll out each ball into a round thin shape. Fry in deep hot oil until golden brown. Drain on absorbent paper and sprinkle with cinnamon and sugar. Pour some thin honey over each round.

CHICHARRONES, the Mexican equivalent of our pork cracklings. Filler's "Bakon Krisps" are actually *chicharrones*. They are delightful to nibble, make a garnish for soups, may be crumbled over *guacamole,* or as a topping for casseroles.

CHILLIS are one of the cornerstones of the Spanish-speaking South American cuisine. But most North Americans are confused about the chilli, even about the spelling.

Part of the confusion arises because the botanical family (capsicum) is large, and its members vary in taste and hotness from sweet and mild to stinging and fiery hot. North Americans are fairly well acquainted with the mild varieties of capsicum: paprika, cayenne, pimiento, red and green sweet bell peppers. But unless we have lived along the Mexican border, we are not likely to know the hotter varieties.

Part of the confusion is due to the various spellings. Oxford's Universal Dictionary gives the English spelling as chilli or chilly. In Spanish it is *chile,* or *chili.* In Mexico it is *chilli.* All these mean the fresh or dried pods of various capsicums. The word "chili" is the form used by American manufacturers for premixed seasoning powders which contain a variety of ingredients plus the capsicum called *chilli ancho,* a red, not-too-hot type.

In this book I use "chillis" to mean the fresh, dried, frozen, or canned pods. When I say "chili" I mean the seasoning powder.

About their hotness, go on the general principle that the smaller the hotter. Since they range in size from ¼ inch to 6 inches, you can see there is a big range. (More than 50 varieties are used in the northern countries of South America.) Color does not indicate hotness. So watch out for chilli *tepines* (small as a pea), chilli *jalapeño* (about 1 inch long), chilli *piquin* (small, brown, and very hot), chilli *serrano* (small, green, very hot, used fresh or pickled), and chilli *chipotle* (long, brown, and so hot one should wear gloves when peeling it).

Easiest of the hot types to obtain usually is chilli *verde,* which comes canned or frozen. They have been peeled before processing, so all you must do is remove seeds and membranes. In the Southwest U.S. you can find fresh chilli *verde,* called Anaheim chilli.

If dealing with any of the fresh, hot varieties do this: they should be blistered by holding on a fork over a flame or electric calrod unit. Then wrap in a wet cloth so they steam. Peel off outer membrane. Slit and remove seeds and inner structural veins holding the seeds. *Basic to taming the hot chilli is peeling, seeding, and deveining.* But don't think of chillis in terms of hotness—rather in terms of a wide gamut of flavors.

Several sauces using hot chillis of one type or another can be bought canned. One is *enchilada* sauce (mildly hot); another is "hot sauce," made of small hot peppers and somewhat resembling Tabasco. Some types of chilli come in cans, pickled or in brine, from Ashley (of Texas) and Clemente Jacques (of Mexico City).

Chilli is used with almost everything except sweets. Dishes of fresh chopped chillis and herbs are placed on the table, some pickled, some fresh, and each person helps himself, using the mix as a garnish or a dipping sauce—a lot or a little or none at all.

When a recipe calls for *chile ancho* or *poblano,* use bell or sweet green peppers. For *chile pasilla,* use fresh green peppers or dried. For *chile serrano* or *jalapeño,* any variety of small red or green hot peppers. Chilli *verde* means canned green chilli peppers. Chilli *mulato* means any hot pepper.

Fresh, not-too-hot chillis may be stuffed with almost anything—cheese, ground meat, ground nuts and rice, boiled beans, and cheese. A popular version is with cheese—usually white, mild cheese best approximated by our Monterey Jack

CHILLIS RELLENOS CON QUESO

*12 chilli poblano (may substitute bell
or green peppers)
¾ pound cheddar cheese
¾ pound Monterey Jack cheese
3 teaspoons salsa jalapeño (below)
5 eggs
½ cup flour
Olive oil for frying*

Remove all seeds and veins from chillis by splitting down middle. Be careful not to pull pepper apart. Mix both cheeses together, add fresh *aji* pepper, or *salsa jalapeño.* If more heat is desired add as much as your taste desires. Place in middle of pepper, and fold over one side, then the other. Make sure it covers the cheese. Roll in flour.

To make the batter, separate the eggs, and whip the whites till they become very fluffy and stiff. Fold in 1 teaspoonful of flour for each egg. Mix the yolks lightly and fold into egg whites. Fold gently. Take stuffed chilli which has been rolled in flour, dip into egg batter, and then fry in deep fat in a heavy skillet about ¾ full of cooking oil at 275° until golden brown. Serve at once with *salsa jalapeño.* Serves 12.

SALSA JALAPENO

*2 tablespoons salad oil
2 onions, diced
2 cloves garlic, chopped
1 No. 2½ can solid pack tomatoes
6 ounces tomato purée
2½ level teaspoons oregano
1 whole jalapeño pepper, chopped*

Heat oil in a skillet with a heavy bottom. Sauté onion and garlic in oil until slightly brown.

Drain tomatoes thoroughly and add to pan together with tomato purée. Before placing the tomatoes in the saucepan, check to see if they are solid. If they are not solid, drain away some of the liquid, then add to the sautéed onions. The sauce should be neither watery nor a thick paste. It should be the consistency of heavy cream. Simmer until mixture thickens, then add chopped pepper and oregano. Stir lightly (sauce should have tomato chunks in it) and store in refrigerator until needed.

Re-heat in a double boiler. Also use sauce as topping for meat and cheese *enchiladas* and egg dishes. Yield: 1 quart sauce—enough to cover about 12 *chillis rellenos*.

Here is a chilli sauce for a plain *tortilla*.

CHIMICHURRI SAUCE

3 fresh green peppers, finely chopped
3 red peppers, finely chopped
10 Catarena dry red peppers, finely chopped
2 medium red onions, finely chopped
1 cloves of garlic, finely chopped
3 tablespoons red wine vinegar
1 teaspoon ground achiote
1 teaspoon paprika or 2 (if no achiote available)
1 teaspoon cilantro chopped
½ cup oil
1 teaspoon chopped parsley
1 teaspoon oregano

In a bowl mix the finely chopped peppers, onions, and garlic. Add vinegar and then *achiote*, paprika, and *cilantro*. Add a little water; the amount will determine the thickness or thinness desired. Add the rest of the ingredients and season to taste. Yield: 1 quart.

SALSA DE CHILLI

This sauce is used with various meat fillings for *tamales*.

1 medium onion, chopped
2 cloves garlic, chopped
½ cup oil
½ cup flour
1½ quarts chicken stock
4 teaspoons chili powder
½ cup tomato purée
Salt
M.s.g.

Sauté onions and garlic in oil. Add flour to make a roux. Add hot chicken stock and tomato purée.

Dissolve chili powder in as much water as needed and pour into saucepan in which chicken stock, onion, etc., is boiling. Reduce heat and simmer about 30 minutes. Strain and season to taste. Yield: 1 quart.

CHORIZO—pork sausages very highly spiced with hot pepper, thyme, or oregano. Common in all Latin American and Spanish cookery.

CILANTRO, or fresh coriander (sometimes called Chinese parsley), is the herb which produces coriander seeds. But the taste of the fresh herb is entirely different from the flavor of the seed. Strangely haunting, curiously Oriental, it is used in soups, stews, sauces. Fresh coriander can often be bought in Mexican groceries or in Chinatown. Or plant coriander seeds.

FLAN. In Spain and in all countries where the Spanish influence is strong, a dessert that we call a caramel custard is most popular.

ORANGE-NUT CUSTARD
(Flan de naranja)

Custard:

1 quart light cream   *1½ teaspoons vanilla*
8 eggs beaten   *3 egg yolks*
½ cup orange juice   *Sugar to taste*

Caramel:

1 cup granulated sugar
1 cup of water
¾ pound sliced almonds

Start by making caramel. Dilute sugar in water, place on fire, reduce until golden brown in color. Add sliced almonds that have been toasted. Pour in custard cups, making sure caramel covers bottom. Let stand until cool.

The custard is prepared by boiling half the cream with the vanilla. Reduce to about 1 cup. Remove from fire. Add the cold remainder of the cream and the rest of the ingredients. Mix well. Fill custard cups in which the caramel has been placed. Bake in oven about 25 minutes at 300°. In case of doubt test with toothpick. Serves 8 to 10.

FRIJOLES deserve your attention. The *frijol* is a bean of at least a dozen different varieties, black, brown, pink, white, speckled. The favorite is a black-hued little fellow called *queretaro*. (Kidney beans will make a fair approximation of *queretaro*.) Easy to find in this country are the *pinto* and the *garbanzo*. Cook as beans are cooked in the United States.

There is a popular and important variation: *frijoles refritos*, or beans re fried. Soft cooked beans are crushed in a frying pan with a fork and fried in pork fat, olive oil, or drippings from roast fowl or bacon. Here is a recipe for 6 persons.

RE-FRIED BEANS
(Frijoles refritos)

1 pound dark beans
2 quarts water
2 tablespoons salt
4 tablespoons fat
1 tablespoon minced onion

Soak beans overnight. Drain off water in which beans have been soaked, and boil in 2 quarts of water and salt until the beans are very tender and have absorbed nearly all the water. Drain and mash. Place fat in skillet and heat until very hot, add beans, cook until the beans are dry and have absorbed the fat. Any beans left over for another day may be fried a second time in somewhat less fat. Bacon drippings add an interesting taste.

Serve cold or hot with a topping such as sour cream, grated cheese, *chicharrones,* or deep fried pieces of *tortillas.*

SOUP OF SEVEN BEANS
(Sopa de siete frijoles)

½ cup each soaked pinto beans, black beans,
kidney beans, chick peas, lentils, navy beans,
dried baby lima beans
1 small onion
4 stalks celery   1 leek
1 clove garlic
2½ quarts chicken stock
1 pound bacon   1 ham bone
8-ounce can tomatoes
¾ pound chorizo meat, skinned
1 bay leaf

Dice the bacon, sauté until fat is rendered. Add chopped vegetables, sauté a few minutes. Add tomatoes, beans, and chicken stock with ham bone. Bring to a boil, lower flame, and simmer till beans are soft.

Remove ham bone and 1 cup of beans. Discard ham bone and reserve the beans to garnish soup.

Put rest of beans and liquid through blender

Mexican cooking is as full of whimsy, fantasy, and new twists on basic recipes as is this room done with Mexican artifacts. Every basic recipe can be varied endlessly.

until all beans are puréed. Sauté *chorizo* meat until cooked, drain off all fat. Return the bean purée to fire; if too thick add a little more chicken stock, bring to boil. Add beans, cooked *chorizo* and season. Serve hot garnished with whole beans and chopped parsley. For 8.

GARBANZOS (known also as chick peas or *ceci*) taste and look more like nuts than beans. Add them to vegetable soup or minestrone or to your own stews. Or serve as a salad, boiled, dressed with a spicy, garlicky French dressing heavily garnished with gobs of chopped parsley along with quartered or sliced tomatoes.

GUACAMOLE is an appetizer, cocktail dunk, a salad, or a sauce for meats. It is made of avocado, onion, chillis, and often tomatoes. Everyone in Mexico and the United States has a favorite recipe. This one is from La Fonda del Sol.

AVOCADO SALAD
(Guacamole)

6 ripe avocados
3 small tomatoes, peeled, seeded and diced
½ teaspoon chopped fresh cilantro
2 finely diced red onions
Juice of 3 lemons
Chopped chilli serrano, or jalapeño sauce
to taste
Salt to taste

Peel avocados. *Guacamole* should be part purée, but with some small pieces of avocado visible. Be sure you don't over-mash the avocado. Add tomato, *cilantro,* and onions to the avocado and mix slightly. Then add lemon juice and chopped chilli. Season with salt, serve cold. A few drops of Tabasco sauce can substitute for the chilli, or 2 teaspoons chili powder.

When served as an appetizer or dip, *guacamole* should be somewhat peppery. In Yucatan and Guatemala, however, it is generally subtle and rather bland, made without any chilli and offered as a palate-cooling sauce in a side dish to cool your mouth after eating hotly flavored foods.

GUAVA PASTE, sometimes called guava cheese, a popular dessert confection, comes in cans or boxes. Serve in strips with cream cheese or a soft, mild white cheese like mozzarella or even a mild Muenster or Monterey Jack.

HUEVOS (eggs) in Mexico are accompanied as often as not by avocados and beans or in a manner reminiscent of Indonesia, with fried rice and bananas. Sometimes they are poached in wine, or, when scrambled, flavored with a touch of cinnamon and a teaspoon of brandy. But the most famous preparation of all is:

HUEVOS RANCHEROS

This is fried or scrambled eggs served on top of a *tortilla* and covered with *ranchero* sauce, a very popular breakfast or lunch dish. *Tortillas* you can secure from a can (Old El Paso brand is good). Lightly fry in a separate pan as needed.

The *ranchero* sauce is the key to all. It can be fiery hot or so tamed that even the most timid will like it:

In a frying pan put 1 tablespoon of oil and 1 teaspoon of minced onion. Stir so the onion will not burn. When transparent, add 1 tomato (peeled and the seeds removed) cut in very small pieces. Salt to taste and add a few drops of Tabasco sauce or a chopped red chilli. Cook another 3 to 5 minutes. Now it is ready to pour over the egg placed on the *tortilla*. Use about 2 tablespoons per egg.

SCRAMBLED EGGS WITH JALAPENO SAUCE

1 tortilla   2 eggs
3 tablespoons jalapeño sauce
Salt

Cut *tortilla* into eighths, melt butter in a saucepan. When butter is hot add the *tortillas*. Fry until slightly crisp. Add beaten eggs and scramble. When eggs are about half cooked, add *jalapeño* sauce and salt. Scramble again but remove from fire before mixture cooks too dry. Serve at once.

MASA HARINA. A flour to make *tortillas, tamales,* etc., made of lime-soaked corn, available in the U. S. from the Quaker Oats Co. *Tortilla* flour can be found at supermarkets in towns or cities where there are sizable Spanish-American groups. Any grocer can obtain it for you through his distributor. Even in hot, humid weather, this flour keeps well. Follow directions on the bag for making *tortillas* and *tamales*.

MOLE—the noblest and most characteristic of all Mexican sauces. There is a saying that every Mexican has two ambitions: to win the national lottery and eat turkey *mole* on his birthday. It is rich, *piquante,* made of chillis, spices, nuts, and bitter chocolate.

In *mole* you will discover chocolate in a new guise, not as a sweet, but to add a depth, a richness, a darkness to many foods like turkey, for instance. You can find canned *mole* in gourmet specialty shops. You have only to add the powdered *mole* to the stock or gravy of chicken or turkey. If you like, step up the chocolate flavor even more by adding perhaps a teaspoon of semi-sweet chocolate bits and ½ teaspoon of aniseed, or ½ teaspoon of anise flavoring. Simmer a few minutes to melt the chocolate and blend the flavors, and serve liberally sprinkled with coarsely chopped salted almonds or peanuts or toasted sesame seeds. Leftover chicken or turkey, or even hard-cooked eggs, may be served with *mole* sauce. Parsleyed rice goes well on the side. *Mole* sauce in cans from Clemente Jacques comes in three heats—fairly mild, hot, and hottest.

NOPALITOS are the leaves of the prickly pear cactus plant cooked, shredded, and served as a vegetable, or as a salad with a vinaigrette sauce or French dressing. Put up in cans by Clemente Jacques.

ORANGE FLOWER WATER. As in Spain, this flavoring is widely used in custards, sweet sauces, and pastries. Can be ordered from any specialty food shop. Use like vanilla.

PEPITAS is a word that refers to any seeds, but generally it means pumpkin or squash seeds which are dried and salted like nuts. They are used extensively in *moles* and other sauces. Also one of the world's most perfect "nibbles," and an imaginative garnish for vegetables.

PILONCILLO is unrefined raw brown cane sugar, widely used even to sweeten coffee. You can approximate the flavor of this soft, moist sugar by adding a little dark molasses to old-fashioned dark brown sugar. Serve a small bowlful spiced with cloves and cinnamon to go along with a demitasse.

CAFE PILONCILLO

¾ cup brown sugar
1 quart water
1 cinnamon stick about 2 inches long

Add sugar to water plus cinnamon stick, bring to a boil, let simmer for about 15 minutes or reduce to about ⅓ the amount started with. *Piloncillo* should be served with strong coffee and hot. Each person takes as much as desired.

QUESADILLAS are small-size turnovers made of *masa* and filled with a variety of things: boiled and fried potatoes, cheese, squash flowers, shredded cooked meat in sauce, slivers of green pepper, chicken *mole*. They are deep-fat fried, often served with a snowy plume of chilled sour cream or yogurt. These differ slightly from *empanadas* which are baked.

SEVICHE: A seafood cocktail of enormous distinction made from flaky white fish or scallops marinated in lime or other citrus juices and delicately flavored with herbs and peppers. Here are two recipes from La Fonda, each serving 6.

SEVICHE

1½ pounds filet of striped bass or any
flaky white fish
1½ cups lemon juice
¾ cup orange juice
2 tablespoons ketchup
1½ green peppers (mild) thinly sliced
1½ red peppers (mild) thinly sliced
1 red onion thinly sliced
½ aji, seeded, chopped fine
About 3 scallions cut fine

Cut filet in 1-inch strips the length of filet. Slice on bias, not too thin. Place in stainless container or earthen bowl. Cover with about 1 cup of lemon juice, marinate overnight.

The next day pour off lemon juice, wash in cold water, drain off all water, return to container it has been marinated in. Pour in remainder of lemon juice, orange juice, ketchup, and thin sliced onion, red and green peppers (save about half of the pepper slices and a little onion for garnishing top). Mix all gently, season. Use as much or as little *aji* as you desire in taste. Garnish top with peppers, onions, and minced scallions.

SEVICHE DE MARISCOS

½ pound sea scallops
1½ cups lemon juice
⅓ cup orange juice
1 teaspoon each red onion, red pepper, and
green pepper, julienne
1 aji pepper
1½ tablespoons ketchup
1 large boiled sweet potato

Marinate scallops in 1 cup lemon juice overnight and prepare next day exactly as with fish in previous recipe. Peel sweet potato and cut in ½-inch slices as an addition to garnishes.

TACOS are U-shaped folded *tortillas* that have been fried in deep fat till crispy. They are then filled with a variety of garnishes. To get them the right shape to receive a filling, place a 1-inch spatula in the middle of the *tortilla* and force it down into the fat, letting the tips show slightly above the level of the fat. Be careful that the ends do not close, or you will have trouble inserting the stuffing. When crisp and golden brown remove from fat and cool. Then spoon into the pocket whatever you plan to use as a filling. *Tacos* are never served hot—only warm.

CHICKEN TACOS

¾ cup cooked diced chicken
¾ cup jalapeño sauce
6 tortillas   ½ cup onion minced
⅓ cup grated dry Monterey Jack cheese
½ cup fine shredded lettuce
1 small fresh tomato diced

Mix, by heating, the chicken with the *jalapeño* sauce. Then spoon into pocket of *taco*. Next sprinkle in a little onion and cheese, then the lettuce across the fold of *taco*. Into each end (at the fold) place some fresh small diced tomato. Once *tacos* are filled they should be served at once. To be eaten in the hand. Follow same procedure with beef or pork filling.

CHICKEN AND GUACAMOLE TACOS

1 cup cooked chicken, diced
2 cups jalapeño sauce
3 ripe avocados, about 1 pound each
6½ ounces fresh diced tomato
4 ounces red onion diced   Juice of 3 lemons
1 teaspoon chopped cilantro
¼ of a small hot fresh pepper
Salt to taste   12 tacos

Peel avocados, remove pits, and mash with a fork. Add rest of ingredients, mix well, add salt to taste. After filling the *tacos*, cover opening with *guacamole* salad from one end to the other.

SHRIMP AND EGG TACOS

1 tablespoon chopped raw onion
2 tablespoons butter
½ pound cooked split shrimp
4 eggs, scrambled
3 tablespoons jalapeño sauce
Shredded lettuce
1 fresh medium size tomato, diced fine

Sauté the onion in butter until cooked, add the cooked shrimp which have been split in half, sauté till shrimps are hot. Add the eggs which have been scrambled. Cook until eggs are dry. Add the *jalapeño* sauce, mix well. Correct the seasoning.

Spoon about 3 tablespoons of filling in each *taco*, and sprinkle some finely shredded lettuce in the opening on top of the filling. Place a little fine-diced fresh tomato in each corner. Serves 4.

TAMALES are made of corn meal usually mixed with chopped meat, more or less hot with chilli, depending on your preference. They are wrapped in corn husks and boiled until ready, and served in their husks at table. You can make them at home of *Masa Harina*.

TOMATO VERDE, otherwise known (and canned in the U.S.A.) as TOMATILLOS. These are not ordinary green unripened tomatoes, but a different botanical variety. They counteract the heat of chillis. In Mexico you are warned always to remove the skin from the green tomato before you use it.

GREEN ENCHILADA SAUCE

(Salsa de tomatillo)

2 medium onions
2 cloves garlic
Scant ½ cup oil
½ cup pepitas (pumpkin seeds)
⅓ cup sesame seeds (toasted)
8 green chillis (canned or frozen, seeded and stemmed)
3 medium (No. 2) cans tomatillos (discard half of the liquid)
½ bunch parsley, chopped
Salt
Beurre manié (butter and flour)

Chop onions and garlic. Sauté in oil, but do not brown. Add *pepitas* and sesame seeds. Sauté a few minutes more. Add green chillis, *tomatillos* and half of its liquid, and chopped parsley. Boil about 5 minutes. Pass through blender, return to the fire and bring to a boil. Add enough butter *manié* to give consistency that will cover *enchilada* when ladled over it. Yield: 1 quart or enough for 10 *enchiladas*.

This spoon rack holds both wooden spoons and twirlers to make chocolate drinks silken smooth and frothy. Racks and twirlers are usually decorative.

TORTILLAS are the standard bread in Spanish-speaking Latin America. The *tortilla* is a thin puffy pancake made of corn. Quantities are eaten at every meal fixed in a variety of ways: plain, sauced, and filled—as with *tacos* and *enchiladas*. They are also used as containers for a variety of other foods. Their preparation, allowing for small regional variations, is as follows:

TORTILLAS

Even though canned and frozen *tortillas* may be good, the true enthusiast longs for the fresh, home-baked taste and fragrance. The aroma of lime-flavored corn baking on the hot griddle is as nostalgic in its way as the yeasty scent of home-baked bread.

The kernels of dry corn are cooked slightly and then allowed to soak overnight (or even a couple of days); raw lime has been placed in the water to cause the outer skin to loosen. When the lime water is poured off, the corn is ground into flour *(masa)* on the *metate*, a grinding stone. See *Masa Harina*, above.

Once the *masa* is ready, the girl making the *tortillas* takes a dampened ball of it and pats it back and forth between her palms until it has the desired circumference and thickness. It is then gently laid on a hot griddle. The *tortilla* cooks in a minute or two, is turned once, sometimes puffs with an air bubble in the middle. A pile of *tortillas* is served wrapped in a napkin to keep them hot.

Each person helps himself to one or two, wraps it around whatever else is on the table—such as chopped meat, cheese, beans, greens, even a small steak—and rolls it or folds it. Holding it in the fingers like a rolled sandwich, one bites, trying to keep the juice of the filling from running out the other end. The *tortilla* is a cousin of the *chapati* of India and Pakistan and other pancakes of the world (see chapter, "The Universal Pancake").

Tortillas will keep for several days, and for a long time in the freezer. To prevent them from sticking together, place a layer of waxed paper between them and keep tightly covered.

TOSTADAS. The easiest way to become acquainted with the true *tortilla* taste of Mexico is through *"Fritos,"* which are actually *tortillas tostadas*. They are authentic *tortillas* cut in strips and fried curly-crisp in deep fat. Either *tortillas* or *tostadas* may be dipped in the following sauce.

TOSTADA SAUCE

1 cup liquid of tomatoes
2 cups solid pack tomatoes
½ cup onions
¼ cup jalapeño sauce
3 teaspoons oregano
Salt to taste
Yield: 1 quart

A Bouquet of Spanish-American Specialties

Unknown to most North Americans is the fact that the South Americans like peanuts as much as we do. And they do more things with them, even making ice cream and saucing chickens.

CHICKEN WITH PEANUT SAUCE

(Pollo con salsa de mani)

4-pound chicken disjointed
Seasoned flour

½ cup shortening
2 tablespoons chopped onions
Pinch of garlic powder
1 clove, put through press
3 cups chicken stock
1 small piece cinnamon stick
½ cup sherry wine
1 teaspoon sugar
¼ cup blanched, chopped almonds
½ cup peanut butter
2 tablespoons corn starch

Dust chicken with flour in which salt and pepper has been added. Sauté chicken in shortening till brown, add onions, sauté a few minutes, add garlic.

Remove all grease from the skillet. Add chicken stock or water, cinnamon stick, sherry, sugar. Simmer about 5 minutes, adding almonds a minute or so before chicken is cooked.

Remove chicken, add peanut butter, simmer a few more minutes. If more stock is necessary add about 1 cup. When peanut butter has blended in add a little corn starch to give body and hold

---

WHAT TO ORDER
Menu-Hopping in Rio de Janeiro

MEAT

PACOCA DO NORTE—dried beef with toasted manioc flour

CHURRASCO—barbecued beef in the manner of Rio Grande do Sul

FEIJOADA CARIOCA—black beans and meat, Rio style

PIRAO—a side dish of manioc flour made with the liquid from cooking meats, fowl, fish, or shrimp

VEGETABLES AND CEREALS

ACARAJE—navy bean purée with shrimp sauce

TUTU—black beans, usually leftovers, recooked with manioc flour and fried sausages

FAROFA—toasted manioc flour, to be sprinkled on any or all dishes or to be eaten by itself

FISH

BACALHAU "DONA TZAURA"—codfish baked with various seasonings

SARAPATAL AMAZONAS—turtle giblets boiled with various seasonings

CARURU MURITIBA—shrimp and okra

BOSSANOVA—shrimp pie

EFO—shrimp with spinach

VATAPA—dried shrimp cooked in oil and coconut milk with white bread. Has many variations, using other proteins.

DESSERTS

FLAVITA—banana cake

CREME DE CAFE—caramelized custard flavored with strong coffee

sauce from separating. Correct seasoning. Serve with white rice. Serves 4.

COLD FISH IN PINE NUT SAUCE

(Pescado frio en salsa de piñón)

1 piece of halibut, about 3 pounds
½ cup white wine
Juice of half a lemon
1 medium red onion sliced
Water   Salt
½ pound cooked shrimp, peeled and deveined

Place fish in shallow pan with wine, lemon juice, sliced onion, and enough water to cover. Bring to a boil and cook till bones can be removed. Be sure not to overcook.

Remove fish from stock it has been cooked in and let cool. Chop shrimp and add to half of pine nut sauce. Filet fish in 2 pieces, being careful not to break fish. Spread the shrimp and pine nut sauce on bottom piece of fish, place other half of fish on top. Cover top of fish with the rest of pine nut sauce.

Make a vinaigrette sauce, and add a mixture of ½ cup each cooked peas, string beans, diced carrots, and potato. Place fish on serving dish, place spoonful of vegetables around fish. Decorate with lemon wedge and fresh parsley.

PINE NUT SAUCE

3 ounces pine nuts (½ cup)
3 hard-cooked egg yolks
1 cup whipping cream
Salt and pepper

Combine all ingredients and mix in a blender. Or grind pine nuts and egg yolks in a food grinder, whip the cream, combine and season. Makes about 1½ cups sauce.

PICKLED BEANS

½ cup vinegar
Scant ½ cup oil
¼ cup tomato juice
Salt and pepper to taste
24 ounces cooked pinto beans
¾ cup diced red onion

Combine vinegar and oil with tomato juice to make dressing, season. Add cooked beans and diced red onions. Marinate about 3 hours before using, or for best results, overnight. Serve with cold meat (6 portions). Decorate top with chopped onion and parsley.

SWEET POTATO AND PINEAPPLE PUDDING

(Camote con piña)

2 cups mashed, cooked sweet potatoes
1 cup crushed pineapple, drained
1 cup sugar
¾ cup blanched almonds, ground very fine

Mix all ingredients, cook over low heat; stir constantly with wooden spoon till bottom of pan may be seen clearly. Place in serving dish; chill.

PUMPKIN BISQUE

1-pound can unseasoned pumpkin
(or 2½ pounds fresh pumpkin, peeled)
4 cups chicken stock, well seasoned
¼ cup minced onion
3 scallions, minced (separate white
and green parts)
½ teaspoon salt   1 cup light cream
¼ cup heavy cream, whipped
2 medium tomatoes, thinly sliced and peeled

Add onion and white part of scallions to chicken stock. If you use fresh pumpkin, add it now. With canned pumpkin, first bring stock to boil, simmer 15 minutes, then add pumpkin. Blend well, bring to boil again, simmer 5 minutes longer. Purée in blender until smooth. Cool; add light cream seasoned to taste. Gently place thin slice of tomato to float in each cup. Decorate slice with rosette of whipped cream. Garnish with minced green scallions. Serves 8 to 10.

FOAM SOUP A LA FONDA

⅔ cup flour
2 teaspoons grated Parmesan cheese
2 ounces butter, melted
3 whole eggs
1½ teaspoons baking powder
3 ounces tomato juice
1½ quarts chicken broth

Mix flour with cheese, add melted butter. Add eggs one at a time, mixing after each egg. Last add baking powder.

The foam should not run but should slowly fall from spoon. Put tomato juice in strong chicken broth; bring to a boil. Season. When boiling, drop the foam by spoonfuls into the broth. Cover and reduce heat. Let simmer about 10 minutes covered. The foam should be very light and fluffy. Sprinkle fresh chopped parsley on top.

Continental
Kitchen

Methods You Can Use

*Many of the deepest secrets of great chefs
are simple—but precise and appropriate—
cookery techniques you can adopt at home*

Rotisserie units, either charcoal or electric, for outdoor use come in many sizes. This one has many kinds of attachments.

Discover the Rotisserie

*The ancient art of the rotating spit
is still the gourmet way with a roast*

For years the U.S.A. lagged behind the rest of the western world in the perfect roasting of meats, fish, and fowl. The lead of other countries was clearly due to their use and mastery of the rotating spit, a method so ancient that its origins are

lost in time. Our attention was focused on ovens that would bake a perfect cake or pie, quite a different technical problem from meat roasting.

Then after the war the U. S. was hit by the barbecue craze, which is to say grilling or broil-

Not all appliances on the market featuring a rotating spit follow the preferred principles given in this chapter. For best results, the fat should not drip into the fire to burn up. In the appliance look for a vertical fire or overhead fire—in any event a heat source out of the line of dripping juices. Also choose a rotisserie with accessories to hold foods of different sizes and shapes. Deluxe models include balancing weights to assure even rotation, and some method of reducing heat to a "keep warm" temperature.

ing over intense heat—heat so intense that all the nourishing juices are sealed (or supposed to be) into the meat by the crust that forms on the surface. But it takes know-how to broil successfully, and a lot of fine meat was spoiled by amateurs (having a lovely time, of course) who didn't know such fine points as preventing fat drippings from falling into the fire and creating a sooty, undesirable deposit, or how to keep the meat from catching fire.

When Americans *en masse* began to travel abroad we saw the rotating spit everywhere: from the ordinary *tavernas* of the Greek islands to the middle and upper class *trattoria* in Italy to the great three-star restaurants listed in France's Michelin Guide. We also tasted what we saw being cooked. "Can this be chicken?" "You mean this is lamb!" we said, looking incredulous. Meats taste more of themselves when spit-roasted.

So the idea began to spread. By 1950 there were two or three U. S. makers of rotisseries that had vertical fire boxes for charcoal, so the drippings fell into a drip pan instead of into the fire, thus permitting basting with all kinds of flavored bastes. By 1965 there were at least 30 manufacturers of properly-designed rotisseries. And 36 oven manufacturers put rotisseries into their top-of-the-line oven models. By now there are so many worthwhile products on the market, using every type of fuel (electricity, gas, charcoal, infra-red), that it is impossible to keep up with them all. There are outdoor units, portable or built-in units for the kitchen, camping units powered by batteries so you won't need to do any hand-turning of the spit.

Let me say, right here, that I am prejudiced in favor of rotisserie roasting. It is more foolproof, produces a juicier, moister result, takes less attention and trouble, is more smoke-free and spatter-free. And it certainly tastes better.

Furthermore, foods do not shrink, but actually tend to swell. The fats drop out but not what the French call *jus,* meaning true meat juices. So little juice drops out that bastings may have to be used, compounded of such as butter, herbs, soy sauce, honey, ginger—whatever you decide is called for. Because the food is rotating in front of the fire, it is kept constantly bathed in the basting, insuring that all sides become done at one time. The rotating sets up a moisture seal, preventing any drying out. This is in contrast to the drying effect of roasting in an air-tight oven, where the relative humidity is bound to be lower than in open air.

All proper rotisseries have the heat source out of the line of fall of the dripping fat. All have a drip pan (or equivalent) that lets the drippings accumulate. The French are quite adamant about basting only with the fat of the drippings—not the *jus.* They think it helps in the browning. Some French cooks think only butter is the proper fat for basting. Other peoples are more open minded.

The myriad possibilities of basting are one of the major assets of cooking on the spit. For it lets you roast many kinds of flavors into the very juices of the meat. Even a fine rib roast, although excellent basted with only its own fat drippings, may be varied in a number of interesting ways.

A basting sauce may be applied to the food before or during the cooking. Prepared meat sauces are not ideal as bastes, for they tend to be strong and are usually intended to cover up lack of taste in poor meat or poorly-cooked meat. And no single baste is perfect for the various types of food you can cook. So experiment, using what I suggest as a starting point. Go on from there to find personal concoctions that please you. A good baste need not be complicated; the most famous are the simplest. But try to use the best ingredients: fresh herbs, good sherry, vermouth, madeira, or whatever.

A good basting sauce needs to be liquid—but not too liquid. It should be easy to apply, yet not fall off too quickly as it runs around the food rotated. The base may be soy sauce (taking the place of salt), vinegar, vermouth, soup stock, or water in which a bouillon cube has been dissolved. Depending on the fattiness of the meat

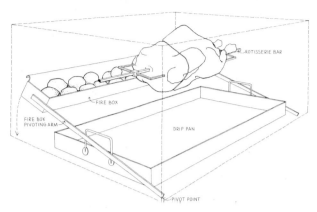

When looking for a proper rotisserie, shop for one that has a heat source which is not directly under the dripping fat. Otherwise the fat burns, depositing sooty smoke on the meat.

or fish, it should also contain some fat: butter, margarine, olive oil, bacon grease, or the drippings from the food being cooked.

In addition, you want seasonings. Best are fresh herbs; next best, dried herbs. The need for salt and pepper varies, depending on the food itself, and if you cook low and slow enough, you'll need very little of either. A meat that is still moist when cooked contains so much flavor that it requires less salt than when dried-out in an oven.

Bases for Basting

Chinese or Japanese soy sauces are an ideal base for any baste. (Chinese soy is saltier than Japanese, so act accordingly.) Dilute 50 per cent with water. Adding honey to a soy baste helps it cling to the meat better, and also helps make a beautiful browning. A little crushed fresh ginger or garlic can add sparkle to this baste—excellent for pork and lamb.

Clear soup stock (such as consommé) is a good base, to which you can add minced herbs. Citrus juice (such as lemon or lime), blended with butter and herbs, is excellent for fish, pheasant, chicken, and capon.

A little sweet (red) vermouth or Blonde Dubon-

Removable spit in the oven is now available in many gas and electric ranges. Spit need not be used when baking, broiling.

An example of a spit-less spit, which is really a flexible basket which takes the shape of the meat, fowl, or fish. Such accessories are essential to the full enjoyment of rotisseries.

This rotisserie uses infra-red rays as its heat source, and cooks about 25% faster as a result. Even with greater heat, instead of drying out, meats remain moist and juicy.

net is a good addition to meat bastes, while the dry (white) vermouth is good for sea foods or fowl. Use red wine for dark meat. Sweet wines such as sherry are good for ham.

The juice in which dried mushrooms have soaked is a superb base. Better still, cook the dried mushrooms in their soaking water for about 20 minutes, sweetening with a sweet sauterne, a little sugar, and soy sauce. Then mince them fine, returning them to their cooking liquid. Add this to the fat drippings of whatever you're cooking, and you have a new taste thrill.

A good mayonnaise is an excellent seasoning for fish and steak. Blend with lemon juice and chopped parsley.

Although the main goal of rotisserie cooking is to retain the taste essence of the food itself, without camouflage or subterfuge, some meats (such as pork) can stand heartier bastes. Here is one that will measure up to the tastes of the stoutest rancher on the Rio Grande.

MEXICAN BARBECUE SAUCE

½ cup olive oil
1 onion, chopped
1 garlic clove
1 chilli pepper, minced, or cayenne pepper
½ tablespoon salt
2 large tomatoes, cut up
2 tablespoons chili powder
¼ cup vinegar
¼ cup water

Heat 1 tablespoon olive oil. Add onion and slowly fry until lightly browned. Add garlic, chili, salt, and tomato and simmer until thickened. Add remaining ingredients and cook 5-8 minutes, stirring constantly.

A light basting of liquor on a roast, about 5 minutes before you take it off, is a time-honored technique. Use bourbon on beef, rum on lamb, gin on pork. Paint the meat lightly with about a jiggerful. If it catches fire, never mind. It will flame for a moment until the alcohol burns off.

Basting should be done with a brush or a glass baster, which is like a big medicine dropper. Don't worry about overdoing the basting.

If you have a spit attachment for your oven, you should leave the oven door open when doing rotisserie cooking. For it is not the temperature of the air around the food that matters; it is the radiant rays of the heat source hitting the food—similar to broiling—that does the cooking. So the surrounding air can be quite cool (room temperature) and yet the meat will continue to cook without becoming dry.

Another reason rotating foods are moister is that gravity does not drain the juices down and out. On a spit, when the fluids start in one direction (downward, of course) suddenly downward becomes upward. Thanks to the rotating, the juices are juggled within the meat, and stay there.

You can cook a 16- to 20-pound prime rib of beef on a rotisserie, and end up with no more than two teaspoons of meat juice in the drip pan. In oven cooking the same size roast would produce at least a cupful of the precious *jus*. (This does not count the fat drippings in both methods.)

Here are a few hints that will make a difference:

1. Have your meat at room temperature. Introducing it to heat from the cold of the refrigerator seems to shock the meat fibers and they draw together, as if in defiance of their rough treatment. The result is not as tender as when meat is warmed to room temperature before cooking.

2. Learn about "coasting." This is a waiting period *after* cooking, but keeping the meat warm. The French take "coasting" for granted.

What does it do? It is hard to describe. The texture of the meat gets firm instead of flabby. The coasting period can be 10 to 25 minutes, depending on your convenience. Let the spit keep rotating, but reduce the heat to a "warming" temperature—100° to 120°. You will need an appliance which has this control or will have to move meat further from heat element on simpler models.

3. You must be able to tell, visually, when the meat is done. A meat thermometer is a most necessary gauge, but the degree of aging makes a big difference. If you follow prescribed timetables slavishly, your results may vary considerably. I am sure you have observed how a professional chef presses steaks with his long-handled fork as he is broiling them. He is not just testing his reflexes.

When meat is first placed in front of the fire, it is spongy and bouncy to the touch. It becomes firmer as the cooking proceeds. It is rare when it stops being spongy. Anyone can acquire the feel of what is rare, medium, and well-done. Practice a little, feeling the response of the meat to pressure. With an open mind and no glass in your hand, you should master this in six tries.

Big roasts are an exception. Only a meat thermometer inserted deep into the roast can tell you about the inside state of things.

When meat is cooked on a rotisserie, in open air, with the heat so placed that no fat falls into the fire to burn and make sooty smoke, it is perfect cooking. Note how meat swells.

BASTES AND MARINADES

Meats and fowl have different textures. Some are loose-pored and others are tightly-pored. So some soak up a marinade faster than others. The time you allow for marinating varies, depending on the size of the piece and the density of the pores. Lamb and mutton are the most tightly-pored, so can be marinated 8 to 12 hours. Beef, especially fine cuts, is loose-pored and drinks up the marinade like a blotter. Marinate steaks only 30 minutes.

Meats with many juices of their own do well to have a baste that includes something sweet, like honey, sugar, a sweet wine. This makes a glaze and seals the pores, keeping in the juices. Even fatty fishes (such as salmon and tuna) do better if basted with a mixture that has a little sweetness for glazing. The fats drip out, but the moist juices (meaning flavor) stay inside.

FOR PORK

1. One-quarter soy sauce, ¼ honey, ½ boiling water, 1 cubic inch shredded fresh ginger. Marinate for 1 to 3 hours, depending on size and thickness of cut. Baste pork with this mixture several times during roasting.

2. Two parts soy, 3 parts sweet wine (such as tokay, sweet sauterne, Mirin). Bring these to a boil and reduce 20 to 30 per cent. Cool and use as a marinade for 2 hours. Baste 2 or 3 times during cooking period.

3. Hoisin (hoy sien) sauce, which is a canned Chinese sauce of considerable complexity. Use straight out of the can as a marinade and baste. If sauce is too thick to run around revolving meat, thin with water.

4. One-half cup soy sauce, ½ cup sherry, 2 cloves garlic crushed, 2 minced scallions, 2 star anise seeds. Bring to a boil and cool. Because star anise is strong, reduce time of marinating. Baste with it periodically.

5. Two tablespoons soy sauce, ½ cup vinegar, ¼ teaspoon chili powder, 2 tablespoons sugar, 2 cloves garlic, mashed, ¼ teaspoon pepper.

FOR MUTTON AND LAMB

Two cloves of crushed garlic, 1 cup soy sauce, 1 cup honey, 2 cups boiling water, 1 cup red wine. Marinate 8 to 12 hours and use a baste during cooking.

FOR BEEF

Small cuts of beef (like steak) can soak up a marinade in 20-30 minutes. Big cuts (like rolled roasts) should be given 30-40 minutes in a marinade. If it is a tough cut, adding wine to the other seasonings helps tenderize it. Here is my pet standby marinade-baste for a tender piece of beef:

One-quarter soy, ¼ honey, ½ boiling water. Sometimes I add 1 clove crushed garlic or the equivalent amount of grated fresh ginger.

FOR CHICKEN OR TURKEY

Salted butter and minced fresh herbs and celery tops—for basting only. Especially good herbs are parsley, thyme, bayleaf. Sometimes add juice of 1 lemon.

FOR DUCK AND SQUAB

One-quarter soy, ¼ honey, ½ boiling water, 1-inch cube of ginger root, grated or minced. Marinate 1 hour and baste several times during roasting.

A roll-around rotisserie-broiling unit that has many attachments and meets the requirements of the most experienced meat cook is shown outdoors. Its heat can be controlled.

Puréeing Heightens Flavor

How expert chefs eliminate indigestible fibers to step up taste by 30 per cent

The foreign cuisines with the most sensitive approach to foodstuffs are very conscious of fibrous tissues. They have discovered there is little, if any, taste in fiber and they take steps to eliminate this woody material before the food is served. The chefs who revolve around the Franco-Italian axis are convinced that a leafy or stringy or husk-coated vegetable tastes more like itself if puréed. That's why you see so frequently on European menus a *purée* of spinach, *purée* of peas or limas, *purée* of corn.

Since different foods have different fibrous content, and it occurs at different places, no blanket rules can be laid down for removing it. The vegetables that improve most markedly are corn, peas, shell beans, kidney beans, and limas. They must be cooked and then puréed in a Foley food mill or passed through a fine sieve. If puréeing with the food mill seems too laborious, try using the blender for the beginning process and then finish by putting through a sieve. Puréeing with a potato ricer removes an amazing amount of fiber—even from a soft thing such as an avocado. (Try this if you are making avocado soup.)

When you examine the residue after puréeing, the outside covering of each kernel feels, to the touch, like ground cellophane. Taste it, too, and you will see at once why it contributes nothing to flavor. It simply HAS no flavor. Even more interesting, the remaining edible parts are so loaded with flavor that they need very little seasoning, hardly even salt. That is, unless they have been overcooked and so have lost their taste in the cooking water.

Simple mashing brings out flavor in foods that are not fibrous, such as strawberries and potatoes. No one can argue that. It even seems that grinding, although the goal is not to remove fiber, heightens flavor. Chuck beef, the best for hamburger, is definitely more flavorsome that way than the same chuck cooked in one piece. And remember peanut butter, the darling of American youth! Is it not more peanut-y than whole peanuts?

Tartar steak, so dear to the Scandinavians, is raw scraped beef, seasoned in various ways. Scraping means drawing out the fleshy part of the meat from the stringy connective tissues, using a blunt

A

B

C

Puréeing Heightens Flavor

How expert chefs eliminate indigestible fibers to step up taste by 30 per cent

The foreign cuisines with the most sensitive approach to foodstuffs are very conscious of fibrous tissues. They have discovered there is little, if any, taste in fiber and they take steps to eliminate this woody material before the food is served. The chefs who revolve around the Franco-Italian axis are convinced that a leafy or stringy or husk-coated vegetable tastes more like itself if puréed. That's why you see so frequently on European menus a *purée* of spinach, *purée* of peas or limas, *purée* of corn.

Since different foods have different fibrous content, and it occurs at different places, no blanket rules can be laid down for removing it. The vegetables that improve most markedly are corn, peas, shell beans, kidney beans, and limas. They must be cooked and then puréed in a Foley food mill or passed through a fine sieve. If puréeing with the food mill seems too laborious, try using the blender for the beginning process and then finish by putting through a sieve. Puréeing with a potato ricer removes an amazing amount of fiber— even from a soft thing such as an avocado. (Try this if you are making avocado soup.)

When you examine the residue after puréeing, the outside covering of each kernel feels, to the touch, like ground cellophane. Taste it, too, and you will see at once why it contributes nothing to flavor. It simply HAS no flavor. Even more interesting, the remaining edible parts are so loaded with flavor that they need very little seasoning, hardly even salt. That is, unless they have been overcooked and so have lost their taste in the cooking water.

Simple mashing brings out flavor in foods that are not fibrous, such as strawberries and potatoes. No one can argue that. It even seems that grinding, although the goal is not to remove fiber, heightens flavor. Chuck beef, the best for hamburger, is definitely more flavorsome that way than the same chuck cooked in one piece. And remember peanut butter, the darling of American youth! Is it not more peanut-y than whole peanuts?

Tartar steak, so dear to the Scandinavians, is raw scraped beef, seasoned in various ways. Scraping means drawing out the fleshy part of the meat from the stringy connective tissues, using a blunt

tool like a kitchen table spoon. Scraped beef is very different from ground beef, in which the fiber still remains, even though cut up fine. Doctors know that scraped beef is more digestible, suitable even in ulcer cases. It also uncovers amazing new flavors.

Some vegetables, such as tomatoes and cucumbers, call only for peeling and seeding. Many countries know these facts. Peeling and seeding is meticulously practiced in Japan, at all social levels, and in all homes and restaurants.

Play around with puréeing, mashing, peeling, seeding, grinding, sieving. Use it to give your own recipes an exciting Continental lift. Or try a classic French *quenelles,* a recipe which depends upon the basic purée flavor principle. This one, a forcemeat of fish, is from Alice B. Toklas, the famous companion of Gertrude Stein and a resident of France for 55 years.

QUENELLES GODIVEAU LYONNAISE

Place in the blender the yolks of 3 eggs with ⅔ cup of flour, 4 tablespoons melted butter. Blend one minute and while blender is still running add ⅔ cup hot milk. Keep blending until perfectly smooth. Place in a small saucepan over medium heat and cook about 6 minutes, stirring constantly. Put aside to cool. This mixture is called *panade.*

Place in the bottom of the blender the whites of 2 eggs, then add ½ pound fat from beef kidney, skin removed, and cut into small cubes. When perfectly smooth remove from the blender with a rubber spatula and replace with ½ pound cubed pike or perch, weighed after bones and skin have been removed. Add ½ teaspoon salt, ¼ teaspoon pepper, ¼ teaspoon nutmeg; in about 3 minutes add the *panade,* and the fat and egg mixture. Blend first at low speed, then at high

speed until perfectly smooth and very fine.

This mixture is now ready to be rolled between floured hands into finger lengths. Poach for 5 minutes in salted water, 1 teaspoon salt to the quart. Be careful the *quenelles* do not stick to the bottom of the pan or together. Remove from water with perforated spoon and place on a kitchen towel to dry; pat them quite dry. They are now ready to be simmered for 10 minutes in whatever sauce is to be served with them.

The *quenelles* may be served around a boiled fish in a cream sauce, or in the juice of a braised chicken, or around a roast veal, or by themselves as an entrée. One recommended sauce is:

SAUCE ROYAL

Prepare a chicken *velouté:* warm 4 cups of chicken bouillon; place 1 cup in the blender along with 4 tablespoons softened buttter, 4 tablespoons flour. Blend till perfectly smooth. Add 3 green onions cut into pieces and blend a few seconds, just long enough to chop the onions. Add the sauce in the blender to the rest ot the heated bouillon and simmer 1 hour, stirring occasionally to prevent scorching.

Place 6 tablespoons truffles (3-ounce tin) along with ¼ cup chicken bouillon into the blender, and blend until the particles practically disappear. As the sauce cooks, gradually add ½ cup chicken bouillon. At the end of the simmering add ½ cup heavy cream. Then strain, replace over heat and stir in the truffles from the blender. When the sauce boils, carefully add the *quenelles.*

Cover and simmer gently for 10 minutes. Then add ⅓ cup butter, cut in small pieces, and 2 tablespoons good, dry sherry. Do not allow the sauce to boil; do not stir, but gently tip the saucepan in all directions. When the butter is melted and the sherry is amalgamated, serve.

D

A. Limas have heavy, "cellophane" husk on each bean. Left, container shows residue.

B. Left, hulls left after puréeing shelled peas. Result: peas unbelievably more tasty.

C. Corn has highest percentage of tasteless fiber. Cut from cob, put through food mill.

D. Even good cuts of beef contain fibrous tissue. Eliminate by scraping with spoon.

The perfect puréeing tool, the Foley food mill. Extracts fiber from foods, even those that have been put through the blender.

Though Greek Oranges look deceptively simple, they provide a taste thrill worthy of the closing note of a very important menu. They really are fixed this way in Greece.

The Continental Way with Fresh Fruits

Garnish them with wines or cordials properly paired for perfect flavor

Certain fruits and certain wines and liquors seem to be made for each other, and the blending of them into perfect union is one of the fine arts of continental cuisine. Yet few desserts are easier to make, including even the classic iced *sorbet*. The entire trick consists of pairing a particular fresh fruit with a wine, liqueur, or rum that complements its flavor (and bourbon shouldn't be left off the list). But which goes with which?

A man who has studied this field more intensively and extensively than almost anyone I know is Alan Lewis, a vice president of Restaurant Associates in New York. So I quote Mr. Lewis:

You have a classic union of fruit with a liqueur when you blend kirsch or Cherry Heering with cherries. You have another when you combine fresh greengage plums with mirabelle, the liqueur that derives from this fruit; or when you bring purple plums together with quetsch, which owes its flavor to the darker plums. When you blend crème de cassis, a potent infusion of black currants, with the currants themselves, you have a rich union to enhance the flavor of the fruit.

I could go on and on calling off such natural partnerships, but I'll stop with curaçao, which many households keep on hand only to add zip to the flavor of fresh oranges. I have a friend who never thought of mixing it with any other fruit until, one day, she discovered that a wide variety of wines, liqueurs, and brandies come in miniature bottles. Containing from one to two ounces

and costing from 25¢ to $1.50, they provide an inexpensive way to experiment, and that's what she has been doing ever since. (Note: Not all states allow sale of these miniatures.)

Although marrying fruits to the spirits from which they derive is the best way to begin, let your curiosity take you on from there. You'll discover that such a voluptuously sweet liqueur as Cherry Heering, or as apricot brandy, can subdue the harsh edges of *any* tart fruit. With a little experimentation, you'll discover that a herbal liqueur can rescue full-blown bananas and other peak-ripe fruits from a cloying sweetness; that sweet peaches, pears, and figs can gain interesting flavor from the anise seed of anisette, from the caraway seed of kümmel, and from the bouquet of herbs in Strega or Galliano.

Try flaming some of your liquored fruits. Small fruits, such as berries, can be flamed raw. Flaming not only makes the dessert more attractive, but heating, even briefly, burns up the alcohol and reveals a truer fruit flavor. Blazing is made easier when you use high-proof liqueurs (see page 183). If you use low-proof liqueurs or wines, it's a good idea to add brandy or rum for better flame. Warming the liqueur before igniting it also helps.

The ideal temperature at which to keep and serve raw fruit is between 75 and 80 degrees, the natural warmth of the summer orchard at the peak of picking. Many people, however, find chilled fruit more refreshing—though I consider this more propaganda than fact.

There are several ways of blending fresh, un-cooked fruit with spirits. Poaching fruit in wines and liqueurs (which is not to be confused with stewing) gives a most delicate flavor to hard-fleshed fruits with stones or pits such as pears, peaches, cherries, nectarines, and apricots.

In the following recipes you can, in most cases, substitute the fruit you happen to have for the one the recipe calls for. If you have any doubt as to the compatibility of your fruit and the wine or liqueur to use, look at the chart on the next page.

Poaching Fresh Fruit

For success in poaching fruit simmer it (with or without skins) a brief 3 to 7 minutes, depending upon ripeness. Remove fruit immediately and put into an iced bowl, since it would continue to cook in its hot liquid even after removal from fire. Chill liquid separately, and pour over fruit before serving.

PEARS IN WHITE WINE

6 ripe perfect pears, whole, peeled or unpeeled,
but with stems intact
1½ pints dry white wine
1½ pints water
½ pound sugar
Sprig of woodruff, optional

Bring water, sugar, and wine to a boil. Add pears, woodruff, and simmer, briefly.

PINEAPPLE AND GRAPE COMPOTE

1 large pineapple
1½ quarts water
½ pound of sugar (more if pineapple is tart)
2 ounces kirsch or framboise
½ pound seedless white grapes

Peel pineapple, remove core, and cut in vertical segments. Bring water and sugar to a boil, then lower flame and add liqueur. Add pineapple and barely simmer as above. Add washed grapes, un-cooked, before chilling. Serves 6.

PURPLE PLUMS IN PORT

12 purple plums
1 quart water
½ pound sugar
6 ounces port wine

Wash plums but do not peel. Bring water, sugar,

and wine to a boil, add plums and barely simmer for from 3 to 7 minutes, depending upon ripeness, or less if skins show signs of breaking. Serves 6.

VARIATIONS OF PLUMS IN PORT

Use the same recipe as above for greengage plums, but substitute 2 ounces of mirabelle for the port.

You can substitute apricots. Then use 2 ounces of apricot brandy for port wine.

You can also substitute 2 ounces of quetsch for port, but add it *after* water and sugar boil.

You can substitute peeled nectarines for plums.

PEACHES IN CASSIS

6 ripe peaches, peeled
1 quart water   ½ pound sugar
2 ounces crème de cassis

Bring water and sugar to a boil, add peaches and liqueur, and barely simmer.

You can substitute two pounds of ripe Bing cherries (pitted) for peaches, and kirsch (4 ounces) for crème de cassis. Serves 6.

PEACHES IN RED WINE

6 ripe whole peaches, peeled
1 quart water   ½ pound sugar
1 cinnamon stick
6 ounces red wine

Bring water and sugar to a boil and add cinnamon stick. Reduce to a simmer, and add peaches, cooking 3 to 7 minutes. Serves 6.

GLAZED ORANGES

6 whole oranges, peeled down to the flesh
1 quart water   ¾ pound sugar
2 ounces Grand Marnier

Shred, julienne-style, the rind of three oranges. Boil water and sugar to make syrup. Add shredded orange peel and simmer a few minutes. Blend in Grand Marnier and pour syrup over oranges. Place in pre-heated (375° F.) oven for five minutes or until oranges are glazed. Serve warm or chilled. Serves 6.

GREEK ORANGES

Here is a somewhat different way to treat oranges —not using any cordial or flaming. It takes more time but the results are startling, and it is well worth the trouble.

Use 1 orange per person if served whole. Use 1½ orange per person if they are to be segmented. Pare off the outer colored part of the skin, carefully avoiding the white part. Then julienne the peel into tiny slivers.

Put this julienne in boiling water, boil for 10 minutes and drain. Have more boiling water ready and again boil for 10 minutes. Again drain and put into fresh boiling water for another 10 minutes. Three boilings, three drainings.

While all this is going on, trim off all the white underskin, and discard. You may leave oranges whole (as in the picture on page 168) or you may remove the pulp, segment by segment.

Make a sugar syrup (1 pound of sugar for 6 oranges plus sufficient water). If you have segmented the oranges, pour any remaining juice into this syrup. Add a few drops of red food coloring to jolly up the general look. Boil this syrup for 10 minutes. Then, while it is still boiling, pour over the oranges which have been placed in a non-metal container. Let stand for 15 minutes. Pour off the syrup and boil it again for 15 more minutes. Finally, pour hot syrup over the oranges. Add the julienne of boiled orange peel.

Cool to room temperature and serve. Better if not refrigerated.

PEACHES BLAZED WITH BOURBON

6 halves of fresh, peeled peaches
1 tablespoon grated orange rind
3 tablespoons butter
3 teaspoons sugar   ½ lemon
2 tablespoons orange marmalade
3 ounces bourbon

Pierce peaches all around with a fork. Blend grated orange rind into butter and heat in a chafing dish. Sauté peaches, gently turning them in butter sauce, and baste. Take care that butter doesn't burn. Sprinkle on sugar, then add a little lemon juice, and continue to baste. When peaches are a golden brown, turn cavity side up and fill opening with marmalade. Sprinkle bourbon over fruit, and ignite. Serve flaming peach with sauce. Serves 6.

Compatible Liquors and Fruits

Anisette:
Melons, raspberries
Apricot Brandy:
Apricots, peaches, tangerines
Aurum:
Apricots, melons, oranges
Blackberry Cordial:
Blackberries, plums, melons
Bourbon:
Peaches, pears
Brandy:
Strawberries, raspberries, peaches, pineapples
Champagne:
Peaches, berries, grapes
Chartreuse:
Grapefruit, pineapples, tangerines
Cherry Heering:
Cherries, grapes, melons
Cointreau:
Oranges, apricots, melons

Crème de Cacao:
Bananas, pears
Crème de Cassis:
Black currants, blackberries, peaches, strawberries
Curaçao:
Oranges, pineapples
Framboise:
Blueberries, currants, grapes, pineapples, raspberries, strawberries
Galliano:
Figs, peaches, pears, baked apples, strawberries
Grand Marnier:
Grapefruits, oranges, tangerines
Kirsch:
Bananas, cherries, melons, peaches, pineapples
Kümmel:
Figs, peaches, pears

Mirabelle:
Berries, greengage plums, nectarines
Peach Brandy:
Bananas, peaches, pineapples
Pear Brandy:
Fresh pineapples, pears
Port:
Berries, nectarines, melons, purple plums, raspberries
Quetsch:
Berries, grapefruits, purple plums
Red Wine:
Peaches, rhubarb, strawberries
Rum:
Bananas
Strega:
Figs, peaches, pears
White Wine:
Apples, pears, purple plums

BROILED PEACHES

6 freestone peaches, halved, pitted
3 tablespoons currant jelly
Brown sugar to taste
Crème de cassis

Fill cavities of peach halves with currant jelly. Sprinkle with brown sugar, and broil lightly until sugar is glazed. Remove to serving plate, and sprinkle with crème de cassis. Serves 6.

STRAWBERRIES IN BORDEAUX

2 pints of strawberries
2 tablespoons sugar
1 pint red Bordeaux wine

Clean and trim berries, sprinkle with sugar, add wine, and let chill before serving. Serves 6.

MELON BALLS WITH LIQUEUR

3 well-ripened honeydew, Spanish, or
Persian melons
Blackberry cordial, aurum, or kirsch
1 pint well-ripened blackberries
Sugar to taste

Set melons aside at room temperature for an hour or so. To prepare, cut one melon in half and scoop out in balls. Drench the melon balls with chosen liqueur. Cut remaining two melons in halves, remove seeds, and heap centers with a mixture of melon balls and berries, sugared to taste. Serves 4.

BANANAS WITH RUM

6 ripe bananas,
peeled and cut in half lengthwise
1 pint heavy cream, whipped
2 ounces dark Jamaican rum

Gently blend rum into the whipped cream and use to garnish bananas, served two halves to a dessert plate. Serves 6.

RASPBERRIES WITH PORT

2 pints raspberries (or strawberries)
4 tablespoons sugar
1 pint heavy cream, whipped
2 ounces white port (or brandy)

Wash and dry berries. Fold sugar into whipped cream, add port or brandy and use to garnish each serving of berries. Serves 6.

CHERRIES WITH CURRANT JELLY

1 pound fresh Bing cherries
1 ounce red currant jelly
2 ounces kirsch

Pit cherries, melt jelly, and mix. Add kirsch, and keep mixture in refrigerator to chill until ready to serve. Serves 4 to 6.

The Classic Sorbet

The great-great-grandfather of ice cream and sherbets was iced, puréed fruit pulp called *sorbet* (pronounced soarbay). It was sweetened with sugar syrup, often enlivened with a little lemon juice. Sometimes, but not always, it was dressed up with a flick of the appropriate fruit liqueur just as it was served. It probably originated in Paris about 1880.

Sorbets were the darlings of the Victorian era. And well they might be, for they are delicious. They owe this deliciousness to the fact they are NOT hard frozen. In texture, *sorbet* should be about the consistency of frosted malted milk or thick cream. They must be served in goblets, parfait glasses, stemmed compotes, or even Pilsener glasses. You would eat the first half of your portion with a spoon, but you would probably drink the last half because it would be quite unfrozen and almost liquid by that time. Hence, use a glass that can perform both ways.

Because *sorbet* is not supposed to be frozen to the crystalline state, eating it does not paralyze your taste buds as modern ice creams and ices do. Consequently, you are better able to appreciate the flavor of whatever it is made of. The quality of the fruit or melon you use becomes very important. Favor, then, fruits that have ripened on the tree or vine.

Another reason *sorbets* are so flavorsome is that the fruit, or melon, is puréed. Puréeing definitely heightens the flavor of anything, and with fruit the gain is even more pronounced, for the juices are freed to be savored more. Some fruits and berries could be puréed in the electric blender. But seedy berries like raspberries, blackberries, and blackcaps should be put through the Foley food mill to remove the seeds. Pineapple should also be put through the Foley food mill to get rid of the woody fiber which is quite noticeable after puréeing in a blender.

Sorbets are easy to make. First, make a simple syrup (¾ quart of boiling water to ¾ quart of sugar). Boil until your testing spoon drops syrup in thread-like strings. Let syrup cool. Then mix with puréed fruit or melon. (See directions below for proportions of fruit and syrup.)

Besides those fruits included in our formulas below, we suggest these: mango, damson plum, cocoa plum, greengage plum, dewberry, blackcap, mulberry, pomegranate, persimmon, Japanese quince, loganberry, Monstera, guava, Indian currant, and cherimoya.

To freeze the *sorbet* mixture, when ready, you can use either an electric ice cream freezer (preferred for a creamier mixture and for its greater convenience) or standard refrigerator trays (after removing grids) in the freezer. Freeze for 30 to 40 minutes or until it is of a viscous texture. If it gets too frozen and set, you can put it back in the blender to be whipped to a foamy consistency. Serve at once.

If it gets too liquid, return to trays to freeze lightly, but not to a hard crystallized state. The time to add liqueur or wine is after the *sorbet* is served in the glasses; but add just a dash, so as not to overwhelm the fresh fruit flavor. Treat the liqueur as a garnish — not a main ingredient.

SUGGESTED COMBINATIONS

RASPBERRY — Kirsch, framboise, white port
STRAWBERRY — Grand Marnier, framboise,
   champagne
PEACH — Benedictine, peach brandy, bourbon,
   champagne
APRICOT — Apricot brandy, Cointreau, white wine
CANTALOUPE — Cognac, Marsala wine
CHERRY — Cherry Heering, madeira
CURRANTS — Crème de cassis, white wine,
   champagne
PLUMS — Mirabelle, Tokay wine

Sorbet, forerunner of ice-cream, is the puréed pulp of fruit (or melon), seasoned and semi-frozen. Never hard-freeze it.

PROPORTIONS FOR BERRIES

For raspberry, blackberry, gooseberry, blueberry, huckleberry, currant, and cherry (all to be strained or sieved for purée and juice only): use 3 pints of fruit purée to a quart of syrup.

PROPORTIONS FOR FLESHY FRUITS (PULP)

For peach, apricot, nectarine, plum, crab apple, quince, and strawberry (all to be peeled or pitted where necessary and puréed): Combine 3 pounds of fruit purée with a quart of syrup.

For cantaloupe, use 3 pounds of sweet meat pulp to ½ pound of sugar. No syrup is used here due to the high water content of melon.

A sparkling tomato aspic, tartly
tasting of vinegar and interestingly
seasoned with herbs and spices, can make
a salad course into a main course.

Add *En Gelée* to Your Repertory

*As the great chefs do it, an aspic becomes
a jellied envelope with flavor*

All the cuisines in the butter-and-fat category make major use of reduced rich stock. When stock is reduced enough it begins to gelatinize and set up like jelly. Out of this characteristic has arisen a key technique in gourmet cookery. The discovery in the past century of unflavored gelatin extended this art even further, permitting jellied dishes to occur at every point in the meal, including the dessert.

Traditionally, before the coming of unflavored gelatin, the jelly (or *gelée)* was of three basic types: made from meat bones and meat, or fish bones and heads, or chicken bones. Its main function is as a binder of other foods. In particular, it makes possible the appetizing use of leftovers.

Since gelatin is a protein, it is a better meat extender than starch or cereal. The numerous delicious potted meats, which are one of the chief dishes throughout those parts of Europe where animal husbandry flourishes, utilize this principle. They are miracles of invention by which poor grades of meat or meat scraps are turned into gourmet fare by enveloping them in an interestingly-flavored gelatin aspic.

Unfortunately, a misuse of aspics in quaintsy tea rooms and in simple-minded recipes for children has put this fine cookery material into disrepute. But if you use it correctly, it gives you a wonderful new tool.

For instance, far too little use has been made of gelatin as a sharply-flavored, tart envelope for sea food. When a dry white wine is incorporated into the liquid, when crisp pieces of celery or water chestnuts are molded in with the fish, when this is served with a really good homemade mayonnaise or with a sauce based on sour cream, you've achieved a triumph of complementary flavors and contrasting textures. Add to this the fact that such a dish can be molded into an interesting shape. You've pleased both the palate and the eye with one stroke.

The Five Basic Types

All gelatinized dishes may be reduced to five basic types. All are made today of unflavored gelatin in a liquid base. The liquid may be stock from meat, fish, or chicken; the juice of vegetables or fruit; wine; coffee; ginger ale; cider; milk or buttermilk; coconut or almond milk. The flavored jelly may contain meat, poultry, game, fish, shellfish, vegetables, fruits, eggs, nuts, or whatever you may have at hand. You can have jellied hors d'oeuvre, soups, salads, or desserts.

Type 1—basic clear jelly. When you add a savory flavor to make it into an appetizer or an entrée, it becomes an Aspic. Or it may be sweet, flavored with wine or fruit juice.

Type 2—with air beaten in to clear basic jelly. These are Whips.

Type 3—with both air and beaten egg whites beaten in. These are the Sponges and Snows.

A really elaborate Swedish banquet includes cold sliced fowl and game in aspic served with a salad.

Photograph courtesy Scandinavian Airlines System

Type 4—with an egg base. *Chaud froid* sauce and Spanish cream or chiffon pie filling.

Type 5—whipped cream base. When combined with a milk base, it is Blanc Mange or Mousse or Parfait or Bavarian cream, etc. Variations of Bavarian cream are the Charlotte, the Trifle, the Ice Box Cake.

I think you should know the traditional way to make jellied meat stock and fish stock at home, so you will have some standard of comparison when you try the short-cut ways found in most present day cookbooks.

HOMEMADE JELLIED MEAT STOCK

2 pounds veal shank
1 calf's foot, boned and blanched
3 pounds chicken bones
1½ pounds beef bones
1 leek   1 onion
2 carrots   2 stalks celery
½ teaspoon pickling spice
¼ teaspoon cracked pepper
1 cup white wine   ¼ cup madeira

Place all of these ingredients but the wines in a

deep pot. Cover with cold water. Place over medium heat, uncovered, and bring to boil. As froth rises to surface, skim it. When liquid begins to boil, cover pot and turn heat low so that liquid just simmers. Allow to cook slowly for 3 hours. Strain stock, discarding all solids. Cool so that fat will solidify on surface and can be removed. Now add the white wine and madeira. Correct for salt. This stock should stand up like gelatin when cold. Yield: about 2 quarts.

HOMEMADE JELLIED FISH STOCK

3 pounds uncooked fish bones and trimmings,
including one or more heads
1 large onion, quartered
1 carrot   Parsley
2 pieces celery with leaves
5 or 6 peppercorns
1 bottle dry white wine
1 quart water
½ envelope unflavored gelatin

Combine all ingredients except gelatin in a deep pan. Bring to a boil. Let simmer gently for one hour. Strain off stock. Discard bones and vegetables. Season with salt. Dissolve gelatin in ½ cup cold water. Add to hot stock. Yield: about 2 quarts.

TOMATO ASPIC

The *gelée* most familiar to Americans is the tomato aspic, which does not use meat or fish stock. A tomato aspic lets you create a cold salad with the ingredients *and* the dressing built in. It can be a side garnish for another cold dish, or it can be the salad itself with no other contents added.

Think of your aspic as a cold sauce. If you wouldn't serve a hot food in a bath of hot tomato juice, then you can be sure that combination won't work well when cold. On the other hand, a well-flavored tomato aspic is to cold cookery just what a well-flavored tomato sauce is to hot cookery. Here are ways to flavor it:

1 envelope unflavored gelatin
¼ cup cold water
2½ cups unseasoned tomato juice
1 teaspoon sugar
⅛ teaspoon ginger
¼ teaspoon salt
1 teaspoon lemon juice

Soften gelatin in cold water. Heat tomato juice and add sugar, ginger, and salt. Combine gelatin

A molded, gelatinized dessert, such as this lemon mousse, shows how the *en gelée* principle applies to any part of menu.

and tomato juice mixture, stirring till gelatin is completely dissolved. When cool, add lemon juice and put in refrigerator to set.

For a different flavor result, omit ginger and lemon juice, but add to the mixture 1 teaspoon basil-flavored wine vinegar.

The intelligent cook will forget all about what *en gelée* can do for the appearance of a dish and concentrate on what it can do for the taste. Until you are completely at home with gelatin cookery, don't bother too much about fancy molds. It is just as nice to pour your aspic mixture into an attractive serving dish, place it in the refrigerator to cool, and serve in the same dish.

Don't make jelly too stiff. The stiffer the jelly, the easier it is to mold, but unfortunately the less desirable it is to eat. When it is allowed to get thick and tough, or when it is poorly flavored, few will enjoy eating it. This is the chief stumbbling block in gelatin cookery.

Fillings for a main entrée can be any cooked food which tastes good cold. The only food not recommended is "mixed" casserole-type dishes. The following are excellent with the appropriate stock: cold beef, either roast or braised, poultry, roast pork, veal, pâté, chicken livers, many vegetables, all kinds of seafood.

The Unspoken Language of Garnishes

They're the signal from the chef to the eater,
and it helps if you know how to read them

The average person probably thinks that the purpose of a garnish is to make a dish look pretty when it is served—a sort of trimming for optical effect. This is not untrue, but it is hardly a fraction of the truth. Most garnishes are important to the taste of the food, either heightening and underlining the taste or offering contrast. The jelly, jam, and pickles used on the average American table with the meat course are an example. Or the chocolate sauce on ice cream. Or the icing on the cake. The old-fashioned drug store sundae was a masterpiece of garnishing.

Various peoples have worked out different systems for garnishing. The Europeans have developed a full-blown system, filling 13 pages of definitions for meat dishes alone in *"Larousse Gastronomique."* In the maize cultures, there are the side dishes of *salsa verde* and other piquant sauces which you may use to garnish with—as much or as little as you care to. But whatever kind of cuisine, the garnishes serve a particular purpose.

Generalizations are always dangerous, but I will head for danger. There are, it seems to me, basically four types of garnishes. (And I am not counting prettification as one of the types.)

1. *The garnish that signals a foodstuff.* It tells what ingredients were used in the cooking. For instance, the contents of a seafood salad, generously dressed in mayonnaise or covered with a jellied *chaud-froid,* cannot be easily recognized. But if the cook puts a few whole shrimps or a few whole lobster claws on top, all can know what to expect. This is especially helpful for people who are allergic to or dislike one or another foodstuff, and who may thus tactfully decline a serving before tasting it. A signal garnish also helps aesthetically, for some of the best-tasting recipes have an appearance that is shapeless, messy—a nothingness. These will gain a great deal from the visual aid of a positive shape or form.

The signal garnish is very helpful at a big buffet party. You don't need to fly lettered pennants from your sandwich trays. Isn't it better to garnish the cucumber sandwiches with a thin slice of cucumber? The signal need not necessarily be edible. Our grandmothers served eggs or chicken pie from ceramic dishes made to look like setting hens. In France, pâtés and civets of rabbit or duck are served from terrines sculpted to resemble what they are supposed to contain. All kinds of amusing whimsy has gone on in this area for centuries.

2. *The garnishes that season by adding another flavor.* They may be flowers, leaves, flames. Then there are the sugar fantasies, the frostings, the icings, the candied confections such as candied violets. Old faithfuls are the branches and leaves of herbs—parsley, dill, cress, lovage, nasturtium. In this group are the twist of lemon peel in the drink, lemon wedges to squeeze over the fish, lime slices in black bean soup, whipped cream on gingerbread, a slice of cheddar cheese on apple pie, the grated cheese in the onion soup, catsup on the hamburger.

Even ice can be a seasoning garnish. Make cubes of strong tea or coffee to use in these iced drinks. As they melt they will strengthen rather than dilute. Fruit punches can be iced with frozen

A good example of classic garniture: potatoes are to be eaten with the fish, the lemon seasons the fish, the greens decorate.

cubes of fruit juice. Even that wonderful cold summer vegetable soup, gazpacho, can be iced with cubes of tomato juice or V8.

3. *The garnish that emphasizes the main ingredient,* helping it make a stronger statement than it would ungarnished. The classic French sauces do this, for they are really reduced essences of the main ingredient. Garnishing also is a good trick for pepping up canned or frozen foods. Commercial products tend to be rather bland, since they must be concocted for a common denominator in taste. Why not add more lobster to canned lobster bisque, or a goodly dollop of real whipped cream to a canned soup? Putting a handful of fresh pea pods in canned or frozen peas does wonders for the flavor.

4. *The garnish that is an accompaniment, whose purpose is to complement and contrast.* When garnishing gets to this stage it begins to change its name and is called *garniture,* at least by the chefs of the international French cuisine.

Through the centuries, cooks and chefs have sought to find the perfect combinations of foods that marry to make a perfect menu. They arrived at certain classic combinations: mushrooms with broiled steak, the penchant of tomatoes and eggplant for lamb, the textural interest of crisp julienne potatoes with sauced fish, the smooth tartness of cauliflower hollandaise with roast beef.

These hallowed affinities are really like thumbnail menus. The theory is that only small quantities of the garnitures should be served with and around the main dish. But oftentimes, especially in Europe and in U. S. restaurants that try to operate in the classical European way, so many of these accompanying garnitures may surround the main dish that it becomes a one-dish meal, eliminating the need to order side dishes of vegetables. With a full classical garniture—there are at least 240 with separate names in the chef's lexicon—you will be lucky to have enough appetite left for a small green salad and a dessert.

A goose, flambéed with cognac at the table just before carving, is a dramatic sight, but the liquor also makes a taste contribution by amalgamating the already present flavors.

Flambé: Spectacular in Fire

How to add flavor with a lovely leaping flame

Flambéing has been developed as both a visual and culinary art in the world's greatest restaurants, whose maîtres d'hôtel, adding ingredients from diverse bottles with tender solicitude, give a virtuoso performance at the chafing dish. A certain amount of drama should always accompany the flaming of food, and the nonprofessional should approach the matter in this spirit, making it a ceremony.

How do you flambé successfully? Working with a dish that fails to ignite is a terrible anticlimax. On the other hand, a flame that smokes the ceiling, singes eyelashes, and threatens draperies is not only unsuccessful but dangerous. Over-flaming the food can ruin it, producing a harsh taste of liquor, obliterating its true flavor.

Follow the two basic rules for flambéing (below) and you can master the technique, which applies to any recipe you want to try. Experiment as much as you want to with flavors, but don't experiment with the technique.

Rule No. 1: Use high-proof spirits. The higher they are, the better. (See list showing the proofs of various liquors and the foods with which they are compatible.) If liqueurs aren't high enough proof to blaze, combine them with others in the 80 to 151-proof range.

Rule No. 2. Use a preheated pan. The food in it must be boiling-hot.

If you use a chafing dish, *crêpes* pan, or other utensil fueled by canned heat or denatured alcohol, put your blazer pan directly over a high flame. Preheating the liquor makes for more successful flaming. To light the liquor, use a taper or a fireplace match, and delay igniting until the sulphur of the match has burned off. If you use a thermostatic pan, preheat it to 300°F. Before adding liquor (which you don't have to preheat in this case), turn control dial down to 200°F.

After mastering these basic rules, there are as many approaches to finesse in flambéing as there are maîtres d'hôtel, captains, and chefs who practice it. Every *flambeur* has developed his own style.

Pointers on which all experts agree: practice on your family as many as three or four times before attempting to wow a table of dinner guests. Learn your recipe by heart; try out different liquors for strength and flavor, and test your cooking unit.

When you perform in front of guests, have a tray beside you that's been stocked in advance with all ingredients and accessories that you will need. Arrange them neatly and artistically for eye appeal.

An important word of caution: Don't pour liquor directly from a bottle into a hot pan. The pouring liquor could ignite. Decant the amount needed and pour from a glass.

Here is a selective list of foods with the spirits that combine best with them for flambéing. Proofs of various liquors are also given:

Check-List for the *Flambé* Artist

DISHES	LIQUORS FOR FLAMBE
Soups:	
Green pea; tomato	Applejack
Black bean	Cointreau
Cream of shrimp	Brandy; rye whiskey
Onion	Brandy
Clam chowder	Bourbon
Fish:	
Seafood; shellfish	Brandy
Lobster	Rum
Fowl:	
Chicken	Brandy with Drambuie or Grand Marnier; peach or apricot brandy
Duck	Brandy with Drambuie or Grand Marnier: Cointreau; gin; rum with kirsch and anisette
Turkey; goose	Brandy with Drambuie or Grand Marnier
Game:	
Pheasant	Brandy with Drambuie or Grand Marnier; applejack
Snipe	Brandy
Guinea hen; partridge; venison	Gin; rum; applejack
Meat:	
Beef; veal; lamb	Brandy and bourbon
Kidneys; chicken livers	Brandy and bourbon
Pork; ham	Brandy with peach or apricot liqueur
Vegetables:	
Artichoke bottoms	Brandy
Mushrooms	Brandy; brandy with kümmel
Candied yams; sweet potatoes	Rum; brandy with curaçao or Grand Marnier
Fruits:	
Apple (baked)	Rum with anisette; bourbon; applejack; ginger-flavored brandy; kirsch
Apricots; nectarines; tangerines	Southern Comfort; kirsch; apricot brandy; Aurum; Cointreau; mirabelle; Chartreuse
Bananas	Gin; rum; peach brandy; kirsch; cognac with Kahlua
Cherries	Kirsch and Cherry Heering; Grand Marnier; maraschino
Dates; figs	Brandy; kümmel; Galliano; Strega
Grapes	Framboise; brandy
Melons	Brandy with anisette; Cointreau with white crème de menthe or blackberry brandy
Oranges	Grand Marnier; Aurum

Peaches	Gin; bourbon and Southern Comfort; brandy; Cointreau; Galliano; kümmel; Strega with white crème de menthe; any fruit brandy
Pears	Bourbon; brandy with crème de cacao; kümmel; pear brandy; Strega; Drambuie
Pineapples	Brandy; Chartreuse; kirsch; framboise; apricot, peach, or pear brandy
Plums	Kirsch with blackberry liqueur; quetsch; sloe gin
Raspberries	Brandy; framboise
Strawberries	Brandy; Cointreau; kirsch; framboise; brandy with crème de fraises

Desserts:

Souffles, omelettes	Grand Marnier: kirsch with peach liqueur or Cherry Heering; applejack; rum
Creams; mousses; ice cream; cakes; pastries	Kirsch; brandy with choice of sweet liqueur
Plum pudding; fruit cakes; mince pie	Brandy; rum
Zabaglione (Sabayon)	Rum; Chartreuse; Grand Marnier; cognac
Crêpes Suzette; other pancakes	Brandy; Grand Marnier; B & B or brandy with choice of sweet liqueur

Coffee:

Café Royale	Cognac
Café Brulot	Brandy
Café Diable	Triple sec; brandy; rum
Café Punchino	Brandy
Café Kirsch	Kirsch with crème de cacao

Proof
(equals 2 times alcoholic content)

Anisette	50-60	Cherry Heering	49	Kahlua	53
Applejack	80	Cointreau	80	Kirsch	80-100
Aurum	78	Cognac	80-84	Kümmel	70-86
B & B (Benedictine & brandy)	86	Crème de cacao	50-60	Liqueur, peach or apricot	60
		Crème de fraises	60		
Bourbon	80-100	Crème de menthe	60	Maraschino	80
Brandy	80-84	Curaçao	60	Mirabelle	90
Brandy, apricot	70-86	Drambuie	80	Quetsch	90
Brandy, blackberry, peach, or ginger	70	Framboise	82-100	Rum	80-151
		Grand Marnier	80	Rye Whiskey	80-86
Chartreuse, yellow	86	Gin	80-94	Strega	80
				Southern Comfort	100
Chartreuse, green	110	Galliano	80	Triple sec	80

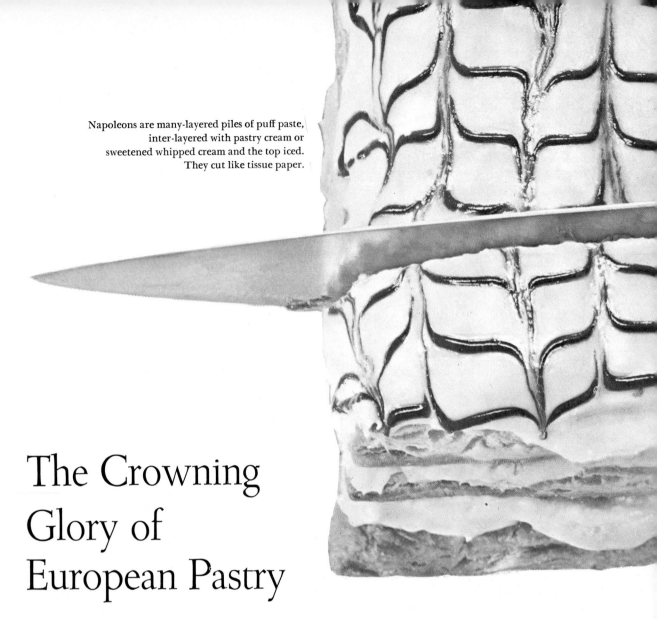

Napoleons are many-layered piles of puff paste, inter-layered with pastry cream or sweetened whipped cream and the top iced. They cut like tissue paper.

The Crowning Glory of European Pastry

It's puff paste, well worth preparing at home for incomparable fresh flakiness

The rest of the world has very little to teach us about pastry. We have assimilated almost all of the ways of the western world. *All but one*.

That is the incomparable, flaky, many-purposed pastry known as puff paste. (The French call it *feuilletée* or *feuilletage*, meaning many-layered or many leaves.) In the United States we generally meet this type of pastry only in restaurants, in the dessert called a "napoleon." But unfortunately most napoleons are made up too far in advance, so the filling tends to make the flaky layers soggy. Many people, unless they have been to Europe, have never had a chance to meet a proper, freshly made and exquisitely crisp puff paste.

People with access to really fine pastry shops can buy desserts, patty shells, or *croissants* made of puff paste. And of course the scant score of

really good restaurants in America frequently have dishes on their menus calling for a flaky patty shell. You can recognize these by such terms as *vol au vent* or *bouchée*, followed by words describing what they are filled with. Common fillers are chicken or sweetbreads bound with a *velouté* sauce. The same really good restaurants would also serve a proper napoleon, as well as smaller, less filling puff pastes such as palmiers, papillons, arcs, sacristans, bow ties, cream horns, and dartois.

Puff paste is not hard to make—that is, the recipe is uncomplicated—but it does require care, precision, a knowledge of technique, and about 3 hours total time. However, if you make three or four batches at the same time, it will take only about 10 minutes longer and you will be stocked for weeks with the aid of the freezer. Puff paste freezes well. Then you'll be ready with patty shells, cheese straws, *croissants,* coverings for casseroles, tart shells and canapé shells—in short, anything that requires a crisp, light, flaky pastry. For the recipe and directions, turn the page.

On your first try, though, make only one batch. Then work up to two batches. One batch chills and rests while you are rolling the other.

Some cooks roll their pastry about ⅛ inch thick, cutting it into sections of the size most useful for their cookery needs. Then they stack the wafer-thin layers between waxed paper, using two sheets of paper between each layer. It is best to lay these stacks on a flat surface like a cooky sheet, so they will freeze flat. Then wrap the precious bundles in heavy-duty aluminum foil for storage.

If you decide to go into puff paste production, you should pre-plan its various uses so as to cut it to correct size and shape before you put it in the freezer. Puff paste, well wrapped, also will keep for several days in the refrigerator, in which case you would do your final rolling and cutting after the sixth "turn" (see next page). If you freeze it, you can hold it as long as three or four months before baking.

In the baking, the general professional opinion is that it's best to place the icy-cold pastry in a very hot oven (500° F.) and reduce the heat by 50° every 5 minutes down to 350°. This makes about 20 minutes in all.

You can also bake at 500° F. throughout; then it will take only 15 minutes. But you may find it necessary to cover the pastry after the first 10 minutes with lightweight aluminum foil to keep it from getting too brown too fast.

Paula Peck differs slightly from the consensus in her book, "The Art of Fine Baking." She says: "Success with puff paste depends on knowing how to bake as well as how to make. Most recipes call for a very hot oven, 450° or more. I find that while puff pastries rise in such a hot oven, the bottoms are invariably too brown, and the centers of large pastries remain uncooked . . . I found a moderate oven of 350° was ideal. It takes longer, but there is no danger of burned bottoms or sides." A beginner should probably follow Mrs. Peck's more cautious advice.

Here are additional pointers as you follow the steps in the picture sequence:

Every time you roll out and fold your dough in threes (prior to folding), you are making more tiny layers of pastry, each of which will rise when you bake them, no matter what shape you use.

When starting to make a turn, *always* place the open end of the dough to your left, as you did on the first turn.

In the last step, use a sharp knife and a sure hand. Never saw at the pastry because this seals the edge and prevents the dough from rising. Lift whatever shape you're cutting with a broad knife or a spatula, and be sure to touch the dough only in the center.

Put whatever you're going to bake on ungreased, chilled cooky sheets and place in the refrigerator for at least 10 minutes so that everything is very cold. Starting to bake in a hot (425°-450° F.) oven "scares" the butter out of unchilled pastry. Butterflies are the easiest things to make from puff paste. Try your hand at them first.

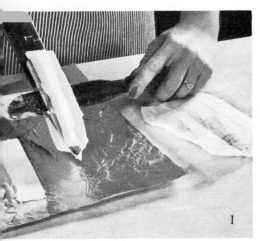

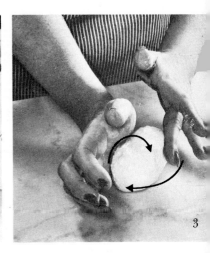

1 Knead 1 pound of butter in ice water till waxy. Then shape into a brick roughly 5″ x 5″ x 1¼″. Cut brick into four equal pieces. Return to refrigerator.

2 In a bowl put 4 cups sifted bread flour and 1 teaspoon salt. Add slowly 1½ cups icy cold water, mixing with a fork. Turn out on floured board.

3 Knead lightly to make sure flour and water are truly blended. Avoid overkneading to prevent developing elasticity in dough. Cover dough and put in the refrigerator for 15 to 20 minutes. Goal: to bring dough and butter to the same temperature and workability, for you must blend them without too much handling.

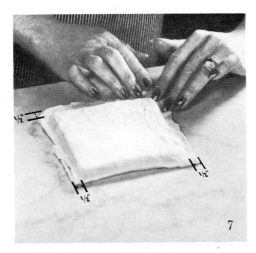

European Pastry:

7 Fold upper half of your dough over the butter, bringing it up snugly to the butter at the fold, and leaving ½″ dough on the other three sides. Pinch edges together firmly. Wrap in foil, refrigerate for 30 minutes.

8 Place chilled dough on floured board, with the edge that was at the bottom (when you pinched the edges together) now turned clockwise to your left. Pound vigorously with rolling pin to spread butter. Refrigerate.

9 Roll dough on well-floured board into a rectangle 8″ x 18″ x ⅓″. Don't roll over ends. Keep thickness uniform.

sometimes an accompaniment of *broyo*, the local variant on corn meal mush. The next one you run across labeled *à la béarnaise* may be completely different. Almost always, however, this description will mean simply that the meat or grilled fish is accompanied by Béarnaise sauce—an egg-butter-wine-herb combination tricky to make successfully—which isn't Béarnaise at all.

Beauharnais, à la *(named in honor of a member of the Beauharnais family)* Accompanied by artichoke bases covered with tiny potatoes bedded in Béarnaise sauce to which tarragon purée has been added. Served chiefly with *filet mignon*.

Bénédictine, à la *(in the Benedictine fashion)* Accompanied with little boat-shaped pastry shells filled with creamed cod. Served with fish or poached eggs.

Bercy, à la *(in the fashion of Bercy)* Smothered in chopped shallots. Found particularly in conjunction with steak, but some fish are also treated this way. Bercy is the Seine-side region of eastern Paris, on the Right bank, where the food warehouses are found.

Berrichonne, à la *(in the fashion of the Berry)* Served with braised cabbage, little onions, chestnuts, and slices of lean bacon. Served with meat, especially mutton. The Berry is the central province whose capital is Bourges.

Bonne-femme, à la *(as the mistress of the house makes it)* When applied to fish, this means cooked with chopped mushrooms. With poultry, it indicates cooked potatoes cut into little ovoid pieces, tiny onions, diced lean bacon, and sometimes mushrooms. *Pommes bonne-femme* is that familiar dessert, baked apples.

Bordelaise, à la *(in the fashion of the Bordeaux region)* May mean: (1) with Bordeaux sauce, a tomato sauce flavored with wine, marrow, butter, shallots, thyme, and nutmeg. (2) with Mirepoix sauce which is made by reducing carrots, onions, celery, and ham to a near liquid and seasoning the result with thyme and laurel.(3) with *cèpes* (mushrooms) that have been cooked in a closed earthenware dish with butter, garlic, parsley, and green-grape juice. (4) with artichokes and potatoes.

Boulangère, à la *(as the baker's wife makes it)* Cooked with chopped potatoes and onions. Usually applied to mutton or lamb, but occasionally to poultry.

Bouquetière, à la *(as the flower-girl makes it)* Accompanied with glazed carrots and turnips cut into small ovoid pieces; peas and diced string beans; cauliflower in Hollandaise sauce or melted butter; and new potatoes.

Bourgeoise, à la *(as the city woman makes it)* With glazed onions and carrots, cut into small ovoid pieces, sometimes plus braised fresh vegetables, celery, lettuce, etc. This often includes calves' feet which have been cooked together with the dish it accompanies, usually braised beef, braised leg of mutton, braised veal or tongue.

Bourguignonne, à la *(in the Burgundy fashion)* Cooked in red wine sauce, with mushrooms, little onions, and diced bacon. Applied especially to large cuts of meat, especially beef—*boeuf à la bourguignonne*, more commonly written *boeuf bourguignon*. A special case is *escargots à la bourguignonne* (snails Burgundy style), which means that they are cooked in white wine and consommé with carrots, onions, shallots, and herbs before being put back into their shells and sealed in with snail butter *(beurre pour escargots)*—butter shallots, garlic, and parsley.

Brabançonne, à la *(in the fashion of Brabant)* The Brabant is the Belgian province of which Brussels is the capital. The dish is prepared with potatoes and braised Belgian endive (also called witloof or broad-leaf chicory in the United States). Large cuts of meat are usually presented in this fashion. A secondary meaning is a dish accompanied by boat-shaped pastry shells filled with Brussels sprouts in a cream sauce and potato croquettes.

Bretonne, à la *(in the fashion of Brittany)* Be prepared for white beans when you meet this label, the exception being dishes so named because they are accompanied by *sauce bretonne*—sauce served with the beans. Most meat dishes, such as shoulder of lamb or mutton, so described will be accompanied by the white beans in their sauce. Fish, such as sole, will probably be lapped in the sauce without the beans. *Purée à la bretonne* thins the beans and their sauce into a soup. *Sauce bretonne* is made of onions, carrots, cel-

ery, leeks, butter, and cream if it is to be served with meat. If it is for fish, white wine is used instead of cream.

Bruxelloise, à la *(in the Brussels fashion)* Accompanied with potatoes and Brussels sprouts.

Cancalaise, à la *(in the fashion of Cancale)* Oysters and shrimp tails in Normandy sauce, served on fish. Cancale is a Breton fishing port noted for its fleshy white oysters.

Cardinal, à la *(with shellfish)* An accompaniment for fish made with sliced truffles, mushrooms and the little shellfish known as Cardinals. Grammarians think this should be written *au cardinal*, since the word is masculine, but the *à la* phrase is so firmly rooted in food terminology that it remains here.

Castiglione, à la *(named in honor of Castiglione)* Served with large mushrooms stuffed with rice, eggplant, and poached marrow. An accompaniment for roasts, etc.

Catalane, à la *(in the Catalan fashion)* Part of Catalonia lies on the French side of the border, and has developed a cuisine of Spanish influence modified by French skill. The term *à la catalane* most often signifies that you will encounter eggplant, tomato, olive oil and, of course, garlic. With large cuts of meat the term signifies an accompaniment of diced eggplant cooked in olive oil, and pilaff of rice with tomato sauce. With eggs, expect them to be cooked in oil with tomatoes and served with separately cooked eggplant, hotly peppered and redolent with garlic. Unless you really like garlic, look out.

Cavour, à la *(named in honor of Cavour, the Italian statesman)* Bedded on polenta (the Italian form of cornmeal mush) and accompanied by grilled mushrooms stuffed with mashed chicken livers and truffle slices. This treatment is applied especially to sweetbreads or veal steak.

Chambord, à la *(as served at the château of Chambord)* An elaborate, complicated, and very rich accompaniment for large fish braised whole, which involves fish patties, fillets of sole, mushrooms, roe, truffle-stuffed olives, and crayfish.

Chanoinesse, à la *(as the deaconess makes it)* Served with tiny carrots in cream and truffles in pastry shells. With sweetbreads, poultry or egg dishes.

Chasseur, à la *(as the hunter likes it)* Cooked with chopped mushrooms, shallots, and white wine. Widely applied to small meat cups, poultry or egg dishes. The *"à la"* often disappears, as in *tournedos chasseur.*

Châtelaine, à la *(as the mistress of the chateau makes it)* With artichoke bases stuffed with chestnuts; braised lettuce, and new potatoes. Goes with large cuts of meat.

Chinonaise, à la *(in the fashion of Chinon—Rabelais' home town)* With little balls of braised green cabbage stuffed with sausage meat, and potatoes powdered with parsley. Served with large cuts of meat.

Clamart, à la *(in the fashion of Clamart)* With artichoke bases filled with tiny peas, and new potatoes. With large or small cuts of meat.

Clermont, à la *(in the fashion of Clermont)* With balls of braised stuffed green cabbage cooked with slices of bacon and potatoes. Served with large cuts of meat.

Colbert, à la *(named in honor of Colbert)* It must be because of the services this eminent minister of Louis XIV rendered to the navy and the merchant marine that his name was given to a method of cooking fish. It means breaded and fried. *Beurre à la Colbert* is a special mixed butter often served on fish so cooked. It includes dissolved meat jelly, tarragon, parsley, and lemon juice.

Conti, à la *(named in honor of the Conti family)* François-Louis, Prince de Conti, was elected King of Poland in 1697 but never sat on its throne. Made with croquettes of mashed lentils and little ovoids of potato browned in butter. It is served with small cuts of meat.

Crécy, à la *(in the fashion of Crécy)* A considerable variety of preparations which carry this tag have one thing in common—they all contain carrots. *Purée Crécy* is a thick carrot soup. Crécy does not refer to the famous battle of 1346, but to a small town not far from Paris famous for the quality of the carrots it grows.

Créole, à la *(in the Creole fashion)* For the French, Creole evokes Martinique and Guadeloupe, their possessions in the West Indies, not Louisiana.

It has two chief meanings: (a) when applied to a main dish, that it is accompanied by a pilaff of rice with stewed sweet peppers and tomatoes; (b) when applied to a dessert, that it probably is made with rice, and in the majority of cases is flavored with orange.

Dauphinoise, à la *(in the fashion of the Dauphiné)* The Dauphiné is one of the Alpine provinces, where a mountain potato of particularly fine quality is grown. Hence this description almost always indicates *pommes de terre dauphinoises* (Dauphiné potatoes)—thinly sliced potatoes moistened with boiled milk and beaten egg, heavily seasoned with salt, pepper, and nutmeg powdered with Gruyère cheese, blessed with a hint of garlic, and baked in the oven. Don't confuse this with *pommes de terre dauphine,* which are balls of dough, mashed potatoes, and egg yolk, deep-fried.

Demi-deuil, à la *(in half-mourning)* A whimsical description inspired by the black-on-white appearance of this preparation—Suprême sauce with truffles. It appears chiefly on boiled fowl and braised sweetbreads.

Diable, à la *(with deviled sauce)* Although this fashion of serving poultry takes its name from the sauce that goes on it, it actually implies an entire cooking process. A chicken cooked *à la diable* is split open along the back, flattened out, and grilled until it is nearly done. It is then coated with breadcrumbs, and returned to the grill to finish cooking. *Sauce à la diable* is a highly pungent concoction which starts out with white wine and vinegar, into which at various stages are incorporated shallots, thyme, bay leaf, pepper, parsley, and Cayenne pepper.

Dieppoise, à la *(in the fashion of Dieppe)* Originating in the Normandy fishing port which gave it its name, this involves cooking fish in white wine with mussels and shrimp tails, and lapping it with a white wine sauce that includes the cooking liquid and more mussels. Particularly good with sole or fried smelt.

Dubarry, à la *(named in honor of Madame Dubarry)* Garnished with cauliflower balls, crusted with cheese, and drenched with Mornay sauce, a variant of béchamel. Served with meat. *Potage Dubarry* is cream of cauliflower soup.

Duchesse, à la *(as the duchess makes it)*

With Duchess potatoes, meaning mashed potatoes with egg yolk, seasoned with a dash of nutmeg.

Duxelles, à la *(as made for the Marquis d' Uxelles)* More often written simply Duxelles, without the *"à la,"* this accompaniment for small cuts of meat is a sort of mushroom hash, with shallots and nutmeg. It was invented by La Varenne, the chef of the Marquis d'Uxelles.

Ecarlate, à l' *(scarlet)* Applied to pickled beef or pork cuts, especially tongue, which through pickling have acquired a red color.

Etuvée, à l' *(stewed)* Indicates that the dish described, whether meat, poultry, fish, vegetables or fruit, has been cooked (but not boiled) in a covered vessel.

Fermière, à la *(as the farmer's wife makes it)* With carrots, turnips, celery, and onions cooked in butter. Served with braised or fried meat.

Financière, à la *(as financiers like it)* Just to prove that there is logic in menu nomenclature, almost indentical with *"à la banquière"* (see above).

Flamande, à la *(in the Flemish fashion)* Most often, an accompaniment of braised cabbage, carrots, cubes of lean bacon, and potatoes, served with large cuts of meat, *Potée à la flamande* is cabbage soup. *Asperges à la flamande* is asparagus served with melted butter and hard-boiled eggs cut in half. You scoop out the yolk of the egg, crush it into the melted butter and use it as a sauce for your asparagus.

Florentine, à la *(in the fashion of Florence)* With spinach. Usually applied to eggs and fish dishes in France. One of the few terms that have crossed frontiers without changing meaning, *alla fiorentino* in Italy also usually indicates spinach, but there it is often attached to dishes like veal and steak.

Forestière, à la *(as the lumberjack's wife makes it)* With the crinkly mushrooms known as *morilles* (morel), spheres of lean bacon, and diced potatoes sautéed in butter, applied to poultry and small cuts of meat.

Française, à la *(in the French fashion)* With little baskets made of baked Duchess potatoes (see above) filled with mixed diced vegetables; asparagus tips; braised lettuce; and cauliflower in Hollandaise sauce. Served with large cuts

of meat. The word *"française"* here presumably refers to the Ile-de-France (island of France), the region of which Paris is the center. The macedoine of vegetables is particularly typical of the Parisian region.

Frascati, à la *(as made at the Frascati restaurant)* Slices of foie gras, green asparagus tips, mushrooms, and truffles, accompanying a roast.

Gasconne, à la *(in the Gascon fashion)* This is applied to a number of dishes which have entered the repertory from Gascon cooking, but there isn't much of a common denominator—except that any Gascon dish is likely to be a lusty treat for trenchermen, and if it involves cooking in fat, the fat is likely to be goose. *Epalue d'agneau à la gasconne* is shoulder of lamb stuffed with chopped ham, bread moistened in consommé, onions, garlic, parsley, egg, herbs and spices, braised in bouillon, and cooked with cabbage, carrots, onions, and quartered potatoes. *Côtes de porc à la gasconne* are pork chops marinated in oil, vinegar, thyme, and garlic, fried in goose fat, smothered in olives, and doused with a rich gravy. *Omelette à la gasconne* adds diced ham, chopped onions, garlic, and parsley to the eggs of the omelette, and cooks it in goose fat.

Gauloise, à la *(in the fashion of Gaul)* This one you aren't likely to meet on French menus in the United States, for it indicates an ingredient little favored here—coxcombs, along with chicken kidneys, used in soups. If you come across the name attached to *vol-au-vent* (flaky pastry shells filled with creamed goodies), there will also be truffles and pickled tongue in a Madeira wine sauce. Don't confuse this term with the *gauloise,* a little cake flavored with apricots and almonds.

Grècque, à la *(in the Greek fashion)* Usually pretty much of a misnomer, for of the various and highly different dishes which bear this description, very few are actually of Greek origin, though more contain ingredients much used in Greece. The only dishes so ticketed which have anything in common are the group of cold hors d'oeuvres *(artichauts*—artichokes—*à la grècque, champignons*—mushrooms—*à la grècque,* etc.). These are pickled in a brine made of water, olive oil, lemon juice, coriander, peppercorns, salt, thyme, bayleaf, fennel, and celery.

Hongroise, à la *(in the Hungarian fashion)* Cooked in cream and seasoned with paprika. Eggs, fish, meat, poultry, and vegetables are all treated in this fashion. There are also various accompaniments for main ingredients which may cause the dish to be labeled *à la hongroise,* which if it is a question of meat usually adds cauliflower to the cream-paprika combination; but when it is a question of boiled or sauté fowl, can signify pilaff of rice and diced tomatoes stewed in butter.

Italienne, à la *(in the Italian fashion)* With finely chopped mushrooms. This term turns up in connection with meat, poultry, fish, and vegetables. When applied to noodles (spaghetti, macaroni, etc.), it means with butter and grated cheese only.

Japonaise, à la *(in the Japanese fashion)* Applied to any dish involving Chinese artichokes. These comestible roots are known in France as *"crosnes du Japon."* Imported from Japan rather than China, their odd-looking name comes from the fact that they were first raised in France in the town of Crosnes, not far from Paris. *Salade à la japonaise* is a special case, another name for *salade Francillon,* a mixture of mussels, potatoes, and truffles of which the invention is attributed to Alexandre Dumas *fils.* The dessert known as a *Japonaise* is a molded ice with tea-flavored mousse inside, and a coating of peach ice cream.

Jardinière, à la *(from the garden)* As the name indicates, this means an accompaniment of fresh vegetables. The classic combination is carrots and turnips, diced or otherwise shaped into small pieces; peas; fresh green beans; and whatever else happens to be in season. Each vegetable is cooked separately (the carrot-turnip combination counting for one) and they are arranged individually around the main item of the dish.

Languedocienne, à la *(in the fashion of Languedoc)* With tomatoes, eggplant, and *cèpes* (mushrooms) cooked in oil, plus garlic in the sauce. Applied to meat or poultry.

Liègeoise, à la *(in the fashion of Liège)* Flavored with juniper berries.

Limousine, à la *(in the fashion of the Limousin)* With red cabbage cut into long strips, cooked in pork fat with chestnuts.

Lorraine, à la *(in the fashion of Lorraine)* With red cabbage braised in red wine, and potatoes.

Lyonnaise, à la *(in the fashion of Lyons)* This term has a variety of meanings, but in general it implies the presence of onions. Thus *omelette à la lyonnaise* is an onion omelet, *pommes de terre lyonnaise* are potatoes sauté with onions, etc.

Mâconnaise, à la *(in the fashion of Mâcon)* Meat cooked with red wine. Mâcon, located between the Burgundy and Beaujolais wine districts, produces good, but not great, wines—the kind you can use for cooking without regretting their loss for drinking.

Madrilène, à la *(in the Madrid fashion)* Applied to various dishes characterized by the use of tomato extract. Its commonest appearance is as *consommé à la madrilène*—a tomato-flavored consommé served cold.

Maraîchère, à la *(as the market gardener's wife makes it)* Braised (or less frequently, roast) meat cooked with carrots, small onions, stuffed cucumbers, and sometimes salsify and potatoes.

Marêchale, à la *(as the marshal's wife makes it)* Applied to veal steak, poultry fillets, or other small cuts, it means breaded and sautéed in butter. It generally implies also that the dish is accompanied by asparagus tips and truffles.

Marigny, à la *(named in honor of Marigny)* With small artichoke bases filled with creamed corn, and new potatoes. Served with small cuts of meat.

Marinière, à la *(as the sailor's wife makes it)* When applied to shellfish, especially mussels, it means cooked in white wine and butter with shallots and herbs. For fish, it means cooked in white wine and accompanied with mussels.

Marocaine, à la *(in the Moroccan fashion)* Accompanied by pilaff or rice flavored with saffron; diced summer squash sautéed in oil; and braised sweet peppers stuffed with chicken. Served with mutton or lamb.

Mascotte, à la *(for good luck)* With artichoke bases sautéed in oil; potatoes cut into small ovoids and sautéed in oil; and truffles slices. Accompanies

small cuts of meat or poultry.

Masséna, à la *(named in honor of Napoleon's Marshal Masséna)* With artichoke bases filled with Béarnaise sauce and poached sliced marrow. Served with small meat cuts.

Matignon, à la *(named in honor of Marshal de Matignon)* With carrots, celery, and onions, stewed with herbs until they have been reduced to a *purée*, and moistened with Madeira wine. A richer version adds ham to this.

Mentonnaise, à la *(in the fashion of Menton)* The last city of any size on the French Riviera before you reach Italy, Menton has developed a preparation applied to a number of dishes, especially fish. It is dominated by tomatoes, black olives, and a richness of garlic.

Milanaise, à la *(in the fashion of Milan)* The northern Italy industrial and operatic capital has given its name to a variety of treatments of meat, notably: (a) accompanied by little earthenware cups filled with macaroni *à la milanaise* (meaning with tomato sauce); (b) accompanied with gnocchi crusted with grated cheese; (c) accompanied with macaroni *à l'italienne* (with butter and cheese); and cooked ham, pickled tongue, mushrooms and truffles, all cut into thin strips and doused with tomato sauce. The first two appear usually with large cuts of meat, the third, with small cuts.

Mirabeau, à la *(named in honor of the early revolutionary orator Mirabeau)* With grilled meat, anchovy fillets laid across the meat, stoned olives, blanched tarragon leaves, and anchovy butter.

Moderne, à la *(in the modern fashion)* Accompanied by little molded mixtures of fresh vegetables (carrots, turnips, peas, string beans, etc.) and braised lettuce, and sometimes also with truffled fish patties and pickled tongue. Served with large cuts of meat.

Monselet, à la *(named in honor of Charles Monselet, a 19th-century gourmet and poet)* This name is given to a large number of dishes whose preparation includes the use of artichoke bases and truffles plus, if the nature of the dish permits, potatoes browned in butter.

Montmorency, à la *(made with Montmorency cherries)* Covers everything which this fruit enters, from *caneton à la Montmorency* (duck with cherries) through *tarte à la Montmorency* (cherry tart) to *glace à la Montmorency* (cherry ice cream). Grown in the Parisian region, the Montmorency is a somewhat bitter cherry, of the type known in France as English cherries.

Mornay, à la *(named in honor of Henri IV's counselor, Philippe de Mornay)* With Mornay sauce, a variety of béchamel crusted with grated cheese, used most often on fish.

Nage, à la *(swimming)* This applies to shellfish, especially crawfish, small lobsters, and spiny lobsters, and means that they have been cooked in water seasoned with spices and herbs, in which they are served, either hot or cold.

Nantua, à la *(in the fashion of Nantua)* Located on a lake 1,500 feet up in the Jura mountains, the city of Nantua is famous for its crawfish and its patties made from lake fish. Only the first is indicated by the term "à la Nantua," which means that crawfish tails will be found in the dish, or that it will be covered with crawfish sauce, used often on fish, shellfish, or eggs.

Niçoise, à la *(in the fashion of Nice)* In general, this indicates a dish strong in tomato and garlic. This is true of *stockfish* (dried cod) *a la niçoise; omelette à la niçoise,* which also includes another Nice favorite, anchovy fillets; *poulet sauté à la niçoise,* stewed chicken; *poularde à la niçoise,* fried chicken; *filets de boeuf à la niçoise* (filet mignon with string beans, new potatoes, and anchovy fillets, doused with a sauce including tomato, garlic, white wine, consommé, and tarragon); but only partly true of *rougets* (red mullet) and *entrecôte* (steak) *à la niçoise,* which are made with tomato but omit the garlic. Exceptions: *gnocchi a la niçoise,* made with potato flour; *sauce à la niçoise,* which is distinguished by anchovy essence and tarragon; and *salade à la niçoise,* a warm-weather favorite of uncooked vegetables—string beans, quartered tomatoes, anchovies, ripe olives, and sometimes capers. When a dish becomes *à la niçoise* by virtue of the side dishes served with it, there are also several possibilities: it is accompanied by (a) stewed tomatoes, braised summer squash, little artichokes cooked in butter, and new potatoes; (b) with stewed tomatoes flavored with garlic, string beans, and new potatoes; or (c) with stewed tomatoes, green or black olives, anchovy filets, and capers. The first two appear with meat and poultry, the last with fish.

Nivernaise, à la *(in the fashion of the Nevers region)* With small glazed onions and carrots cut into little ovoid shapes. Served with meat.

Normande, à la *(in the fashion of Normandy)* A variable term which indicates the appearance of at least one of the three great foods of this region—milk, apples, seafood—often two, and rarely, all three. The only one that comes to mind at the moment which uses all three is *matelote à la normande,* a salt-water fish stew, which is flavored with burning Calvados (applejack), and contains butter and cream. Small cuts of meat and poultry *à la normande* include two of these ingredients—the cooking juices are washed away from the sides of the pan with cider, and combined with Calvados and cream to make the accompanying sauce, while *perdreau à la normande* (Normandy partridge) beds the bird on apples and douses it in cream. *Sauce à la normande* has both cream and cider in it, and goes on eggs, fish, or chicken. The dessert, *soufflé à la normande,* is flavored with Calvados and has bits of apple in it. Seafood alone characterizes the preparation of fish *à la normande,* which means with poached oysters, shrimp tails, smelts, mushrooms, and slices of truffle. But as *sauce à la normande* is often added too, this brings together all three of Normandy's gastronomic glories.

Orientale, à l' *(in Oriental fashion)* Preparations, chiefly of fish, eggs, or vegetables, involving tomato with saffron (or occasionally garlic instead of saffron) and often including gumbo (okra).

Orly, à l' *(in the fashion of Orly)* Refers to fillets of fish which have been dipped in a light dough, deep-fried, and are served with tomato sauce presented separately. Why this method is attributed to the Paris suburb chiefly famous for its airport, the writer has no idea.

Parisienne, à la *(in the fashion of Paris)* Astonishing as it may seem to tourists who associate Paris with rich food, the typical Parisian meal is simple and the favorite dish of Parisians is nothing

more esoteric than steak with French fried potatoes. Hence *à la parisienne* denotes the appearance of Parisian potatoes—the smallest you can find, sautéed in butter, glazed by application of veal consommé, and powdered with chopped parsley. There will usually be some other vegetable with the potatoes, most often braised lettuce or quartered artichokes. Similarly, *potage parisien* is vegetable soup containing potatoes, leeks, and carrots.

Paysanne, à la *(as peasants like it)* Applied to meat or poultry, usually braised, with carrots, turnips, onions, celery, lean bacon, and potatoes cut into ovoid shape.

Périgourdine, à la *(in the fashion of Périgord)* Périgord is the truffle center of France, and any dish so described is all but certain to have truffles in it. This is also *foie gras* country, so the chances are about fifty-fifty that you will meet *foie gras* as well. *Oeufs à la périgourdine* are hard-boiled eggs stuffed with truffled *foie gras*. *Poularde à la périgourdine* is roast chicken also stuffed with both. *Filet de boeuf à la périgourdine* is roast beef with truffles tucked into slits cut in the meat, served surrounded by little rafts of *foie gras*. In *poularde truffée à la périgourdine* the stuffed chicken is buried for several days in truffle peels to steep it in truffle flavor. *Poulet sauté à la périgourdine* is chicken fried with truffles. *Tournedos à la périgourdine* also omits *foie gras*, the filet mignon appearing on a raft of toast, crowned with butter-fried truffles and soaked in Madeira sauce. Finally *cèpes à la périgourdine* doesn't even include truffles, the mushrooms being cooked with diced bacon, parsley, garlic, and grape juice—but this mushroom is also so ubiquitous in Périgord cooking that its presence alone suffices to label the dish.

Piémontaise, à la *(in the fashion of Piedmont)* Accompanied with rice mixed with grated white truffles. White truffles are a specialty of northern Italy, the French variety being black. This appears with both meat and poultry dishes.

Poulette, à la *(pullet style)* The name presumably is a reference to similar sauces used in chicken fricassees, though it applies chiefly to specialty meats, like kidneys. It means that the dish, after cooking, is combined with

a cream and egg sauce, and is usually served with little onions and mushrooms.

Princesse, à la *(as the princess makes it)* With asparagus tips and truffles. Usually accompanies poultry, sweetbreads, or others into the filling of pastry shell.

Provençale, à la *(in the fashion of Provence)* Any dish so described is almost sure to contain tomatoes and plenty of garlic. In the rare cases when the tomato disappears, the garlic invariably remains. Thus roast pork *à la provençale* for once doesn't have the tomatoes, but is steeped in a bath of olive oil, garlic, and herbs before going into the oven. But *daube de boeuf à la provençale* (beef stew) and *boeuf bouilli à la provençale* include both tomatoes and garlic. So does fried chicken, Provençal style. Eggplant also appears often in Provençal dishes—poached eggs Provençal style, covered with garlic and tomato sauce, are served with diced eggplant. When a dish is labled *à la provençale* because of its accompanying side dishes, this usually means that it is served either with eggplant stuffed with tomato paste, string beans, and potatoes; or with Provençal tomatoes—cooked in olive oil, flavored with garlic, and sprinkled with parsley. If it is *à la provençale* because it is served with Provençal sauce there are several sauces so named. The most common is a white wine-tomato-garlic sauce which appears on almost everything warm—eggs, fish, meat, poultry, vegetables. For cold dishes (especially hard-boiled egg), capers, pickles, and plenty of garlic. There is also a garlic sauce—*sauce à l'ail à la provençale*—a cream sauce involving consommé, egg yolks, butter, lemon juice, herbs, and the garlic.

Richelieu, à la *(named in honor of Cardinal Richelieu)* The general meaning is an accompaniment of tomatoes, stuffed mushrooms, braised lettuce, and potatoes browned in butter, which normally appears with meat dishes. Completely unrelated is *filet de sole à la Richelieu*, a favorite preparation of this fish often applied also to others, which means that after they have been soaked in egg, breaded, and cooked in butter, they are served with melted butter seasoned with pepper, lemon juice, and chopped parsley and truffles. There is also a cake known as a Richelieu.

Sarrasine, à la It would be romantic to translate this "as the Saracen women make it," and it seems justified by one of the two accompaniments for large cuts of meat which this indicates—rice baskets filled with tomato extract and sweet peppers, with a thin slice of fried onion on top, which certainly has Oriental overtones. However, the other half is a sort of buckwheat scone—and the French word for buckwheat (also called "black wheat") happens to be the same as the word for Saracen. So *"à la sarrasine"* means only "with buckwheat."

Savoyarde, à la *(in the fashion of Savoy)* Like its neighboring Alpine province of Dauphiné (see above), Savoy is strong on potatoes and not much else, except cheese, so that this tag here also indicates the presence of potatoes. *Pommes de terre à la savoyarde* differ from the Dauphiné dish only in using consommé where the Dauphiné uses milk. *Omelette à la savoyarde* is a potato-cheese omelette, thus combining both of the region's chief food products.

Souvarov, à la *(named in honor of the 18th century Russian General Souvorov —or Souvarov, as it is also spelled)* This means poultry or game birds cooked in a coating of dough and served with *foie gras* and truffles. There are also little cookies called Souvarovs.

Strasbourgeoise, à la *(in the Strasbourg fashion)* The capital of Alsace boasts its own sausage, akin to the frankfurter, so any dish labelled this way is usually accompanied by Strasbourg sausages. The chances are good that there will be sauerkraut also (see *à l'alsacienne*, above). A second meaning is a dish accompanied by sauerkraut, chunks of lean breast of pork braised with sauerkraut (a specifically Strasbourg touch), and slices of *foie gras* sautéed in butter (Strasbourg is a *foie gras* center).

Toscan, à la *(in the fashion of Tuscany)* With large macaroni, diced and mixed with purée of *foie gras;* and truffles, cut into large dices and sautéed in butter. Served with veal steak, sweetbreads, or breast of chicken.

Valenciennes, à la *(in the fashion of Valenciennes)* With rice cooked with chopped sweet peppers. Served with small cuts of meat and poultry. Valenciennes is the famous lace making city. It has no other connection with rice.

Where to Buy Unusual Foods by Mail

Most are available in the specialty shops of large cities and in ethnic neighborhoods—but if you can't find them, use this directory

If you live in or near a metropolitan center, you will find gourmet grocery stores that carry a wide assortment of foreign foodstuffs and specialties. But if you are not so located, there are a number of stores specializing in mail order to which you can turn. Large department stores as well often have food departments which specialize in foreign delicacies, and they generally print catalogues for which you may write.

All the stores listed below have catalogues which they will send on request. Some carry specialties of many countries, so they cannot be classified by country.

Old Denmark, 135 E. 57th St., N.Y., N.Y. 10022. Specializes in Scandinavian, but also carries foods from all of Europe. No minimum price on size of order.

Kassos Bros., 570 9th Avenue, N.Y., N.Y. 10036. Greek specialties. Minimum order, $5.

Manganaro Foods, 488 Ninth Avenue, N.Y., N.Y. 10018. Foods from Italy, France, Switzerland, Ireland, Netherlands. No minimum price on size of order.

Paprika-Weiss, 1646 Second Avenue, N. Y., N.Y. 10028. Specialties of Central Europe, including Hungarian, Austrian, German, Swiss, Yugoslavian, Czechoslovakian. Minimum order, $3.

Casa Moneo, 219 West 14th Street, N.Y., N.Y. 10011. Spanish and Mexican specialties. Minimum order, $5.

La Perferida, 177 S. Water Street, Chicago, Ill. Specializes in Puerto Rican, Cuban, and Mexican foods. Minimum order, $10.

Cheese of All Nations, 235 Fulton Street, N.Y., N.Y. 10007. No minimum price on size of order.

Index of Recipes

General Index